HARRY DODSON'S
PRACTICAL KITCHEN GARDEN

HARRY DODSON'S
PRACTICAL KITCHEN GARDEN

HARRY DODSON
AND JENNIFER DAVIES

BCA

LONDON · NEW YORK · SYDNEY · TORONTO

This edition published 1992 by BCA
by arrangement with BBC Books,
a division of BBC Enterprises Limited,
Woodlands, 80 Wood Lane, London W12 0TT

First published 1992
© Harry Dodson and Jennifer Davies 1992

CN 3186

Illustrated by Will Giles and Sandra Pond

Set in 11/13pt Garamond by Ace Filmsetting Ltd, Frome
Printed and bound in Great Britain by Richard Clay Ltd, St Ives plc
Colour separations by Technik Ltd, Berkhamsted
Jacket printed by Belmont Press Ltd, Northampton

PICTURE CREDITS · David Clark for BBC page 119; Bruce Coleman pages 71 (Eric Crichton), 95 *bottom* (John Fennell), 115 (John Fennell) & 126 (Eric Crichton); Jennifer Davies pages 19, 40, 57 *both*, 61, 74 *both*, 76, 81, 84, 93 *left*, 94, 99, 111 *left*, 120, 130, 133 *bottom*, 159, 179, 194 & 197; East Sussex County Library page 10 left; Robert Hill for BBC pages 12, 22, 26–8, *all*, 34, 37 *left*, 38–9, 43, 55, 58, 59, 63, 78, 86, 103, 111 *right*, 113 *all*, 114 *top*, 122, 132, 137 *both*, 138, 145, 146, 151, 153, 160, 162, 170 *top*, 171, 174, 175, 185, 187, 195, 198, 199, 204–5 *all*, 206 *all left*, 210 & 218–9; John Jefford for BBC pages 70, 98, 101 *right*, 142, 154–5, 158, 165, 180, 206 *right* & 207; John Perkins for BBC pages 30, 42, 47, 64, 93 *right*, 101 *left*, 117, 128, 150, 182, 184 & 202; Photos Horticultural pages 48–9 *all*, 50, 51, 52, 54, 62, 66, 67, 72, 75 *both*, 79, 80, 83, 87, 89, 95 *top*, 102, 108 *both*, 110 *both*, 114 *bottom*, 124, 133 *top*, 134, 136, 139 *both*, 140, 163, 166, 167, 170 *bottom*, 178 & 190; David Secombe for BBC pages 7, 14, 37 *right*, 92 & 106; The Earl of Selborne page 8 *bottom left*; Harry Smith Horticultural Photographic Collection pages 68, 82, 90, 123, 127 & 135; Topham Picture Source page 109.

The photograph on page 9 *right* is from *The Sussex County Magazine* Vol. IX No. 10, October 1935.

BBC Books would like to thank Harry Dodson and Fred Norris Jnr for the loan of family photographs.

The front cover photograph was taken by David Secombe for BBC Books.

Contents

	· INTRODUCTION ·	PAGE 7

CHAPTER ONE　　　　· *VEGETABLE GARDEN BASICS* ·　　　　PAGE 13
Soil – Digging – Manures and fertilisers – Sowing and planting vegetables –
Crop rotation – Intercropping

CHAPTER TWO　　　· *OBTAINING VEGETABLES OUT OF SEASON* ·　　　PAGE 33
Using hotbeds – Pots – Coldframes – Cloches

CHAPTER THREE　　　　　　· *SALAD CROPS* ·　　　　　　PAGE 41
Tomatoes – Cucumbers – Lettuce – Radishes – Chives – Spring Onions –
Mustard and Cress – Lamb's Lettuce – American Land Cress

CHAPTER FOUR　　　　　· *ROOTS AND TUBERS* ·　　　　　PAGE 53
Jerusalem Artichokes – Chinese Artichokes – Beetroot – Carrots – Celeriac –
Kohl Rabi – Parsnips – Potatoes – Salsify and Scorzonera – Swedes – Turnips

CHAPTER FIVE　　　　　　· *BRASSICAS* ·　　　　　　PAGE 69
Brussels Sprouts – Broccoli – Cabbages – Savoys – Coleworts – Couve
Tronchuda – Calabrese – Cauliflowers – Kales

CHAPTER SIX　　　　· *SPINACH, FLORENCE FENNEL*　　　　PAGE 77
AND GLOBE ARTICHOKES ·
Roundleaf or Prickly Spinach – Perpetual or Winter Spinach – New Zealand
Spinach – Seakale Beet – Rhubarb Chard – Good King Henry –
Florence Fennel – Globe Artichokes

CHAPTER SEVEN　　　· *PEAS, BEANS AND SWEETCORN* ·　　　PAGE 85
Garden Peas – Purple-podded Peas – Sugar Peas – Asparagus or Winged
Peas – Broad Beans – Runner Beans – French Beans – Haricot Beans –
Butter Beans – Ornamental Beans and odd Peas – Sweetcorn

CHAPTER EIGHT　　　　· *ONIONS AND LEEKS* ·　　　　PAGE 97
Onions – Welsh Onions – Egyptian Onions – Shallots –
Cocktail Onions – Leeks

CHAPTER NINE	· VEGETABLES FOR FORCING AND BLANCHING ·	PAGE 105
	Dandelions – Chicory – Asparagus – Endives – Rhubarb – Seakale – Celery – Cardoons – Mushrooms	

CHAPTER TEN	· MARROWS, COURGETTES, SQUASHES AND PUMPKINS ·	PAGE 121

CHAPTER ELEVEN	· AUBERGINES AND CAPSICUMS ·	PAGE 125

CHAPTER TWELVE	· HERBS ·	PAGE 129
	Angelica – Balm – Basil – Borage – Caraway – Chervil – Dill – Fennel – Garlic – Hamburg Parsley – Horseradish – Marjoram – Mint – Oregano – Parsley – Rosemary – Rue – Sage – Savory – Sorrel – Tarragon – Thyme	

CHAPTER THIRTEEN	· INTRODUCTION TO FRUIT ·	PAGE 141
	Forms of tree – How to wire a wall – How to erect a fence to support espaliers or cordons – Heeling-in – General instructions on planting and pruning	

CHAPTER FOURTEEN	· TREE FRUIT ·	PAGE 149
	Apples – Pears – Cherries – Plums and Gages – Peaches and Nectarines – Figs	

CHAPTER FIFTEEN	· SOFT FRUIT ·	PAGE 177
	Raspberries – Gooseberries – Currants – Loganberries – Strawberries	

CHAPTER SIXTEEN	· GRAPES AND MELONS ·	PAGE 189

CHAPTER SEVENTEEN	· STORING AND SAVING ·	PAGE 201
	Making a root store and a clamp for vegetables – Picking and storing Apples and Pears – Saving and storing seed – Storing herbs	

CHAPTER EIGHTEEN	· A BRIEF INTRODUCTION TO SHOWING ·	PAGE 209
	Planning ahead – Preparation – At the show	

· LIST OF SUPPLIERS ·	PAGE 214

· INDEX ·	PAGE 219

Introduction

Since making the BBC television series *The Victorian Kitchen Garden* which showed crops in an old walled garden being raised as they used to be, I'm often asked for advice on traditional gardening methods. In fact it's become apparent that many of the skills I learnt from a young garden boy upwards still have a value. For example, not long ago I was asked how to plait up Onions on a string for storing. Old-time gardeners used to make a lovely job of that – all those Onions

strung a different size to each string, so that when the time came to use them you could see at a glance the ones you wanted. Making hotbeds to bring forward vegetables is another traditional method which still seems to fascinate. It's certainly energy-saving, the heat simply coming from fermented manure! I also get asked how to put together home-made composts, how to prune Figs and how to look after fruit under glass. On this last point more people nowadays have glasshouses and conservatories than they did, say, twenty years ago, and they want to know how to grow Peaches, Nectarines and Grapes in them.

The queries about Onion ropes and hotbeds and fruit under glass are answered in this book together with, I hope, enough practical information to help everyone who wants to grow their own fruit and vegetables. The book has one other element which perhaps makes it a bit different from other gardening books. It's that, in many cases, as well as giving the method of how to do things *today* I've described how they *used* to be done. This I know interests many people. Only last Christmas I received a card from a lady who kindly said that what she liked in the television programmes were my personal reminiscences! Well, I'm lucky on that score, because I've a deep well to draw from. My father was a gardener at Byfleet in Surrey, but on his death, when I was just six years old, my mother went back to my grandparents. They lived on the Selborne estate at Blackmoor in Hampshire, and there I spent many of my boyhood days with my mother's brother, Fred Norris. Fred was head gardener to the Earl and Countess of Selborne and *his* uncle had been head gardener before him.

Uncle Fred taught me all the rudiments of gardening. I learned them in between being the garden's gofer (going for this, going for that), scrubbing pots and cleaning boxes. But I could

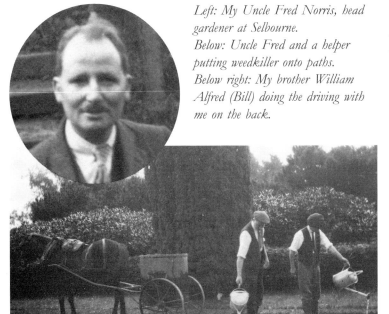

Left: My Uncle Fred Norris, head gardener at Selbourne.
Below: Uncle Fred and a helper putting weedkiller onto paths.
Below right: My brother William Alfred (Bill) doing the driving with me on the back.

Right: Uncle Fred and me photographed with an onion crop to be proud of.
Far right: Stansted Park in Hampshire where I was the garden's 'gofer' (going for this, going for that).

thin a bunch of Grapes and tie a Peach tree long before I left Blackmoor school. The school was only a couple of hundred yards from our cottage, so I didn't have far to go, but there were lots of little hamlets on the estate and some pupils had a long walk morning and afternoon.

Uncle Fred's training paid off because in 1930 I was made head garden boy at the school for the three years before I left. Pupils learned gardening when they got to Captain Adlam's class. Lessons took place on half a day a week in summer and usually the same in winter but then mainly indoors, although some of us older boys did winter work outside on our own, such as compost making and digging. There were two boys to each of the boys' plots and two girls to each of the girls' plots. The boys' gardens were four times bigger than the girls' gardens, and whereas the girls grew flowers, the boys grew mainly vegetables. There were bush Apples and Plums at the end of the boys' plots but this area wasn't very productive as the fruit was often stolen before it was mature!

All boys grew the same items, and their gardens were joined one to another and the line of crop was sown or planted in one straight line across them. During the producing period, vegetables could be bought at the school and from the purchase money Captain Adlam bought all the seeds, plants and sundries needed for the next year's gardening.

The school taught boys how to dig, sow, make compost, lift, store and gather produce and keep a garden tidy. But most of the lads who had fathers or other relatives working on Blackmoor estate already knew how to look after a garden because estate workers took lots of pride in their plots as doing so meant cash saving to them. Estate cottages had large gardens and many cottagers kept a pig in a sty provided by the estate, or chickens, or both. It was a way of life you don't see today. From October through to January on evenings when there was a moon you could scarcely go through the village of Blackmoor or the small surrounding hamlets without hearing

someone sawing wood up or digging in their garden, so lads got the hang of gardening early.

I went from being garden boy for Uncle Fred to garden boy to the Rector of Blackmoor. At that time he also employed two full-time gardeners and a part-time one. After two years I left as it was the Rector's custom to keep a boy only two years because then his wage would have had to go up. Also by that time a boy would need to move on to better himself.

After a twelve-month stint on pleasure-ground and general garden work at Headley in Hampshire I saw an advertisement for an improver journeyman in the *Gardener's Chronicle*. The *Chronicle* was the bible of all gardeners and young journeymen in those days and cost 6d (2½p) a week, quite a big hole in your pocket money. The job was at Stansted Park, Rowlands Castle, Hampshire, in the kitchen gardens of the Earl of Bessborough. I was taken on as the boy directly under the kitchen garden foreman. (There was a foreman to each department of the garden.) You went with

the foreman on all the jobs, fetched the tools, washed them and hung them up, collected vegetables with him and were general dogsbody. That's how I learned the job.

I lived in a bothy. That's the name given to the house young, unmarried gardeners occupied. This was in a yard where there was also a little forcing pit and an enormous stoke hole for the garden's heating boiler. Every morning the head bothy boy had to go out and ring the bell on the stoke-hole chimney, and when it rang you had to be out of that bothy and away. Woe betide anybody who wasn't down at the bottom of the frame yard by the time the head gardener, Mr Tomalin, got there to see all his staff!

Mr Tomalin always told boys that he would keep them for eighteen months to two years and at the end of that time of service, if progress had been satisfactory, he would place them in one of the best jobs, or one of the best of so many, in the country. All the head gardeners who were high up the scale were in contact with one another. They used to meet at shows where they judged or at Royal Horticultural Society committee meetings and they would pass on the names of young gardeners who wanted to better themselves. The post of journeyman at Ashburnham Place near Battle, Sussex, came up and Mr Tomalin did all the writing and fixing for me. I went for an interview and got the job, though it was a foregone conclusion that I would.

The head gardener at Ashburnham was Mr Creasy and the garden was enormous and very old. I've never come across glasshouses anywhere so ancient: they were probably made by the estate carpenter in days gone by. When I got there the pineapple pits were derelict, but there were still a great many vines. There was also a very elaborate tool shed where each man had his own pegs for his tools which you were not allowed to touch or use and which, of course, were kept in immaculate condition. They were all polished and oiled and looked lovely.

At Ashburnham we didn't work in departments; we all worked under the inside foreman and mostly worked together. That was very good training because you got the opportunity to do all the fruit and pot plants and also to work in the 'flowering house'. This was always staged up with lots of flowering plants for Lady Katherine Ashburnham to see. At that time I was hoping to get on the list for Windsor gardens, but Hitler had

Left: Ashburnham Place where I worked before the war.
Above: I joined the Royal Sussex Regiment.

Right: My wedding day. My mates at Nuneham tied stinging nettles to watering cans filled with confetti. When we walked out of the church, the cans were turned upside down.
Far right: Just married.
Page 12: Chilton Gardens – still my pride and joy.

other things in mind and before I knew where I was I was in the Royal Sussex Regiment serving in France.

When eventually I was discharged from the army I went to work as general foreman in the gardens at Leigh Park in Hampshire. It was the home of Miss Fitzwyram but when war broke out it was taken over for HMS *Vernon*'s Mines Design Department. I was working on food production. There were a thousand people to be fed each day in the canteen there. I couldn't leave until I got Admiralty permission and when that was granted I went to work for Lord Harcourt at Nuneham Park, Oxford. I was there two years and that's where I met Jane, the girl I was to marry. Because

I was general foreman at Nuneham Park and couldn't get any higher and because I wanted to get married, I advertised for a head gardener's job, putting in the advert 'to be married when suited'. It was a term often used in those days as usually the job you were in was for a single man and you lived with the other gardeners in the bothy. Sometimes, of course, you could get married and move into a cottage on the same estate, but usually a man wanted promotion so he would advertise whatever his credentials were, whatever department he wanted, and the advertisement would end with the words 'to be married when suited'. It was quite simple and it was well understood at that time.

Despite there being twenty-six other applicants I got the job of head gardener at Chilton in Berkshire. It was 1947 and I was twenty-seven. I was reputed to be one of the youngest men in the country with a job of the size and importance of Chilton. The kitchen garden had four Peach houses, three vineries, a Rose house, flowering block, Carnation house, tropical house, four Melon houses, hotpits, coldframes and nearly five hundred cloches. By 1967, however, things had begun to wind down. The price of oil had escalated and it wasn't economical to heat the glasshouses any longer. Eventually the gardens were turned over to me to run as a commercial nursery.

Then in 1984 the BBC came along and I started a new career demonstrating on television the skills I had learned from my work in kitchen gardens over the years. As I mentioned, I'm now known for being 'the Victorian gardener', but I'm not really that old – it's just that I remember how the old boys used to do things in kitchen gardens!

Vegetable · Garden · Basics

Soil – Digging – Manures and fertilisers –
Sowing and planting vegetables – Crop rotation –
Intercropping

CHAPTER ONE
Vegetable Garden Basics

A good garden's built on basics. The first is soil fertile enough to grow crops well and the second is the knowledge of how to make the soil fertile if it isn't. Other basics are knowing how to prepare ground for crops, how to sow, plant and feed them and which vegetables will follow on best on ground left vacant by others. If your garden's small you might also treat as basic the knowledge of how to get several vegetable crops from one piece of ground but all at the same time.

Soil

Every garden that I've worked in *had* to produce fruits and vegetables, and so over the years its soil was dug and manured to make it productive. In the beginning achieving fertility wasn't easy, especially with the light, sandy soil at Blackmoor and the equally difficult heavy loam at Stansted Park, but years of work produced a dark, crumbly, fertile growing medium at both places.

Garden soil falls into roughly four main categories: clay, sandy soil, chalky soil and, best of all, medium loam. (Heavy loam borders on clay and light loam is generally pasture land broken down with manure and compost to make it easier to work.)

Left: Some useful garden tools including a few like the potato ridger (far right) not so well-known today.

HOW TO RECOGNISE TYPES OF SOIL
■ Clay
Clay soil is heavy and difficult to dig. Its close-packed nature restricts roots and air. Clay holds moisture well but needs plenty of 'opening' material worked into it. If this isn't done it becomes hard and cracks and is difficult to sow, hoe and till in summer. Clay soil is often a problem in the gardens of new houses where the land has been left like a building site. On a day when it's fine but the soil's not too dry, a piece of clay squeezed in the hand (the 'hand test') will become like putty or Plasticine. Improve clay soil by incorporating into it farmyard manure, leaf soil and coarse grit. Years ago the heaps of gritty waste swept by the 'beat man' who cleared the roads was used. Instead, today, you can buy and add coarse ⅛in (3mm) grit.
■ Sandy soil
Sandy soil is, as its name suggests, mostly made up of sand grains which make it very porous and allow water to run out of it too easily. If you do the 'hand test' on this type of soil it won't bind together but will run through your fingers. Improve it by digging in farmyard manure, coarse peat and compost and other materials of a water-holding nature.
■ Chalky soil
Chalky soil has no goodness in it and drains too quickly. You can recognise it by its whitish

appearance. The weeds groundsel and chickweed flourish on it. Improve chalky soil by digging in plenty of compost, which will give it the nutrient content it lacks.

If you've got any of the above three kinds of soil it'll take several years and hard work to get it to the ideal which is:

■ **Medium loam**

Medium loam is dark and when it's turned over you can find traces of compost and farmyard manure in it. Squeeze a bit in your hand, open your palm, touch lightly with the ball of your thumb and it should crumble down or break in two.

Digging

You dig to:

(a) incorporate farmyard manure or compost into the soil to help make it more fertile and also more capable of retaining moisture;

(b) dispose of light annual weeds and spent crops;

(c) break up compacted ground, assist drainage and give plants a free root run.

The main time for digging is in autumn when crops are cleared and when, if your soil is a heavy clay, it can be thrown up roughly so that over the winter frosts can help to break it down. Start your digging as soon as crops have been cleared: the more you can get done by Christmas, the better, particularly if the ground is heavy and it looks as if it's going to be a wet winter.

In my young days digging was a major autumn and winter job for kitchen garden staff. At that time nearly everyone used a spade. Few people use one today – in fact, the tool was almost forgotten at Chilton after I fixed up the outside staff with flat-tined forks. They are much lighter to use and do the same job on all but the lightest of land.

If you *are* using a spade, digging is much less laborious if you hold it in the right way. Place your

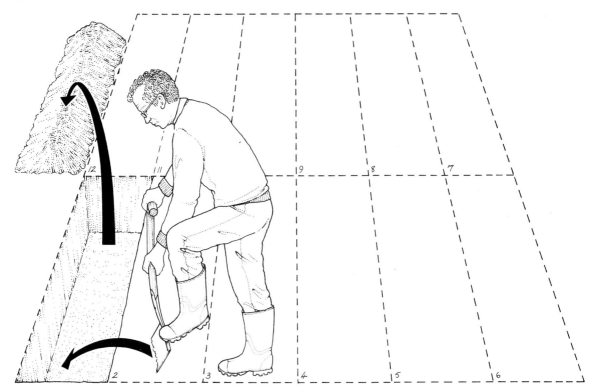

Ordinary digging

right hand on the top of the handle, then place your left hand a little way down the shaft into a comfortable position. Have your foot ready to press the blade down: it should be driven straight down into the soil, not at an angle. Slide your left hand down to a comfortable position, then lift the soil up and turn it over. The spit (which is a layer of soil a spade-blade deep) shouldn't be too wide. If it is, it makes unnecessarily heavy work. A width of 8–9in (20–23cm) is as much as anyone can carry on lifting for several hours of digging.

ORDINARY DIGGING

The method for ordinary digging is to take a trench out before you start, which enables manure put in to be well dug in. Remember that the soil has to be pushed forward and over as you dig, burying all weeds (except perennials like thistle and dock, because these will grow again). The soil from the starting trench has to be removed by wheelbarrow to the end of the land where the digging will finish, and you will use this to fill in your last trench, so leaving all the plot level.

MOCK TRENCHING

You can give root crops a greater depth in which to grow by breaking up hard subsoil. One way to do so is by mock trenching. This is like ordinary digging in that you open up a trench and barrow the soil to the other end of the plot where you'll finish. Then you step into the trench and dig down another spit, but instead of lifting this soil out of the trench you break it up and leave it in the bottom. If the land is poor, dig in compost or farmyard manure. Get back out of the trench and turn the next top spit over, then step in and break up the bottom as before. Carry on over the entire plot in this way, making sure that the finished digging looks good and level.

Right: Mock trenching. Stage 1: open up a trench and wheel the soil to the end of the plot. Stage 2: step into the trench and dig the soil over another spit deep, adding manure if needed.

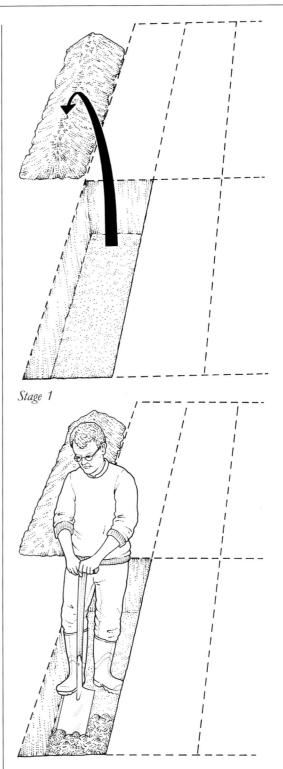

Stage 1

Stage 2

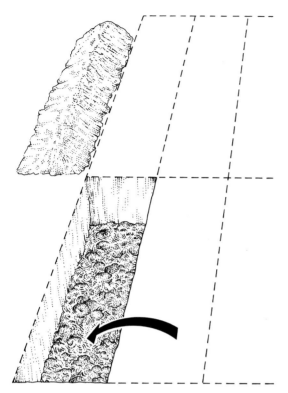

Stage 3: step out of the trench and turn the next spit over. Repeat Stage 2. Continue until you fill the last trench with the soil from the first.

TRENCHING

Trenching, which is another way of creating a greater depth of soil for root crops, requires the removal of a trench two spits – or 2ft (60cm) – wide and one full spit deep. Dig over the bottom a further full spit deep, incorporating any compost or manure, then throw the next two spits over on to this, shovelling out the loose crumb at the bottom of the first spit otherwise you will lose your trench.

RIDGING SINGLE SPIT

A good method of digging land which needs the frost to get into it to make it easier to work in the spring, particularly if you're planning to sow Carrots, is ridging single spit. To do this take out a trench two spits wide and work in any compost needed. Then begin ridging by throwing one spit onto the ground to the left of the trench and the next to the right, something like edging up a path. Alternatively one spit can be thrown on top of the other. The finished plot viewed from the end should look like a plot of ridged-up Potatoes (minus, of course, the potatoes!).

DOUBLE RIDGING

Finally there's double ridging. I learnt to do this at Stansted Park where it was practised because it's good for very sticky soil – and the ground at Stansted *was* sticky, as I've cause to remember. One spring I was forking up the fruit border ready for sowing Brassicas and Lettuce when it began to rain. I had only a yard left to do and it wasn't heavy rain, so I carried on. When I had finished the foreman and Mr Tomalin, the head gardener, grumbled that the ground wouldn't work any sense for the rest of that year. What they meant was that it would dry out hard and be difficult to hoe or drill. As it turned out they were right, for instead of being nice and friable it had become like a putty pot and, of course, as it was spring, there was no chance of frost coming to break it down.

You do double ridging in much the same way as trenching. Use a spade or fork to mark out a width of 2ft (60cm) across the patch of ground. Then take out a trench where you want to begin. The trench should be 2ft (60cm) wide and 1ft (30cm) deep. Dig the bottom of the open trench over to a depth of a further 1ft (30cm) working in compost if needed or placing a layer of compost on top of the bottom layer and then turning the next top of soil over onto this. Shovel the crumb out and form the ridge by placing half the soil to your left and half to your right. This method makes quite big ridges. If the land that you are working is very heavy and sticky, adding a dressing of coarse grit, lime or wood ash is beneficial. Throw it between the top and bottom layers of each ridge.

Right: Soil preparation at Chilton.

USING MANURE INSTEAD OF DIGGING

During the Second World War a Mr F. C. King was head gardener at Levens Hall, South Westmorland. He reckoned that you didn't need to dig a garden at all. Instead you cleared off your crops, spread well-prepared compost or very old farmyard manure 2–3in (5–7.5cm) deep over the garden, sowed and planted into that and you got good crops. The theory behind this was that the earthworms pulled the manure down and aerated the garden and also that well-made compost was weed free and in turn suppressed weed growth, rather as bark mulch does today. There were many articles about this in the *Gardener's Chronicle* magazine at the time, but it's something I've not tried.

Manures and Fertilisers

Manures and fertilisers give nutrients to crops. Farmyard manure and compost also help to alter the soil structure and make it better at holding moisture.

FARMYARD MANURE

Farmyard manure is the soiled litter from penned-up animals. It's excellent for making the soil friable and easy to work and is also a good source of plant food because it contains the three essential nutrients, nitrogen, phosphorus (in the form of phosphoric acid) and potash.

Farmyard manure is usually applied during the winter months. It's best when dug in 9–12in (23–30cm) deep. That way it will hold moisture, a particularly useful quality if the soil is light. Farmyard manure brings most benefit to the soil if applied every other year. If this can't be managed, it should certainly be dug in every three years otherwise crops will suffer, become small,

and, in some cases, not be worth the labour of growing them.

On light land, apart from digging in this manure, it can be an advantage to work into the top 4–6in (10–15cm) some well-rotted compost or very old farmyard manure which has reached the state at which it all crumbles down.

In addition to being an invaluable fertiliser, farmyard manure also makes a good mulch for newly planted trees and shrubs. It's especially good for walled fruit which dries out quickly. The best time to apply the mulch is in the months of April, May and June when it will conserve the moisture already in the ground. It's a good idea to water the mulch in too. If the weather turns very dry and an unmulched tree looks as though it's suffering, give it a good soak and put mulch on straight away.

Country dwellers can generally get hold of farmyard manure without difficulty, but if you live in a town or city it might be less easy. However, I expect that if you ask around or look in the Yellow Pages you will succeed in locating a riding stable or even a city farm which would be willing to sell you some and help arrange its transport.

BAG FERTILISERS

Bag fertilisers are useful because unlike farmyard manure they don't need to be stacked or wheeled, just simply emptied from a bag into a bucket and spread. Also, of course, you can dig the ground without the hindrance of having to work in farmyard manure. Bag fertilisers can be divided into two categories, straight and complete. Straight fertilisers release a particular basic plant nutrient, whereas complete fertilisers contain the three essential nutrients, nitrogen, phosphorus and potassium, that plants need for healthy growth.

I use bag fertilisers on flower crops and as a supplement to farmyard manure. It's also effective on ground which was heavily dressed with farmyard manure the previous year: use 2–4oz per sq yd (50–100g per sq m) of complete fertiliser, either purchased or made up from straight fertilisers, to produce good Lettuce, Carrots, Parsnips, Beet, Radish and Turnips. The complete fertiliser that I use for this is one which has stood by me over the years. It's 3.2.1:

3lb (1.5kg) sulphate of ammonia (nitrogen),
2lb (1kg) superphosphate and
1lb (500g) sulphate of potash.

You can make a larger amount, but always keep to the same ratio of 3.2.1.

This is suitable for a wide range of flowers, fruit and vegetables and can be used any time during the growing season to give crops a boost. In dry weather it should be well watered in.

SOME USEFUL STRAIGHT FERTILISERS

■ Dried blood
Expensive but a good form of nitrogen for crops where size matters, such as Onions, Celery, Leeks and Runner Beans. Use very sparingly. Soak it in a hessian bag in a tank of water for several days, then dilute this down to the colour of weak tea and apply as needed.

■ Bone meal
Use for almost any planting job. May be included in potting composts and used for top dressing fruit borders and pot plants.

■ Hoof and horn
Much the same as bone meal, but especially useful when planting fruit trees. Both give off nitrogen over a long period because, of course, bone takes years to rot away.

■ Fish meal
Pretty good for anything on a long-term basis. When I was at Leigh Park all the pike died in the pond and they were given to the head gardener. We dug them into a vegetable border and I remember that they also produced some wonderful Dahlias!

■ Nitrochalk
Supplies nitrogen and lime. Helps ferment the compost heap and is good for Black Currants.

■ Soot
Soot contains a small amount of nitrogen. Soot water is good for Chrysanthemums and Cinerarias and is also a useful insecticide. To make soot water buy soot from a chimney sweep, put it in a hessian bag and steep it in a tank of water. If the soot is fresh it needs to soak for a few days as it will be very dry. Before using, dilute until it looks like weak tea.

■ Seaweed
Useful for digging in to manure the soil generally. Helps to make it easy to work and supplies some nutrients.

■ Spent mushroom compost
As seaweed (above).

'SPECIAL' FERTILISERS

In pre-war days sundries firms sold ready-made bag fertilisers specifically for certain crops. Old-time gardeners and foremen used to swear by them. One known as Le Fruitier, which was for fruit and vegetables, was a household word. Clay's Fertiliser was another popular product: black, stinking stuff, but good for anything. Then there was Bentley's Vitalizer or Thomson's Vine Fertiliser – the list was endless. None is obtainable today. They've disappeared because the big private gardens which grew Peaches, Grapes and Carnations have gone.

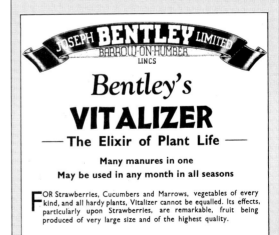

COMPOST

Compost created from vegetable waste is a valuable fertiliser that I first learned to make at school. In autumn we collected leaves in the woods at the back of the school and with them made a large, square heap in which were interspersed layers of vegetable waste. The leaves produced heat and we had to turn the heap a few times during the winter – it was better than school lessons! The heaps were made like small ricks and were sometimes over a year old before being used. By that time you could cut them down with a spade. Good 'compo' it was, dark brown in colour and clean to handle.

As boys my brother and I had our own garden at home and even we used to make compo. It was only on a small scale but we knew its benefits, especially for the soil around Blackmoor which was light and sandy and needed something to help it hold moisture. We used to go out on the road and shovel up the farm horses' droppings; there was seldom a day in winter when these animals didn't pass the cottage.

How to make compost

Spent crop greenery, grass mowings and trimmings, vegetable peelings, bracken and straw can all go on to a compost heap. You can also add leaves from trees (especially Oak and Beech), but personally I prefer to put these into a pile on their own and leave them to rot down to make leaf soil (see p. 24). If you are able to make the heap really ferment like a steaming mound of farmyard manure, even perennial weeds can be added because the heat, as well as helping to break everything down quickly, will kill them.

Put all this refuse in either a bin-like affair made of wood, or between sheets of tin, or in a brick compound – in fact, between anything which will

Adding a layer of manure to the compost heap.

keep the heat in the heap. If possible, arrange the different sorts of rubbish in layers. Old potting soil or any garden soil or loam added to the layers is useful, especially if worms are present. Coarse material, such as herbaceous and brassica stumps, should be chopped up and put in between something which will generate heat like fresh farmyard manure, green grass or autumn leaves picked up damp. The same material should be put around the sides of the heap because it will keep in the heat and quickly break down the tougher contents. You can buy compost-activating compounds which also have the latter effect.

After fermentation has died down the heap can be turned with advantage because exposure to the air helps to speed up the process of decomposition. Turn the inside of the heap to the outside and the outside inside, adding a little activator if needed. In winter the heap should be covered, especially on top, to keep out the rain and keep in the heat. One method of doing this is with a few inches of soil, patted down.

LIQUID FARMYARD MANURE

Liquid manure is good for fruit trees, including those in pots, Celery, Tomatoes, Cucumbers, Melons . . . the list is endless. Old estate gardens always had a tank of this on the go because the basic ingredients (fresh cow pats or sheep droppings) were easily obtainable on the estate. Of the two manures, sheep droppings make the stronger solution. Years ago it was the job of the garden's pot boy to collect them in the park or home paddock. A large garden used to need two or three bags to make enough liquid to see it through the growing season from April to September.

To make liquid manure put the fresh droppings into a hessian bag and stand this in a tank of water. Two or three days is the usual time to allow it to soak, then you give it a prod and a swish round and by that time the water is nicely permeated. You can use it in varying strengths. Diluted to look like weak tea it's good for newly planted fruit trees which do not have much root. When it resembles strong tea it's excellent for mature fruit trees carrying a heavy crop.

GREEN MANURE

Green manure is certain crops grown on a patch of ground and then dug into it while they're still green. Some examples of green manure crops are Mustard, Rye Grass, Clover, Winter Tares, Lupins, Trefoil and Comfrey. The crops put nutrients and eventually humus into the soil and those with fibrous roots help to make the soil easier to work. Some green manures have the added advantage that while the crop is growing it spreads over the ground like a blanket and suppresses weeds.

Crop waste can also be treated as green manure if it's dug in early enough: for example, the tops of Carrots, Beetroot, Spinach and Parsnips; and Brassica and Lettuce leaves. In fact scientists say that all crop waste dug in provides some use in the ground, but I think it must be very small.

When I was a schoolboy a large mass of Mustard used to be grown between the Apple trees on the Blackmoor estate. To benefit the trees the Mustard was ploughed in while it was still green. That was a job I did, as it needed a lad because of the closeness of the work. For a few weeks after the Apple crop had been cleared I had to lead two horses at plough between the 'breaks' (the spaces between the rows of trees). A weight on a chain going before the plough shield dragged the Mustard down and the shield covered the Mustard as it went along.

Mustard was grown elsewhere on the estate too because it was said to be a deterrent to wireworm when it was ploughed in. Clover roots were also ploughed in, not only to give fibre to the ground but because they added nitrogen to the soil – Clover, like all legumes, has small nitrifying nodes on its roots.

From the above you'll gather that my early learnings about green manure were on a large scale. It was only during the Second World War that I began to hear of it being recommended for small gardens.

Sowing and Planting Vegetables

SOWING

Sowing is done:
- in containers under cover;
- out of doors, either directly into the ground where the vegetables will mature or into a seed bed from which young plants can be transferred to their permanent position.

Sowing under cover

Vegetables are sown under cover for a number of reasons:

(a) to have young plants ready to put out in spring to get an early crop (e.g. early Cauliflower and Lettuce sown in February/early March);

(b) to give some plants a good start – useful perhaps, in an area that's wet (e.g. Peas and Beans sown in January/February, planted out in late April);

(c) to make sure that plants come to maturity (e.g. Celeriac and Celery have to be planted under glass in March/early April or they'll never be ready);

(d) to protect tender crops (e.g. Aubergines and Capsicums).

The staples of indoor sowing are composts, both in which to sow the seed and to grow on seedlings and plants. When I was a boy you couldn't buy ready-made compost. In big private gardens the basic ingredient for it, loam, was found on the estate. The site from which the loam was to be taken was chosen by the foreman or his understudy. Garden labourers cut it out in blocks about 6–9in (15–23cm) on each side, the depth depending on the class of loam and depth of fibre. Of course, the parks around mansions were good, unused pieces of land which had been manured by grazing cattle and sheep, and so usually produced excellent loam. This was carted back to the gardens by the estate's carter, or sometimes by a carter loaned by the estate farm. Many large gardens in those days had a garden pony and a carter who could do useful jobs around the gardens.

When the loam arrived at the garden the turves were stacked upside down in neat heaps or stacks (the name used depended on the area or county you were in) usually about 4ft (1.2m) high and 6ft (1.8m) wide and as long as you wanted. The stacks were often left for several months before being used. In some places well-rotted farmyard manure was put between each layer of turves when the stack was made. Two such heaps were here in the yard at Chilton when I took over. They had been beautifully stacked and were in excellent condition. The amount needed was cut down with a spade and chopped as fine as required, depending on the plants to be grown in it and the size of pot: 9, 10 and 12in (23, 25 and 30cm) pots would have larger pieces than 5 or 7in (13 or 18cm) ones. Of course, some gardens didn't have this parkland turf available, so they had to buy in. A favourite loam on the market then was Kettering Loam.

Gardeners in those days had as many different ideas for a good potting mixture as there were hours in a day. But all the old boys used to say that potting compost should be 'porous, but also rich sweet and durable'. The many different mixings often amounted to much the same thing or provided the same results and continued to do so until commercially made-up compost came along.

Loam composts have now mostly been replaced by peat ones which a lot of people find easier to handle and more convenient. However, I still prefer to make up my own. The basics in it are loam, farmyard manure and leaf mould. The leaf mould is easy enough to make. You just gather tree leaves when they're damp and freshly fallen: if they're collected when dry, they won't rot down properly. Most varieties make satisfactory mould but Oak and Beech leaves are the best if you can get them. Just leave them in a heap for at least 12 months before use. In addition to being an ingredient of potting compost, leaf mould can be used for mulching shrubs and can be mixed into flower beds.

My Uncle Fred always had several heaps of leaf mould being made and several ready. They were in secluded spots behind Rhododendron clumps and under the trees planted for shelter belts in the pleasure grounds at Blackmoor. Some of these compo makings were half under the ground in specially dug holes 10 × 10ft (3 × 3m) in area and 2–3ft (60cm–1m) deep. The heaps were a neat and tidy sight to see, just like the loam stacks and the dung heaps. The men who worked in gardens years ago had the knack and skill not only to make a useful product, but also to make the area in which it was kept look as if it belonged to someone who cared.

How to Make Loam-Based Composts
A useful and simple mix for seed sowing:
½ bushel (18 litres) sterilised loam
¼ bushel (9 litres) granulated peat
¼ bushel (9 litres) coarse sand graded up to ⅛in (3mm)
about ½oz (15g) superphosphate
½oz (15g) ground chalk or limestone
Leaf mould can be used instead of peat. No other bag fertilisers should be used.

A mix for pricking out seedlings:
1 barrow well-matured loam, put through a ½in (1cm) riddle
½ barrow grit or sand graded up to ⅛in (3mm)
5in (13cm) pot bone meal
This makes a good compost for a wide range of annuals and for vegetable seedlings such as Brassicas, Lettuce and Tomatoes.

A mix for potting on:
At each potting-on stage the mixture can be of a coarser nature. That is, the loam can be cut down with a spade and then given a few more chops when it's on the ground. Dried manure can also be added, chopped into pieces the size of a walnut. Mix these with coarse grit, leaf mould, hoof and horn (or crushed bone) and soot. Allow to stand for a few days before use.

MAKE-SHIFT STERILISER
When I was at Leigh Park in Hampshire it was too far to my lodgings each lunch hour so on cold days I made a fire to sit by. One day it occurred to me that the fire could do another job. I found a galvanised bath about a foot deep and 2 ft 6 inches across the top. Using bricks for supports, I placed it over the fire and poured in water up to a level of 3 inches. Then I added old potting soil filling the bath to 3 inches from the top. The fire quickly turned the water to steam. I found that left all day with an old wet bag on top to trap the steam, the soil sterilised nicely. By doing this I could use the same soil over and over again!

When and How to Sow Seed in Pots and Trays
Allow a month to six weeks between sowing and planting out. If you live in an area which often gets a frost in the first fortnight in May, don't sow too early in April.

Use either ready-made seed-sowing compost or make you own (see left). If you use ready-made it'll be so porous that there will be no need to crock the containers, but if you use your own put some curved pieces of broken flower pot over the drainage holes to keep it free. Cover the pieces with some rough material like the bits left over in the sieve when you've sieved for fine soil. Be prepared for home-made compost to be fairly heavy. I can remember when it was almost more than you could do to carry two large made-up seed boxes!

Fill pots to within 1in (2.5cm) of their rim and trays to within ½in (1cm) of their top *(a)*, then water thoroughly so that the compost has sufficient moisture to germinate seed before it needs watering again *(b)*. This is much better than the pot drying out and having to be rewatered, often too late, as lack of water at seedling stage is fatal. Leave for a while to drain before sowing.

Peas can be sown ten or a dozen to a 5in (13cm) pot and Beans one to a 3 or 3½in (7.5 or 9cm) pot or thirty to a standard seed tray. Smaller seeds need to be sown thinly to allow room for the seed leaves to develop. Some seeds are so fine that it's a job to see them. With these it'll help if you put some silver sand in the packet before you start to shake the seeds out *(c)*.

After sowing sprinkle a very thin layer of the same compost over the top of the container *(d)*. It needs to be just enough to cover the seed, and in fact its depth will depend on the size of the seed. Don't firm it down; just leave it. That way the seeds can breathe freely and it's less likely that they'll damp off. When I was a lad no one realised that it was best to do this and the surfaces of sown containers were firmed down with little pieces of board on a handle or with the base of another smaller pot. It used to be part of the ritual which took a man half a day to sow a dozen boxes. Now I sow the same amount in less than an hour!

To get the seeds to germinate you can either put the container into a propagating case or keep it in a warm glasshouse. If you do the latter, lay a pane of glass over the container *(e)*. All vegetable seeds benefit from this. Also put a sheet of newspaper over the glass *(f)*. The glass will keep the moisture in and the newspaper will shade the container from the sun and give the thinly covered seeds darkness to help germination. Each morning, if there's heavy condensation on the glass, turn it over or take it off and shake it. On warm days, to stop droplets falling on the compost, this will probably need doing in the afternoon as well.

As soon as most of the seeds have germinated and are clear of the soil, take the glass off. In fact, if they're only just coming through it pays to take the glass off for a few hours in the day and put it on again at night.

Tomato seeds will take a few more days than most vegetables to germinate. After germination Brassica and Lettuce seedlings should be put as near the light as possible and grown in a normal temperature.

a

b

c

d

e

f

Pricking off

The aim of pricking off is to allow seedlings more room to grow. Do it as soon as the seed leaves are clear of the soil and you can get hold of them.

You'll need bought or home-made compost, a dibber a bit bigger than a pencil and seed trays or 3–3½in (7.5–9cm) pots. A standard seed tray will take thirty Brassicas and forty of most other vegetables. If you're using pots, put one seedling to a pot.

The dibber should give a hole sufficiently deep and large to stop the tap root doubling up. Pop the seedling into the hole. To produce a nice, sturdy seedling the seed leaf should be as near the soil as possible. Fill in the soil round the top of the hole by a slight touch with the dibber and then tap the sides of the container with your fists. This shakes the soil level and down around the roots.

Immediately after pricking out, water with a fine-rose can. If the sun is shining, put paper over the top to stop the seedlings scorching and to cut down on watering – a good thing, as they don't want much until they begin to make root.

Sowing out of doors

The best conditions for sowing seed out of doors are when you can break down the soil reasonably freely and within an hour or two walk across it without it sticking to your boots. Another test is to pick up a piece and squeeze it in your hand. If it crumbles when you touch it with your thumb, conditions are right. You will usually find such conditions in March and April; in June, July and August you might have to water the drills first. If you do, make the drills deeper than normal because, as you water, dry soil will inevitably get knocked into the bottom.

In summer avoid sowing in thundery weather, for a heavy shower of rain will beat down and compact the surface of the ground and in the humid conditions the seed will rot.

Left: My method of sowing seeds in trays.
Overleaf: Sowing on an outside border.

Preparing the ground

For spring sowings the ground will have been dug in the previous autumn or winter. Tread it down firmly to get all the lumps out and rake it to a fine tilth. The smaller the seed you intend to grow, the greater assistance it'll get from finely raked tilth. Peas and Beans don't need so fine a finish as Carrots and Lettuce.

Sowing vegetables where they will mature

Using a garden rod (see p. 29), measure out the distances between the rows, e.g., 1½–2ft (45–60cm) between rows of Cabbages, 12–15in (30–38cm) between rows of Carrots. Mark first along the top of the row, placing sticks as you go, then along the bottom. It makes a more workmanlike job to do this first rather than to sow a row and then measure out for another, and it also saves time as you're not carrying the measuring rod up and down each row.

Next, push one end of a garden line into the ground against the stick which marks the top of the first row and run the string down to the stick which marks the bottom of that row *(a)*. When you push the other end in, pull the string really tight, because the weight of soil, especially if you're making big drills, will push against it. Also make sure that the string is touching the ground all the way up the row. If for any reason there's a dip in the ground and the string is above it, get a brick and weigh the string down until it touches the earth. If you don't do this you'll get a bow in the drill when you draw it out.

Choose a tool with a good sharp corner to it (the usual one for this job is a triangle hoe) and, touching the string the whole way down, start to draw your drill for the seed *(b)*. There's an art in drawing a drill. Hold the tool firmly and draw only 1–1½ft (30–45cm) at a time, and when you put the tool down to restart the drill place it about 3in (7.5cm) back into the bit you've just drawn. That way you are more likely to keep the line straight.

After you've drawn the drills, sow the seed in them as thinly and continuously as possible. If you're not very expert at doing this you can buy a little gadget which you can adjust to dispense the size of seed you want to sow. It makes a good job. I think there's nothing worse than to sow 1oz where only ½oz is needed.

When all the drills are sown, scuffle the seeds in. Do this by putting a foot either side of the drill and shuffling your feet up its length *(c)*. Then lightly rake the surface in the direction of the drills so that the seed's not disturbed.

a

b

c

Sowing a seed bed

A seed bed is useful for Lettuce and Brassicas. Choose an open spot, because if the bed's in shade half the day the seedlings will become drawn. I think that the best place is in a favourable border and close to a path where it's handy to get at.

Make the drills close together and when the plants are big enough transfer them to their permanent planting ground.

ALTERNATIVE METHOD OF SOWING VEGETABLES WHERE THEY WILL MATURE

There's an alternative method of sowing which saves seed and also saves time thinning. It's chiefly done with Lettuce, but you can also do it with Parsnip and Onion.

Mark out the ground as if for seed sowing (see p. 28) and sow two or three seeds at each mark. When the seedlings come up, leave the strongest at each station but remove the other one or two.

MAKING A MEASURING ROD

This is simple to make and more useful than a ruler. I've two 10ft (3m) rods for outside work which fit into the coldframes. Inside staff used to have 5ft (1.5m) rods.

To make a rod you will need a piece of timber ¾in (2cm) thick, 2in (5cm) wide and long enough to suit the size of your garden. With an ordinary ruler and a pencil draw lines along the length of it to mark off 1ft, 6in and 3in (or 30cm, 15cm and 7.5cm if you're metrically minded). Next, using either a saw or a chisel, score straight across the rod to mark 1ft (30cm) and half-way across to mark 6in (15cm), and just make a small mark for 3in (7.5cm). Do this right along the length of the rod.

Thinning

When seedlings come up, even if you've tried to sow them thinly the chances are that they'll need thinning out. This means pulling up some so that the remainder are far enough from each other to be able to develop unhindered into full-sized plants.

In all cases it's best to thin after a shower of rain because then the unwanted plants will pull out easily and not disturb the rest of the bed. Water after thinning to settle the soil back round the plants that are left. If you need to thin and there's no sign of rain, water beforehand. When you've finished thinning, water again to settle the soil back.

Thin Parsnips, main crop Carrots (early Carrots won't need thinning) and Beet as soon as their rough leaves develop. Parsnips need to be thinned to 4–5in (10–13cm) apart, Carrots to 2in (5cm), Beetroot to 3–4in (7.5–10cm) – especially if they're for showing or you want decent roots for storing – and Turnips and Onions to 4in (10cm). The smallest Lettuces should be 6in (15cm) apart and the largest 12in (30cm).

In some cases early pullings can help to cut down thinning. For instance, you can leave Beetroot unthinned and instead pull some while they're small and use them in salad. The remaining ones will then have room to get bigger. *Don't,* however, do this with Carrots, because if you leave them and then disturb the soil it will let the Carrot root fly into the bed. Thin Carrots at rough-leaf stage.

PLANTING OUT

Mark out the rows as for seed sowing (see p. 28) and also measure and mark with a stick the planting place of each plant in the first row. When the first row is planted you can use it as your guide for the other rows. Plant the second row either directly opposite or in a dog leg so that whichever way you look at the patch you will see straight lines.

If you're planting bare-root, say, Lettuce or

Brassicas pulled from an outside seed bed, use a dibber or setting stick. Push it into the ground 3–4in (7.5–10cm), depending on the amount of leg on the plant. Let the roots drop right into the hole and give the top a prod or two with the dibber to shake the soil down around the root. In most conditions it then pays to water the plants because this settles the soil.

If you're planting from stock grown in a box or pot, use a trowel. Take out a planting hole big enough to avoid your having to push the plant into it. The hole should be large enough to accommodate the ball of soil on each plant and have sufficient room for you to work soil round it. The ball of soil should be moist before planting and you've got to take care not to break it because this will damage the roots and check the plant's growth. Plant firmly, pressing in with your fingers. Water to settle the soil.

> ### USING AN AWKWARD CORNER
> If the piece of ground you've been working on is wider at one end than the other, after measuring out the vegetable rows top and bottom, fill in the awkward corner with Rhubarb or Jerusalem Artichokes, or herbs such as Sage, Thyme or Rosemary. Any of these will occupy the area for some time and will efficiently use up a short piece of ground instead of a good long piece.

Planting out.

Crop Rotation

Growing the same vegetable every year on the same ground usually leads to a poor crop and disease, so each year it's sensible to move the site of each type. The exceptions to this rule are Onions and Runner Beans which I've known people grow successfully on the same spot year after year, but this is because they've dug large quantities of fresh manure into the soil each year.

The usual form of rotation is to follow a long-term crop which likes a generous supply of manure, such as Beans, Onions, Celery and Potatoes, with a short-term crop like Carrots, Parsnips, Beetroot, Lettuce, Radish and Turnips. All the vegetables in the second list grow well in the residue of goodness left from the first year's manuring.

Tall late-crop Peas (such as 'Gradus' or 'Ne Plus Ultra') do really well on old Celery trenches. Spring Cabbage is usually planted on ground which has grown Onions. Strawberries can follow on the Potato ground. Brassica land is often earmarked for a Potato crop.

How to Work Crop Rotation

PLOT 1 Vegetables move to Plot 2 in the second year and to Plot 3 in the third year.	(WELL-MANURED FIRST YEAR) BROAD BEANS, RUNNER BEANS, PEAS (Runner Beans and Peas can be intercropped with Lettuce, Spinach, Beet and Radish) ONIONS SHALLOTS TOMATOES CELERY POTATOES	Pea plot when cleared can be followed by Leeks. Onions followed by spring Cabbage. Shallots by winter Lettuce.
PLOT 2 Vegetables move to Plot 3 in the second year and to Plot 1 in the third year.	(WELL-MANURED SECOND YEAR) POTATOES* CARROTS† BEET PARSNIPS† TURNIPS	Early Potatoes can be followed by late sowings of Carrots, Turnips and Lettuce.
PLOT 3 Vegetables move to Plot 1 in the second year and to Plot 2 in the third year.	(WELL-MANURED THIRD YEAR) ALL THE BRASSICAS‡ (Sprouts planted at 2½ × 2½ft (75 × 75cm) can be intercropped with early Beet, Carrots and Lettuce) ROUNDLEAF and PERPETUAL SPINACH if wanted, from late summer. You'll get your first picking of Spinach in the following spring from the Perpetual	

MARROWS can fit on any plot.
A catch crop of TURNIPS, CARROTS, BEET, LETTUCE and ROUND-LEAF SPINACH can also fit on any plot.
* Potatoes appreciate well-rotted compost or farm-yard manure but not fresh farmyard manure. Apply an average size forkful to the yard.
† Don't work fresh manure into the plot for Carrots and Parsnips.
‡ Brassicas don't need fresh farmyard manure; they do well on the previous year's manured plot.

A form of rotation I've never forgotten was one practised at Stansted Park. In this a plot was fairly well dunged and planted with Potatoes. Strawberries followed and stayed there for two years. After the second year's crop they were chopped off at ground level with a spade and drills 3in (7.5cm) deep and 2ft (60cm) apart were drawn out with a triangle hoe. Broccoli was planted in the drills at 2ft (60cm) intervals. This cropped in April/May and after cropping the stumps were removed and Celery trenches were dug 6ft (1.8m) apart. Manure was dug in for the Celery. Come the end of the season, as Celery was lifted, marker sticks were placed in the middle of each trench. This was so that you could line up your next crop dead centre of the trench. The ground was then lightly levelled over with a fork and the trenches grew the following year's Pea crop. Because the trenches were 6in (15cm) apart you could grow Lettuce, Cauliflower, Beet and Turnips between the Pea rows. It was a lovely form of rotation which produced excellent crops and saved a tremendous amount of winter digging.

Intercropping

There are two ways of growing vegetables. You can grow them on their own so that there's just one crop in a patch of ground at a time, or you can put several different crops on the same piece of ground at the same time. This second method is known as intercropping. I think intercropping is a very time-consuming practice because you're trying to get two crops off quickly one after the other, both from more or less the same sowing or planting date. For instance, on a hotbed we used to sow Carrots 7–8in (18–20cm) apart and plant between each a forcing Lettuce. I always felt that I could have got twice as many Carrots without the Lettuce! Another example was as follows. At the end of February or in early March I used to mark the ground out for ½ acre (0.1 hectare) of Sprouts. They were to be planted a yard apart either way, but before they went in Lettuce and Carrots were often sown and these were followed by Radish, Beetroot and Spinach. Oh, it looked good and produced good crops, but in a wet season it also produced a weed problem which was difficult to control and sometimes the Sprouts smothered the last of the Beetroot and Spinach.

When I was a boy old cottagers used to intercrop their Potatoes with winter Cabbage or Kale. They didn't always get a good crop of greens because these were often drawn up through being smothered by the Potatoes. The method did have its advantages, though. The soil at Blackmoor was sandy and if there was any moisture anywhere it was probably at the bottom of the Potato ridge. Also the Potato foliage protected the Cabbage and Kale from the sun and the pigeons. By the time the Potatoes were lifted the pigeons had turned their attention to the harvest fields!

Obtaining·Vegetables Out·of·Season

Using hotbeds – Pots – Coldframes – Cloches

CHAPTER TWO
Obtaining Vegetables Out of Season
Using hotbeds — Pots — Coldframes — Cloches

In my job I was always expected to produce succulent, young vegetables for the table long before their natural cropping season. Here at Chilton I had to have dwarf French Beans, new Potatoes and Strawberries ready in time for Cheltenham Gold Cup Week (mid-March), be cutting spring Cabbage and picking Gooseberries at Whitsun and bring on Cauliflowers for eating from mid-April.

There are four ways of growing vegetables to get them to crop out of their natural season:
- on a hotbed
- in pots under glass
- in a coldframe
- under cloches

Hotbeds

A hotbed is a bed of soil kept warm because it is laid on top of fermenting manure. Vegetables grown in the bed are ready a month to six weeks earlier than those sown in an outside border.

I had my first experience of making a hotbed when I worked for the parson at Blackmoor. In a border backed by a wall we had to dig an enormous hole at least the width of two lights (glass-paned tops) and 3ft (1m) deep. The hole was filled with manure, 6ft (1.8m) of it, 3ft (1m) in the

Left: Pots of forced Peas.

hole and the same rising above it. Manure was plentiful in the rectory garden and was, no doubt, a gift to the parson, for it came from the carthorse stables on the Blackmoor estate. We put mounds of soil on to the manure and covered the bed with two frame bases topped by lights. On the mounds the parson used to raise his Melon crop, three plants to each frame. They were sown in April and were ready for eating in July or early August.

If I make a hotbed now I do so in one of my garden frames. The frames here are 4½ft (1.37m) wide and 8½ft (2.6m) long. Each has a brick base, slopes towards the south and is covered by a glass light which slides into place. I fill the frame to within 15in (38cm) of the top with fermenting farmyard manure. This is left until it has sunk, then I cap it with 6–9in (15–23cm) of soil – the depth depends on the crop: for example, Carrots or Beet need 9in (23cm) but Lettuce or Turnips only 6in (15cm). A few days after completion the temperature of the bed rises considerably, and to avoid scorching seeds or plants I don't put any in until the temperature drops. A good way of testing the temperature is the simple stick method. With this you push a stick into the soil when you make the bed. Experience helps a lot, but I reckon that if the stick end which has been in the soil feels as warm as new-drawn milk (approximately 60 or 70°F) when you pull it out, the bed has cooled sufficiently to be sown.

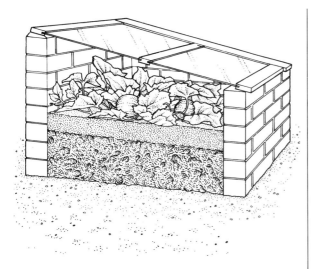

How to make a traditional hotbed.

Before sowing it's best to lay a board down on the surface of the bed. You can kneel on this without disturbing the soil. You need small-handled tools for working in such a confined space. A stick does as a drill, and if I'm sowing Carrot seed in a shallow drill I use the back of my hand to backfill and the back of a broken-handled rake to firm it lightly.

On a cold morning condensation on the inside of the glass light covering the bed is a good indication that the bed is holding its heat.

You can make a hotbed on leaves instead of manure: they don't get so hot as manure and will give a steadier heat. Make sure that the leaves you gather up to make the hotbed are damp. Dry leaves won't ferment.

'ECONOMY' GLASS TOPS FOR HOTBEDS

If you haven't got a proper glass top for your hotbed and you are sowing Marrows or Cucumbers, you can place jam jars over the individual plants to keep the heat in. This method forwards them by about a fortnight.

Forwarding Vegetables by Sowing in Pots

DWARF FRENCH BEANS

We used to forward dwarf French Beans in the Peach and vine houses because they need a constant temperature of 55–60°F (12.7–15.5°C). The method of growing them is to fill a 12in (30cm) pot not quite two-thirds full with compost and sow into it ten to twelve seeds. After sowing put a covering of compost over the Beans. When the Bean shoots reach the top of the pot, top dress to bring the soil up to 1–1½in (2.4–4cm) from the top of the pot. When the plants have reached 6in (15cm) in height they need a bit of brushwood or pieces from the head of a besom broom stuck in as supports. The besom looks quite picturesque but I prefer to use four canes because they make picking easier!

In my heyday we used to grow a Bean called 'The Prince' which I think you can still buy. There used to be no Bean to touch it. When forced it made a nice little slim Bean, but when planted outside it was just like another flat pod, the old 'Canadian Wonder'.

PEAS

In my experience Peas were never grown in pots on such a large scale as Beans. However, early varieties were frequently sown in pots and then planted out. These would crop two or three weeks earlier than those sown outside. The method was to sow half a dozen to a 5in (13cm) pot and put the pots in a warm glasshouse – 55–60°F (12.7–15.5°C) – to germinate in February. Anyone doing it today should transfer the pots to a cooler house when the Peas are a few inches high because you shouldn't force Peas too much. If you do they'll run up to twice their height. Like beans, they will need supports and I often use sticks of Hazel pushed in near the edge of the pot. Also remember to be generous with airing them (ventilating the house).

Peas supported by Hazel sticks.

POTATOES

The method for forcing Potatoes is one tuber to a 9in (23cm) pot or two to a 12in (30cm) pot. Half-fill the pot with soil, put in the Potato(es) and just cover over when the haulm reaches the top of the pot. Top dress to within 1½in (4cm) of the top of the pot when the haulm is 9in (23cm) tall and put stakes in to support it.

Potatoes will tolerate 55–60°F (12.7–15.5°C) until they are 12in (30cm) high, then they should be moved to a cooler house. You can also force Potatoes on a mild hotbed or in an ordinary unheated frame.

CAULIFLOWERS

In the autumn sow Cauliflower seed in seed boxes and germinate in a cold glasshouse. Pot off into 3½in (9cm) pots and over-winter in a cold house. Pot into finals – that is, 9, 10 or 12in (23, 25 or 30cm) pots – in February. Cauliflowers should be ready for cutting in April/May.

This vegetable can also be forced in an un-heated frame provided that it is on a favourable site and has enough height to accommodate a full-size cauliflower. However, I think it's better to grow Cauliflowers in a cold glasshouse because it's easier to air than a coldframe.

Forwarding Vegetables in Coldframes

The best coldframe for forcing vegetables is one so situated that it faces south to catch the sun. Of course, a mobile coldframe is as good because you can carry this to a warm south-facing part of the garden. You can raise early Carrots, Lettuce, Beet and Potatoes in a coldframe. Parsley sown in August in a frame will give you a crop all winter. On frosty nights, to protect the plants, it's best to cover the top of the frame with rush mats or old bits of carpet.

Above: Frame-grown Peas and Lettuce.
Overleaf: A birds eye view of glasshouses and coldframes at Chilton.

Using Cloches

I first saw cloches in Doctor Trotter's garden. He lived at Pond End Cottage, Blackmoor. It wasn't a large garden, but was very well run with one gardener and a garden boy. I could see the cloches from the road and they fascinated me because there weren't any in Uncle Fred's gardens; in fact cloches didn't seem to have a place in the large gardens. That being so, I was a bit taken aback when in 1947 I got the head gardener's job at Chilton and came to find 200yd of cloches staring me in the face. They'd been bought to help boost the Dig for Victory war effort and had been used only for growing early Lettuce. I was asked to use them over a longer period and to sow other crops. I gathered all the information I could and found that I liked them for crop production, and within two years the 200yd of cloches had become 400yd!

The cloches were the sort known as Grower's Barn. Each one spanned 2ft (60cm) of ground lengthways and was 2ft (60cm) wide. It was constructed like a mini-barn made from four panes of glass. Two 2 × 1ft (60 × 30cm) panes formed the roof and two 2ft × 9in (60 × 23cm) formed the sides. If you intend growing vegetables under cloches there is one firm that still makes the Grower's Barn type (see list of suppliers on p. 214). Alternatively it might be well worth your while to advertise for the wire frames of old ones because I'm sure there are many around doing nothing. The rust is easy to get off the frames and glass cut to size can be slipped into them.

For cloche culture the ground has to be in good heart with plenty of well-rotted manure dug into it. The tilth for seed sowing should be very fine and the top 3–4in (7.5–10cm) of a consistency that holds moisture. Good, fertile soil with plenty of peat, leaf soil or well-rotted manure incorporated cuts down on the labour of watering because you can simply water over the cloche without bothering to lift it. The sideways movement of water in good soil is approximately 12in (30cm), so water

dropped on either side will creep underneath the cloche to span the 2ft (60cm) base.

If you put a cloche into position a few weeks before using it, the ground beneath warms up. For January and February sowings put the cloche on prepared ground in late November or early December – certainly before Christmas. Five rows of early Carrots sown beneath a cloche in January or early February should give small Carrots for bunching by late April or early May. Beetroot, three rows beneath a cloche, will be ready by late May. Nine cabbage-type Lettuces (three to a row) under a Grower's Barn can be over-wintered and will be ready for cutting by Easter, and over-wintered Peas (for example, 'Meteor') will be ready for picking in early May. Then the cloches can be moved to Marrows, Runner Beans, dwarf French Beans and Sweetcorn. In summer they can move again to cover Melons and Cucumbers.

The uses of glass cloches are endless (early Strawberries love them), and although labour and breakages rule them out for commercial use, I recommend anyone with a vegetable garden to use them. Grower's Barn cloches have several advantages over the modern polythene types:
(a) A row won't blow away in a gale.
(b) You can remove single cloches (often you have to remove a complete length of polythene).
(c) You can air them without fear that the opening will cause the wind to lift them.
(d) They have more headroom.

A row of Grower's Barn cloches.

Salad·Crops

Tomatoes — Cucumbers — Lettuce — Radishes — Chives —
Spring Onions — Mustard and Cress — Lamb's Lettuce —
American Land Cress

CHAPTER THREE
Salad Crops

I think there's nothing to touch your own home-grown produce in the salad bowl, especially Tomatoes and Lettuce which give off an appetising smell that you never get from those bought in a shop. Of salad crops, Tomatoes, Cucumber and Lettuce (in that order) are the most costly to grow and require the most attention if you want to keep up a continuous supply.

Above: Trusses of glasshouse-grown Tomatoes.
Left: In times gone by the old varieties of Cucumber needed glass straight-jackets to help them to grow straight.

Tomatoes

Suggested varieties, for the greenhouse: 'Alicante'; 'Ailsa Craig'; 'Moneymaker'; 'Shirley'; 'Angela'; 'Harbinger' (this is a good late cultivar which also stores). For growing outdoors: 'Alicante'; 'Outdoor Girl'; 'Ailsa Craig'.

SOWING AND PLANTING IN A GREENHOUSE
In a heated greenhouse you can grow your own Tomatoes from seed. Sow in January to February in 60°F (15.5°C) in a peaty compost, allowing just a few seeds to a 4–5½in (10–14cm) pot and covering with compost. Ideally put the pots in a propagator, or just cover the top of each pot with a pane of glass. As soon as the seed leaves are large enough to handle pot off into 3½in (9cm) pots. When the plants are 6–9in (15–23cm) high, plant or pot into their final cropping position.

If you're using a cold greenhouse it's best to buy your plants from a garden centre and plant them in early April or mid-March if you live in a warm part of the country.

PLANTING OUTSIDE IN THE GARDEN
There are two ways of planting Tomatoes outdoors:
(a) Dig a trench 1ft (30cm) deep and the same wide. Dig manure into the bottom of the trench,

much as when preparing for Celery (see p. 115). Plant the Tomato seedlings 2ft (60cm) apart and cover the top of the trench with Grower's Barn cloches (see p. 40), one cloche to a plant. The plants will be 2ft (60cm) high before they outgrow the space and by that time the weather will be warm enough to remove the cloches. This method gives the plants a month's start over those planted by method (b).

(b) At the end of May plant out in a warm spot, preferably against a south-facing wall or fence.

SOIL

Don't attempt to grow Tomatoes in the same soil or compost year after year because this will lead to the soil becoming sick and also to the plants becoming diseased. This applies to outdoor crops and is even more important for indoor ones where the root run is limited and the soil not 'weathered'. Change the soil even if you're only going to substitute plain soil from the vegetable garden. You can fill in the hole from which you took it with the spent soil of last year's Tomato crop. Add to the fresh soil some compost and wood ash which will supply the potash Tomatoes need to avoid getting greenback, a horrible yellow-green piece in the fruit.

A grow bag will hold three plants, but if your Tomato variety is a strong grower just two to a bag is better. If you're using any soil other than peat compost, plant firmly. Peat compost, however, mustn't be firm; it will find its own firmness when it fills with roots. Water in.

CULTURE

Greenhouse Tomatoes will need airing on all warm days from the middle of May onwards and the air must be increased as the outdoor temperature rises. Leave night air on (that is, ventilate at night) too, because the fall in temperature at night will make condensation form on the Tomatoes if the house is shut up. This wouldn't matter with Cucumbers or Melons, but on Tomatoes it causes a pale, moon-like shape called ghost spot and,

more serious, if you're selling the Tomatoes, russeting on the skin, resulting from the sun warming the condensation the next day and scalding the fruit. The russeting also prevents ripening and can cause light cracks in the Tomatoes.

To encourage a good set in greenhouse-grown Tomatoes, go over the blossoms with a rabbit's tail or fine hair brush. The best time to do this is at noon when the sun is at its highest and the pollen should have dried sufficiently to move freely. After pollinating, damp the house down by spraying water on to the floor (some growers even give the plant a light damp over) and shut the house up for ten minutes. This creates a moist growing temperature, enabling the pollen to run and do its job. Outdoor Tomatoes can be pollinated by tapping with a cane at noon, but if you keep an eye open you'll probably see that insects are doing the pollinating for you.

Continue to tie the plants to canes as they grow and remove all the side shoots as they appear. This stops the plant becoming all growth and not much fruit.

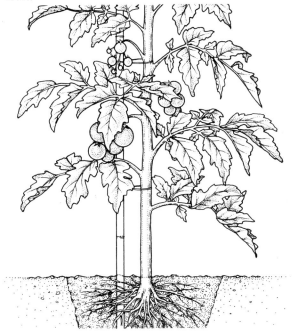

Trench Tomato plant supported by cane.

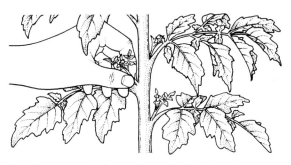

On Tomatoes, pinch out the small side shoots between the stem and the leaf joint. This will help fruit to set.

Do not feed until two trusses are set. Feeding before then encourages rank growth. After two trusses are set feed regularly with a brand product such as Tomerite and/or liquid farmyard manure (see p. 23) well watered in. You'll generally find that Tomatoes grown outside in well-prepared soil won't need as much feeding as those in a glasshouse, but if you're watering them it's no trouble to add a drop of feed to the water.

Keep an eye open for whitefly on indoor Tomatoes. These pests are generally only a problem on an outside crop if it's a very warm summer.

Cucumbers

A young Cucumber formed part of my morning routine when I was a garden lad to Lord Bessborough at Stansted Park. Always I had to take one, together with a bunch of Borage, to the butler. I had to have them in the butler's pantry by 11am and as an incentive I was given a piece of cake if I arrived on time. The blue flowers of the Borage were for the butler to drop on to the surface of claret, which was served in a silver cup, and the Cucumber was for decorating the outside of the cup.

If you're thinking of growing Cucumbers it's best to sow and plant female plants only. You can buy packets which contain only seed for female plants. If you sow male and female together you have the trouble of removing the male flowers to stop them pollinating the female and making the

Cucumbers taste bitter, a condition known as bitterpit.

'Improved Telegraph' is a good greenhouse Cucumber. Also 'Femspot' and 'Femdam'. The latter two are all-female cultivars.

SOWING AND PLANTING IN A HEATED GREENHOUSE

In January and February sow Cucumber seed on its edge in a 3 or 3½in (7.5 or 9cm) pot. Place in a propagator at 60°F (15.5°C) or cover with a pane of glass. When the seed leaves are large enough to handle, transfer to the final growing position, either one plant to a grow bag or one plant to a 10–12in (25–30cm) pot. Pot-planted Cucumbers can be trained as cordons, preferably in a house of their own. Cucumbers need fresh soil or compost for each year or crop.

CULTURE

Cordons produce early fruits and are easy to manage. Train the leaders to a cane or wire. Pinch out all side shoots beyond one leaf, but do not pinch out the leader until it can go no further in the house. Feed each week with liquid farmyard manure (see p. 23) or a general-purpose fertiliser such as Growmore.

Allocate one Cucumber plant to one grow bag.

Ridge Cucumbers

Ridge Cucumbers can be planted out of doors. Any good garden soil is suitable, and the best position is in a coldframe or beneath a cloche. Keep them fed and watered and they will see you through until the first frosts. They're easier to grow than greenhouse Cucumbers because you don't have to train them.

'Masterpiece' is a good variety.

Bush Cucumbers

Last year I grew a Bush Cucumber. It was something I'd never grown before and is something like a Bush Marrow. It needed exactly the same soil and treatment as a Ridge Cucumber. The variety I grew was 'Bush Champion' and I was pleasantly surprised at how well it did!

Lettuce

In my young days there was no Lettuce variety which would 'head' in winter, yet head gardeners were still expected to provide Lettuce during this season. To get over the problem my uncle used to grow boxes of thinly sown Lettuce in the greenhouses. The result was really no more than leaves which he cut off with his knife, but they could be bunched up and sent to the cook, so served the purpose. Mr Stannard, under whom I worked when I was employed by Lord Harcourt, got his winter Lettuce by always having a batch or two grown in pots placed on shelves in the fruit houses. For cutting in early spring gardeners grew 'Stansted Park'. You could sow it *in situ* in the autumn, then thin it or plant it out at approximately 10–12in (25–30cm) intervals. It was hardy and formed quite an attractive head in March and April, but compared to today's Lettuce it was as tough as old boots – no wonder it has disappeared!

There are some wonderful varieties available today, something to suit everyone, including those who like Lettuce with red leaves. Here are a few suggestions: 'Little Gem', a small Cos, for cutting in April and May/June; 'Lobjoits Green Cos' which, sown in March/April, takes some beating for June cutting; 'Lake Nyah', a fine Lettuce for July and August, which is ready ten to twelve weeks after sowing; and 'Valdor', which, sown outdoors in September, is hardy enough to over-winter in favourable areas and will give you a first cutting at Easter.

SUCCESSIONAL SOWING

If early Lettuce is required the first sowing can be in October under cloches or in a coldframe. For this I recommend 'May Queen'. If the seedlings are in a frame they need airing during the winter on favourable days, but this isn't necessary if they're under a cloche. Most years this sowing will give you Lettuce by Easter. Sow the same variety again in February under glass and prick out into boxes. In March or April the seedlings will be ready to plant out in the garden.

The first outside sowing of Lettuce can be made from the end of March. Sow in ½in (1cm) drills, spacing the drills 6in (15cm) apart. For a continuous supply a sowing should be made every two to three weeks right through to late July/early August. In hot spells sow in a pan or pot and place somewhere cool, because the seed will not germinate in high temperatures.

GENERAL CULTIVATION

Lettuce will grow on any plot which has been manured within the last year or two. The plants need water in dry spells and should be kept clear of weeds. Sow little and often.

A GUIDE TO PLANTING DISTANCES
Small types such as 'Little Gem'
6in (15cm) between each plant; 12in (30cm) between rows to allow room to keep them clean and to cut them

Right: When planting, space out Lettuce plants according to the variety.

Butterheads

9in (23cm) between each plant; 12in (30cm) between rows

Modern curly types

12in (30cm) between each plant; 15in (38cm) between rows

Large Cos like 'Lobjoit'

12in (30cm) between each plant; 12in (30cm) between rows.

Right: Butterhead Lettuce. Below: Cos Lettuce.

Radishes

Growing Radishes was one of my jobs when I first started in the kitchen garden. It might have seemed a small crop but it was much in demand in those days. The first sowing was on a mild hotbed, the second in a coldframe, and from the first week of April a bit was sown out of doors every fortnight. The time-honoured variety was 'French Breakfast' and its white top still looks good in the salad bowl. 'Cherry Belle', which is round and a nice bright scarlet, is a much more modern and quick-maturing Radish. 'Saxa Short Top Forcer' is a useful variety for gardeners requiring a long season of production.

SOWING

'Saxa Short Top Forcer' can be sown under frames and cloches at the end of February. It will be ready in a month to six weeks, depending on the weather. I used to reckon on a month when I was planting it for taking to show at Chelsea in late May. From late March/early April sow Radishes on outside ground. There are two ways to do this: (a) Make drills ½–1in (1–2.5cm) deep. Sow thinly in drills, placing the seeds approximately ½in (1cm) apart. The drills may be V-shaped or wide-bottomed, like this:

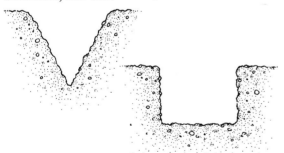

(b) Broadcast on the surface of finely raked soil. Water afterwards with a fine-rose can to settle the seeds.

Whichever method you choose, sow every two weeks on any piece of reasonably weed-free ground. Half a square yard would meet most families' requirements.

'French Breakfast' Radish.

GENERAL CULTIVATION

Radishes often need protecting from birds, especially house sparrows. In dry weather keep them watered, otherwise they quickly become hot-flavoured and woolly in the middle.

Winter Radishes

If you like to eat Radishes all year round, grow Winter Radishes. Sow them in July on early Potato ground or on any plot which has been cleared of an early crop. The usual method is to sow thinly in a V-shaped drill 1in (2.5cm) deep. Keep watered in dry weather and free from weeds.

I like the globe best: 'Round Black Spanish'. There's also a long oval called 'China Rose' which is quite good, being crisp and tender. 'Mino' is a long white, also crisp, which brightens up the winter salad bowl.

Winter Radishes are hardy but I believe in safety first, so I lift them in December and store them in sand or peat somewhere cool and dry. Besides, on winter days it's easier to take a few from a store than scratching around in snow and frost!

Chives

Chives is a perennial plant mostly grown in the herb garden. Its spear-like green leaves have an onion flavour, useful in early spring and autumn when it is difficult to produce young Spring Onions.

SOWING

If you intend the plants to stay in the same spot for a couple of years or more, they will need a bit of land which has previously been manured for another crop. In April to June make drills 12–15in (30–38cm) apart and sow the seed in small pinches 12in (30cm) apart. These in due course will make nice clumps. I reckon six to ten clumps would reach sufficient size in two years to supply the average household.

CULTIVATION

Keep free of weeds and watered in very dry spells. Gather your Chives by clearing one clump at a time: that way you will always have fresh, young, green leaves for use. If any of the clumps flower because you haven't cut enough or are not bothered with them, it's best to remove the dead flower heads before they seed otherwise they will seed all over the garden and become a nuisance.

During the winter you can cover the clumps with a cloche which will prolong their season of use up until Christmas. A cloche covering in the spring will give you early supplies.

Spring Onions

You can sow 'Ispikura' between February and April. It is an Onion which remains usable for a long time and is useful for flavouring mixed vegetable dishes. 'White Lisbon' is a good variety for later sowing.

SOWING

Most Spring Onions should be sown during March and April. For an early crop choose a

Above: Spring Onions. Below right: Lamb's Lettuce.

south-facing plot. The soil doesn't have to be rich. Make the drills ¾in (2cm) deep and 12in (30cm) apart. Sow the seed thinly.

CULTIVATION

Keep the Spring Onions hoed after they have germinated. Usually no water is required. Pull when young. If the ground is wet you can pull out the biggest Onions without trouble, but if it's dry it pays to clear a section of the row to save disturbing those you do not need for a while.

Mustard and Cress

Despite the fact that Mustard and Cress is easy to grow, it doesn't seem so popular as it used to be.

SOWING

A seed box is probably the easiest place to raise a crop. Fill it with a 1in (2.5cm) layer of soil or compost. Water well with a fine-rose can and allow to drain, then sow the seeds on the surface and very lightly press them into the soil. There's no need to cover them with soil because sufficient will stick to the young seedlings. Also covering the seeds with soil will lead to it getting into the young seedlings and making them gritty. Put a pane of glass and a sheet of newspaper over the seed box.

CULTIVATION
Remove the paper and glass when the seedlings are ½in (1cm) high, put the box in full light and keep the soil moist. When ready, cut with a knife.

MUSTARD AND CRESS CONES
I used to include Mustard and Cress among the vegetables I exhibited at London shows. On the day I left Chilton the Mustard and Cress would be barely sprouting, but it finished its growing well in the tent at Chelsea or in the Royal Horticultural Society Hall, depending on where the show was being held!

As well as growing it in standard seed boxes I always used to exhibit several large cones of it. These were made of wire and filled with nice green moss. The moss was made wet and then each cone was rolled over a piece of newspaper which had

Mustard and Cress seeds spread over it. When the cone had got a good covering of seed a sheet of newspaper was wrapped round it until the seed germinated. The paper was taken off and the cone stood in a light place and turned round twice a day to avoid one side growing faster than the other. The cones made a fine display at shows.

Dandelion, Endive and Chicory

See p. 107, Dandelion; p. 108, Chicory; p. 110, Endive.

Lamb's Lettuce (Corn Salad)

It's doubtful whether many people grow Lamb's Lettuce today or have even heard of it. It was grown a lot in pre-war days because at that time there weren't reliable winter Lettuces. In early autumn it was often cut off at ground level, but when winter came on it had to be picked over for the biggest leaves which had resprouted. The

garden underlings had this task and it was a miserable job, what with the leaves being so small and the mornings so cold. A few rows weren't cut down but were left for spring cutting.

SOWING

Sow in July to August in a sheltered border. Make the drills no deeper than 1in (2.5cm) and set the rows 12in (30cm) apart. Sow thinly.

CULTIVATION

Keep clean of weeds and water well if July and August are dry.

To give it protection in winter Lamb's Lettuce can be grown in a coldframe. To avoid 'damping' setting in, air the frame on all favourable days.

American Land Cress

American Land Cress is an oddity I grew for years here at Chilton. It covered the winter gap when ordinary Watercress wasn't available and was used in winter salads and for garnishing meat dishes. It was grown on a corner of land into which well-rotted farmyard manure had been worked. Prior to sowing the ground was trodden quite firm.

SOWING

I used to sow in June or July in shallow drills 9in (23cm) apart and then thin the young plants to 6in (15cm) apart.

CULTIVATION

Once it becomes established you have only to keep Land Cress in check, because after two years it takes over, like couch grass. It's even become a weed on some of the garden paths here.

In summer this Cress has a little credit to its

American Land Cress.

name because it bears a small yellow flower for weeks on end, but for eating gather it in winter and early spring by breaking off pieces about 3in (7.5cm) long. I've always thought American Land Cress hot and bitter, but the cook used it so of course it had to be maintained. It's surprising what oddities were grown in estate gardens; most of them had something seldom seen elsewhere.

Many other items are used in salad that are not really salad veg: for example, Carrots, Peas and Beet. See the appropriate chapters for information on these.

Roots·and·Tubers

Jerusalem Artichokes – Chinese Artichokes – Beetroot –
Carrots – Celeriac – Kohl Rabi – Parsnips –
Potatoes – Salsify and Scorzonera – Swedes – Turnips

CHAPTER FOUR
Roots and Tubers

Roots and tubers are what I call bulk vegetables. They were important in estate kitchen gardens. Big patches of them were grown because they formed the mainstay of meals for the house staff, the lodge keepers and the garden bothy boys.

Bulk veg had to be supplied all through the winter and, to make sure that there was always sufficient, main crops were grown and not touched until it was time to lift them for storing. Today we usually keep pulling from a patch and then store what's left.

Jerusalem Artichokes

The Jerusalem Artichoke is the only vegetable I know which can be neglected year after year; be grown in any odd corner; is tolerant of dry weather; doesn't mind frost; need never be completely lifted and can even be scratched out and almost eaten to death by pheasants but will *still*, without any human aid, reproduce itself and produce a crop if you require it. As well as all these virtues I've known the vegetable to have various uses. Spaced 9in (23cm) apart, the plants form a screen to protect other crops; planted in woodland they provide pheasants with cover, a dusting ground and feed (I've sold hundredweights for cover and feed); and lastly but most importantly, in my young days the cooks on private estates always demanded Jerusalem Artichokes in winter.

My mother, who did her fair share of cooking, preferred them to Potatoes, and my Uncle Fred, the head gardener, used to keep her supplied. Myself, I thought them awful smoky things.

Like all crops Jerusalem Artichokes respond to a little extra attention. Here at Chilton we always used to plant a few under good attention on the end of the Potato patch. There they received the same dressing of well-rotted farmyard manure as the Potatoes and also in late May or early June had a complete dressing – 3–4oz per sq yd (75–100g per sq m) – of a fertiliser like Growmore.

Above: A basket of Jerusalem Artichokes.
Facing page: Lifting early Potatoes.

We planted the ground up in February or March with good-sized tubers, placing them at 2–2½ft (60–75cm) intervals in rows 2–3ft (60cm–1m) apart. In dry spells they were watered and in August the tops were cut off, leaving each one with around 4–5ft (1.2–1.5m) of stem and foliage. Cutting the tops helped build up the tubers – not necessary, of course, if they'd been grown as a screen.

They made tremendous plants and gave an excellent crop which was lifted and put into store with the Potatoes. Storing them was a better system than having to dig out of doors for them on a cold, frosty morning. They had to be washed before being sent to the cook, although of course it used to be the scullery maid who had to deal with them; in fact, I nicknamed them 'Kitchen Maid's Delight' because they were just the opposite, being knobbly old things!

For anyone who's growing Artichokes in an odd corner I'd advise each spring that you cut down all the stems left from the previous year. Fork out any perennial weeds and, where you've had your fill, roughly level off the ground and throw on a little compost or farmyard manure. Treated this way they will go on yielding for years.

As to varieties, Jerusalem Artichoke tubers used to be available from seedsmen either white or rose-coloured; I've still got both. One rose-coloured one I have, called 'Spindle', is easier to clean than other sorts. However, the thing I've noticed about this vegetable is that it's difficult to get a true stock. You buy a variety and then after a year or two it breaks up and is no longer true.

Chinese Artichokes

Many large old kitchen gardens grew Chinese Artichokes. They helped swell the wide range of vegetables demanded by the cook. Chinese Artichokes have small, pearly-white tubers no bigger than a man's little finger – in fact, they're often smaller – and look like round, white nuts joined together. They're lovely fried in butter.

They should be planted in lightish soil, preferably in a border or in a corner where the spot can be remembered or marked so that they're not dug up accidentally. There's a danger of this happening as the foliage, growing to between 1½ and 2ft (45 and 60cm) high, looks like a straggly weed. Twice since I've been here at Chilton I've lost my stock to careless hoers and tractor drivers! An ideal spot for them is in a coldframe, especially if it contains a spent hotbed: they love the conditions.

CULTIVATION
Prepare for planting by raking or lightly forking a good dressing of well-rotted leaf soil into the bed. In March or April plant the tubers in broad-bottomed drills about 3in (7.5cm) deep and 12in (30cm) apart. Lay the tubers flat in the drills, leaving a space between each one of 4–6in (10–15cm). Cover with well-rotted leaf soil or old potting soil (I don't like peat as the results never seem the same). Keep very free from weeds at all times and well-watered in dry weather.

The Artichokes should be ready for use between November and January. They're hardy and those left in the ground usually start into growth again by late February or early March.

LIFTING
Take half a bucket of clean water with you when preparing to lift Chinese Artichokes for immediate use. Lift them carefully and go through the soil to find all the small tubers. As you discover a handful, drop them into the water. When you've dug sufficient, tip them out of the bucket on to a fine sieve and wash them off immediately with a jet of water from a hosepipe; they'll come up a lovely pearly white. If you don't do this but leave the soil to dry on them, they'll be impossible to clean because of their size and shape. This trick was something I learnt early as gardeners knew that clean Chinese Artichokes pleased the cook!

I still have a good stock of Chinese Artichokes and, to make their cultivation easy, keep them in a coldframe. We dig what we require, level over

Left: When you lift Chinese Artichokes drop them straight into a bucket of water.

the frame in spring and dress with old potting soil put through a fine riddle and 2–4oz (50–100g) bone meal. That, together with water and no weeds, is all they ask for.

Beetroot

Beetroot is in demand the year round. The earliest crop with us is from hotbeds in frames. The beds are prepared in February and the seed is sown late in the same month. It's sown thinly in drills which are 12in (30cm) apart and 1in (2.5cm) deep. The seedlings are thinned to 3in (7.5cm) apart when they are 1–1½in (2.5–4cm) high.

In frames the plants need to be kept well watered and, when the days warm up, freely aired. the plants' requirements are warmth, water and air, and if these are all met the beetroot is ready in late April and early May.

The following are recommended varieties: 'Boltardy' is a fine early Beet; 'Detroit' and 'Moneta' are good for summer and autumn; 'Cheltenham Greentop' (semi-long) stores well; 'Golden Ball Beet' adds golden yellow to a salad.

GROWING IN A WARM BORDER
In a warm border Beetroot can be sown under cloches in late February. Sow thinly in drills 1–1½in (2.5–4cm) deep, two rows to a Grower's Barn cloche (see p. 40). Thin as above. The Beetroot should be ready in late May.

GROWING IN OPEN GROUND
Late March/early April is the earliest time that seed can be sown out of doors. Sow in a good piece of ground which for the previous crop has received a dressing of farmyard manure.

This early outdoor crop seldom needs thinning; just pull the biggest roots first and carry on until the crop is cleared. We generally clear our first sowing out of doors by late June/early July.

Above: A trug of long Beetroot and 'Snowball' Turnips. Far right: 'Amsterdam Forcing' Carrots.

Lettuce or dwarf French Beans can follow in the same piece of ground.

MAIN-CROP BEET

Sow main-crop Beet by the end of May on ground well prepared and raked down to a fine tilth. Draw drills 12in (30cm) apart and approximately 1½in (4cm) deep. If conditions are dry, water the drills before sowing the seed thinly. Watering first aids germination and it's better than watering over sown seed. When the seedlings appear you should, of course, water overhead if the soil is dry. I seldom thin the resultant seedlings, but if good ball Beet are required either for the kitchen or exhibition, thin to at least 3–4in (7.5–10cm) distance between each plant.

Long Beet needs a good depth of soil, otherwise treatment is the same as above. Long Beet was universally grown and stored at one time but now it appears that it's grown only in certain areas. I have always preferred the cylindrical root to the long one because it gives lots of even-sized rings when its cooked and cut up.

Whichever type is grown, keep the plants clear of weeds. Be careful not to cut the roots with the hoe because they'll become unusable if you do.

If you like young, small Beet about the size of a golf ball, make a sowing in July. These are lovely served hot with pepper, salt and a knob of butter.

Lift Beet in late September and October and store in a frost-proof shed or in sand which is on the dry side rather than the wet side. Ordinary builders' sand will do but not sand grit. If you have a lot to store and are short of room, put some in a heap out of doors and cover with straw, then cover the straw with 9–10in (23–25cm) of soil.

Carrots

It's not always easy to get a good crop of Carrots. They need ground which was well manured for a previous crop and it seems to take several years, particularly if it's newly broken up maiden ground, to build up a plot that will grow a good crop. However well you prepare them, though, there are certain plots which will not produce Carrots as well as others. I know that on one piece of land I grew a really striking-looking lot, but when they were pulled they were all top and no bottom. That bit of land never did produce good Carrots!

I find Carrots interesting to grow because they can be produced over such a long season. Our first sowings here are under glass and done by 19 January, and as nice, small, young Carrots are as much in demand at Christmas as in May, our latest sowing is between 26 and 29 July.

As to varieties, 'Amsterdam Forcing' and 'Early Nantes' are good early Carrots. 'Autumn King' can still be obtained for winter use. It makes a fair root, as does 'The Favourite'.

PREPARING THE GROUND AND SOWING

The ground should be well dug, broken down to a fine tilth and firmly trodden before raking over. To sow Carrots, draw shallow drills 1–1½in (2.5–4cm) deep in lines 12in (30cm) apart. Sow the seed thinly and scuff the soil in over the drill with your feet in a steady, controlled shuffle. The way to do this is to move the soil first with the left foot, then with the right foot until you get to the end of the row. You can lightly tread over it afterwards. Then lightly rake over the whole bed, making sure that you pull the rake in the same direction that the drills run – that way no seed will be moved from the drills.

THINNING

Modern varieties, which are quick-maturing, small and cylindrical, have been developed to suit supermarkets. They're practically useless for storing but do have the virtue that they rarely need thinning – a blessing when I remember the hours I've spent on all fours thinning Carrots to 2–3in (5–7.5cm) apart.

CARROT FLY

The Carrot fly lays its eggs on the collar of young Carrots and the eggs hatch into grubs which tunnel into the roots. Carrot seed sown in late June often misses the fly, but for earlier sowings try the following effective treatment when the Carrots are a few inches high. Pour a gill (150ml) of paraffin into a bucket of sand, let the bucket stand overnight and then broadcast it over the Carrot bed.

CROP ROTATION ON CARROT GROUND

In my heyday I was able to grow Carrots year after year in a border which fronted a range of vineries. The earliest sowing was made under cloches and the crop was cleared by late June. Well-rotted compost or farmyard manure was rotavated in and a crop of Lettuce, dwarf French Beans or sometimes autumn Cauliflowers followed on after the carrots.

Then in October or November when the ground was cleared it was well dug, trodden and raked and a top dressing of old potting soil was put through a fine sieve and spread over it. This dressing was allowed to weather for a few weeks and then, in early December, the ground was covered with cloches. Carrot seed was sown under the cloches in any favourable spell after 20 January. This gave me Carrots to pull by late April/early May.

STORING

Main-crop Carrots are stored between late September and early October. I always store them in a shed in sand (see p. 204) and cover the heap with straw; I don't like peat for covering.

GROWING CARROTS FOR SHOWS

In our exhibiting days we used to get a crowbar with a parsnip-like tip on the end and with it bore holes in the ground up to 3ft (1m) deep. The top of the hole was about 4–5in (10–13cm) across. Each hole was filled up with finely sieved old potting soil which had been mixed with leaf soil and sand. It took two men to fill the holes: one gently poured the compost in while the other, with the aid of a long stick, made sure that there were no pockets of air. Two or three seeds were sown in each hole and thinned out when the first rough leaf appeared. The strongest plant was left in each hole.

Two other ways of growing Carrots for exhibition are as follows:

(a) Fill a deep wooden frame with the same compost as above. Lightly firm it and sow two or three seeds approximately every 9 sq in (58 sq cm). Thin out to the strongest plant in each 9 sq in (58 sq cm).

(b) Break up a piece of ground the size of the base of a large drainpipe and stand the pipe vertically on top. Fill with the same compost as described in (a) above. How many seeds you sow in the top of the pipe depends on its diameter: if this is 12in (30cm), sow ten or a dozen.

Celeriac

Celeriac is a very useful root vegetable for winter use. It is ideal cooked in soups and stews, or eaten raw, either grated with cheese or like the bottom end of a stick of celery. I think it should be grown much more widely than one sees it, although it never was grown in great quantities anywhere when I was a young gardener. We grew it here at Chilton for a few years on a fairly large scale because it was needed for soups.

'Tellus' is a good variety.

Celeriac.

SOWING UNDER GLASS

Sow from February to early March in a temperature of 60°F (15.5°C). Depending on how many plants you require, put compost into a pot or seed box and water it well before sowing. Sow thinly and gently press the seed into the compost surface. Perhaps an easier method for beginners is to cover the seed very lightly. Either place the container in a temperature-controlled propagator at 60°F (15.5°C) or stand it on a bench in a heated greenhouse and cover it with a pane of glass. Turn the glass each morning to prevent condensation falling on the seed. Remove it when seedlings appear and place their container in a light position.

As soon as they've developed good seed leaves, prick off into a standard seed tray, forty to a tray; if the number you have is small, place each single seedling in a 3in (7.5cm) pot. The best compost to prick them off into is old potting soil put through a ½in (1cm) sieve. To each bucketful of soil add one-third of a bucketful of leaf soil or peat, a little grit and a handful of bone meal and mix well.

After pricking off, water in and keep at 60°F (15.5°C) until the first rough leaf forms. At this stage transfer the plants to an unheated greenhouse or coldframe and take care to give them air freely on warm days. If they're in a coldframe, by late May the lights can be left off at night.

In early June prepare to plant out on to a piece of ground which has been heavily dressed with manure or compost, two water-retaining materials. The water requirement of Celeriac, like Celery, is great. Tread the soil firm and plant 15in (38cm) apart either way. I find that this distance gives good results and allows ample room for weed control. Keep clean of weeds, well watered and fed; liquid animal manure is a good feed for Celeriac. Spray with soot water (see p. 21) to ward off leaf miner, which can be troublesome.

From mid-July I like to pull off the bottom leaves regularly. This keeps a neat 'stand' of foliage on top and also helps the formation of the bulb.

Undefoliated plant

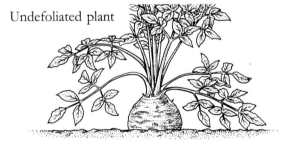

I like to keep mine like this

Lift from mid- to late October and store in a frost-proof shed in dry sand (see p. 204).

Kohl Rabi

During the Second World War I had German prisoners-of-war working under me both in the gardens at Nuneham Park, Oxford, and also when I came to Chilton. In each case, when the time came for them to be sent home, the one item they desperately wanted to take with them was Kohl Rabi seed! They obviously loved this vegetable, but I've always felt it has a strong taste, something between that of a Cabbage and that of a Turnip. I think it's best when young and small, certainly no larger than a golf ball. In fact, when I had to take it to cooks in mansion kitchens they wanted it even smaller than that. I found a good use for it which doesn't involve its taste at all and that was as part of the Gold Medal exhibits of vegetables I used to stage at Royal Horticultural Society shows. Kohl Rabi's colour and shape, and the fact that it was something different, always appealed to the public.

Kohl Rabi is fine if you're seeking a change of vegetable – and you may like the flavour – but if you've only a small garden I'd recommend you

grow instead 'Early Milan' or 'Golden Ball' Turnip. 'Golden Ball' has the bonus that it stores well. Another useful variety of Turnip to try would be 'Green Top Stone' because you can get some spring greens from it. See also p. 68.

I have grown two sorts of Kohl Rabi: 'Purple Vienna' and 'Green Vienna'. I prefer the latter.

CULTIVATION

Any piece of ground which will grow Turnips is suitable for Kohl Rabi. Sow as thinly as possible in open ground from April to mid-July in shallow drills 12in (30cm) apart. Hoe as soon as the seedlings can be seen. Thin early (that is, as soon as the first rough leaf develops) to approximately 4–5in (10–13cm) between each plant. At this stage, if pigeons or pheasants are likely to be a problem, protect the young plants: it's my experience that these particular birds love Kohl Rabi more than Turnips! Keep free of weeds and use when young, because if Kohl Rabi gets to tennis-ball size it's good only for animal feed and, unlike a good autumn Turnip, it can't be stored.

Hamburg Parsley

See p. 135.

Parsnips

Parsnips are a truly lovely vegetable for eating during the winter months. At one time they were grown on a large scale by country folk. I especially remember the big bed of Parsnips my grandfather used to grow, but never was one allowed to be eaten from that bed until he'd brewed his annual quota of Parsnip wine. Jolly good it was too. I must admit that I probably thought the wine better than the cooked vegetable when I was younger, but bothy life taught me to eat what was put in front of me and today I wouldn't feel that winter was

Left: Kohl Rabi, Purple and White Vienna.
Right: 'Hollow Crown' Parsnips.

winter without Parsnips. I'd recommend the varieties 'Tender and True' and 'Improved Hollow Crown'. 'White Gem' is a good short-rooted cultivar.

CULTIVATION

The ground intended for Parsnips should ideally be a well-cultivated plot which was manured for the previous year's crop. It should be deeply dug before Christmas if possible and allowed to winter.

Sowing can take place at any time between late February and April. In old kitchen gardens Parsnip seed used to be one of the first sown, often in February, but I have sown in April and had a good crop. Choose a favourable day for sowing so that the ground can be raked down to a fine tilth and firmly trod without it sticking to you boots. Also try to make it a day when there's very little wind or breeze, because the seed is so light it easily blows away. I usually dress the ground before sowing with 3–4oz per sq yd (75–100g per sq m) of potash. This seems to help prevent canker,

although nowadays Parsnip canker isn't the problem it was when I was young.

Draw drills approximately 1in (2.5cm) deep and 15in (38cm) apart (although 12in (30cm) is wide enough for small-rooted varieties or for April sowings. Parsnip seed is flat and not easy to sow by hand, but pains should be taken to sow it as continuously and thinly as possible. Scuffle in the seed with your feet, then lightly draw a rake over the ground, drawing in the same direction as the drills.

Seed can take a month or more to germinate, but as soon as possible after the seedlings show up get to work with your hoe to stop weeds overtaking what will be, for a few weeks, slow-growing young plants. Little else remains to be done apart from thinning the seedlings to 4–5in (10–13cm) apart. Keep hoed until the foliage covers the ground.

Parsnips can be left in the ground all winter and dug as required; in fact, their flavour seems to be improved if you do this. Of course, in the gardens of private estates we always lifted some and put them in the root store in case a heavy frost or fall of snow made it impossible to dig when the cook asked for Parsnips. That would have been terrible!

Potatoes

Where I was brought up, what was known as Ware Potatoes (that is, for eating and not for seed) were readily obtainable in greengrocers or from the estate farms, but most private gardens big or small still grew them on a large scale. I've even known some cottagers produce so many that they had to make a storage clamp for them in the garden.

BUYING SEED
Although it's all right to save a few Potatoes for seed it doesn't always work out that they're free from disease, particularly if the season has been a wet one. I think it pays to buy seed Potatoes which have been grown under controlled conditions in Scotland or Ireland, and you can easily get these

from a garden centre. You'll also find that bought-in seed Potatoes, having been grown on soil in a different part of the country, are more vigorous than home-grown and saved ones.

Potato varieties worth considering are:
Earlies
'Suttons Foremost', 'Pentland Javelin', 'Arran Pilot' (a good oldie still worth growing).
Lates
'King Edward', Désirée' (keeps a long time), 'Golden Wonder'.

STORING SEED
A Potato has a definite 'eye' end and a definite stalk end. Lay the seed Potatoes in a box, each Potato with its eye end uppermost. You mustn't place the box anywhere warm or dark because that will encourage poor, weak shoots on the tubers. Instead put it in a dry, airy shed, greenhouse or old coldframe. That way you'll get nice, strong shoots.

A basket of Arran Pilot Potatoes.

64

GROWING A VERY EARLY CROP

A few early Potatoes can always be grown in a coldframe, where planting can take place in late January/early February. If they make good headway while frosts continue, be prepared to cover them to protect them on cold nights. From April onwards air freely on warm days, closing up at nights. Water from time to time or leave the lights off on rainy days in April, but remember to close at night. You should be able to dig your first Potatoes in early May.

USUAL PLANTING TIMES

Earlies can be planted in sheltered spots in late March/early April; mid-season cultivars by mid- to late April; and maincrops, depending on the area where you live, in late April/early May. I don't believe in planting Potatoes too early as I think that if they get caught by frost they never really recover and don't give such a good crop as a frost-free patch.

PREPARING THE GROUND

Potatoes will grow in a wide range of soil types but the land will reward you with a good crop if it's well prepared before planting. The preparation shouldn't be skimped. Dig or fork to the full depth of your spade or fork and work in generous amounts of well-rotted farmyard manure or your own compost. Try to do this before Christmas, especially if you're going to plant mid-season cultivars. In addition to well-manured soil, maincrop Potatoes appreciate a dressing of 3.2.1 fertiliser (see p. 21) at the rate of 2–4oz per sq yd (50–100g per sq m); or, if you're going to sprinkle it along a trench, then use about 1½lb (750g) per 30yd (27m) run.

If maincrop Potatoes are to follow on in a piece of ground which has spent brassicas on it, such as Kale, Sprouts or January Cabbage, these can be cleared off during February and early March. This ground still needs compo or farmyard manure and must be well dug as Potatoes like loose soil.

DIGGING AND PLANTING IN ONE

If you want to do two jobs in one, you can dig the ground and plant Potatoes in it at the same time. This was a practice old cottagers had down to a fine art. Their traditional Potato-planting day was Good Friday because that was a holiday (as was Ascension Day) if you worked on the Selborne estate – the Selborne family was religious.

Dig a trench, putting manure in it and digging it in in the usual way. Then go back to the beginning of the trench, make a mark on its face with your spade and pull some soil back down into it to form a ledge beneath the mark. Press your Potato into the mark.

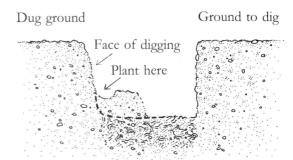

Dug ground   Ground to dig

Face of digging
Plant here

Continue to the end of the row, placing early or mid-season Potatoes at 12in (30cm) intervals, or maincrop ones at 15in (38cm) intervals. Then get two sticks and mark on each 2ft (60cm) – the distance required between rows of early or mid-season Potatoes – or 2½ft (75cm) – the distance needed between rows of maincrop Potatoes and attach a line to the sticks. Lay the sticks on the ground, one at either end of the row, and measure back 2 or 2½ft (60 or 75cm), as appropriate, on the undug ground. Dig back to this line and plant again in the face of your digging. Continue in this way until your planting is finished.

PLANTING IN PREVIOUSLY DUG GROUND

If you're planting Potatoes in ground which has been previously dug, you can plant with a Potato dibber or take out a hole with a largish trowel.

Either way each Potato should be covered with 4–5in (10–13cm) of soil. One other method is to use a triangle hoe to draw drills 4–5in (10–13cm) deep.

GENERAL CULTIVATION

All Potato crops require regular hoeing in the early stages and you certainly need clean land before you earth them up. Earth-up when the crop is 8–9in (20–23cm) high, simply drawing the soil on either side of the row to form a ridge. This extra topping of soil helps to block the light and prevents the top ends of the tubers turning green, something which often happens if the ground is left flat. Earthing-up is extra work but well worth the effort.

After earthing-up spray with a copper or Bordeaux mixture using a fine-rose watering can. This will help to ward off Potato blight, a disease which rots the haulm and gets into the tubers.

FOLLOW-ON CROPS

Land cleared of early Potatoes makes excellent ground for winter greens, January Cabbage, Savoys and late Leeks.

Mid-season Potato ground is good for Lettuce, Radish and the sowing of spring Cabbage seed.

STORING MAINCROP POTATOES

Don't lift maincrop Potatoes until the haulms have died down. Dig up carefully, put to one side damaged and diseased tubers and leave the good ones for an hour to dry off before storing. Store them in a frost-proof shed.

Salsify (Salsafy) and Scorzonera

Few people grow either Salsify or Scorzonera and even fewer know what they are, which is a pity because both are simple to cultivate.

Salsify has a long, tapering, white root. It's sometimes called 'vegetable oyster' because it's supposed to taste like the shellfish. When scraped and cut up it should be put straight away into water with added lemon juice or vinegar to stop it discolouring. It can be boiled and served with melted butter or white sauce.

Scorzonera came originally from Spain. It's a carrot-shaped root, black outside and white inside. You prepare and cook it in the same way as Salsify. Some old cookery and gardening books state that you can even use its leaves in a salad.

Ground which grows Parsnips will suit both Salsify and Scorzonera. Sow seed from April to May. Prepare the ground in the usual way, raking down and treading firm. Draw drills 1–1½in (2.5–4cm) deep, a minimum of 12in (30cm) and a maximum of 15in (38cm) apart. Cover the seed carefully and rake nicely, going in the direction of the drills.

Above: Scorzonera. Right: Salsify.

The germinating seedlings are very thin and weak-looking, something like grass, so it's important to hoe as soon as possible otherwise the weeds will smother them and it'll be an awful job to find them. When the seedlings are 3–4in (7.5–10cm) high they should be thinned to 3–4in (7.5–10cm) apart and kept clean of weeds. Pests usually leave these vegetables alone.

Both Salsify and Scorzonera are best left in the ground in the winter and lifted as required. However, if really bad weather threatens, lift a few and put them in sand in a shed – nothing's more tiresome than to have a vegetable you can't get at because it's frost- or snow-bound!

Swedes

I never was convinced that Swedes have a place in the garden. The conditions are too soft for them. A tougher life in the field produces excellent ones, especially if the land is stony. Acres and acres of Swedes were grown in my home area in the

Swede 'Marian'.

1920s and 1930s. They were intended for cow and sheep feed, but many found their way into the cooking pots of local cottagers. Two useful varieties of Swede are 'Acme Purple' and 'Marian'.

Swedes need sowing in June on firm ground in shallow drills in the same way as Turnips, but place the drills 15–18in (38–45cm) apart. Thin the seedlings out to 8in (20cm) apart. Swedes store better than Turnips.

Turnips

Turnips are good food, cooked on their own or in a stew. In the 1930s young Turnips the size of a golf ball were grown in succession, but these days the demand isn't so great.

Turnips are easy and undemanding to grow. They'll flourish on any piece of land which has had a dressing of manure in the last two years. The varieties 'Milan' and 'Purple Top Milan' make worthwhile crops in a coldframe or under cloches if sown in early March. From the end of March these two can be sown in open ground successionally until July.

We used to sow 'Golden Ball', a good Turnip which stores well, in late May/early June. 'Green Top' was sown in July so that it gave a supply of spring greens. The greens are a bit on the strong side but they used to be very popular served with boiled pork, particularly among country folk who kept a pig for eating. 'Early Snowball' is a good white variety that produces a root the size of a tennis ball.

SOWING

The ground should be raked down to a fine tilth and trodden firm. Draw drills 1in (2.5cm) deep and 12in (30cm) apart. Sow the seed very thinly. It germinates freely so will need thinning to 4in (10cm) apart as soon as possible.

The early crop generally misses the root fly. Try a few 'Milan' plants as an early crop and use them when quite small. In dry weather Turnips aren't easy to produce, so keep them watered.

Brassicas

Brussels Sprouts – Broccoli – Cabbages – Savoys –
Coleworts – Couve Tronchuda – Calabrese –
Cauliflowers – Kales

CHAPTER FIVE
Brassicas

When I came to Chilton in 1947 the gardens grew an acre of various brassicas. These were both for home consumption and for selling. I sold thousands of plants, my best customers being the farming families and their workers who came in wet spells when they couldn't get on with hay-making. They wanted Sprouts, Curly Kale, Sprouting Broccoli, good hardy winter Cabbage and a few Savoys. Of course, the strains I was growing and selling were much improved on the picture-packet seeds the locals could purchase in those days. They quickly understood this and by coming to me saved themselves the bother of raising their own as well as enjoying a better-quality product at the end of the day.

Brassicas have taken giant strides in quality in recent years. The seed breeders have really done a good job on them. However, to suit commercial growers who like a quick turn-round – that is, a crop with every plant in it ready simultaneously so that it can be harvested all at once – a lot of modern brassicas, particularly Cabbages and Cauliflowers, are bred to make a head more or less at the same time. To avoid this happening in your own garden it's best to choose a variety which will crop variably, and hang the crop over a time.

All brassicas need more or less the same type of ground, protection and raising. Garden centres sell insecticides to help with pest control. The most interesting factor to me in growing brassicas is the importance of practising different sowing dates to keep up a succession.

Brussels Sprouts

EARLY CROPS
There are two ways of growing early Sprouts. The first is to sow in the autumn and over-winter in a seed bed. Plant out in March (especially the Bedford cultivars) for cropping in October.

Above: Brussels Sprouts.
Facing page: Ornamental Kale, more used by flower arrangers than cooks but a talking point in any vegetable garden.

The second method is to sow in a coldframe in late February/early March. Sow thinly in drills approximately 9in (23cm) apart. Keep the frame closed until germination takes place, then give air freely. By mid-April the lights can be taken off. Plant out at the end of April approximately 20in (50cm) apart. The crop should be ready in late October, although some modern F1 hybrids can turn in a bit earlier. For early Sprouts I'd choose 'Fillbasket' or 'Roodnerf – Early Button'. 'Ashwell's Strain' will provide a long picking season. Other general good varieties are 'United'; 'Peer Gynt'; 'Wigeon' or any of the 'Bedford' strain.

MAIN SOWING
Preparation of ground

The procedure described below applies to the preparation of ground for main sowings of all brassicas.

The main sowing of Brussels Sprouts can take place in open ground from mid-March to mid-April, depending on the area and the weather. I feel that it's never any use being too rigid with sowing dates for the chosen ones can be wet or the ground unworkable through frost, so it's better to wait until a favourable spell.

The sowing site should be open. Any land that has not been manured for one or two years does well as ground which is too strong at seedling stage produces a rank, lanky plant which is much too soft. The site should be raked down to a fine tilth and drills drawn out approximately 12in (30cm) apart (a flat bottom to the drill produces the best plants). Sow the seed thinly and cover in with the back of a rake or your feet, than lightly rake over the bed for appearance's sake, taking care to pull the rake in the same direction as the rows. Label each row so that you can easily identify the seedlings when the time comes to plant them out – I know that many people find it difficult to tell a Cabbage from a Kale or a Cauliflower from a Sprout in the early stages.

If birds are a problem, protect with a net. Hoe as soon as the rows show a clear drill of seedlings.

Keep hoed and water if it's dry in early May. The plants will be ready for planting out in June.

Planting out
Plant Sprouts out on to land which was manured the previous year. Set out at not less than 2ft (60cm) either way. Vigorous varieties will need 2½ft (75cm) either way, although small gardens can't afford to be this generous so, if yours falls into this category, stick to small, compact cultivars. Plant firmly. Between the wider spacings Lettuce, Radish and early Turnips can be grown as an intercrop (see p. 32).

Broccoli

Sow from mid-March to mid-April. Prepare the sowing bed as instructed for Brussels Sprouts (see left). Plants will be ready for planting out in June. Sprouting Broccoli needs a good, firm piece of land manured for a previous crop. Plant out 2ft (60cm) either way.

'Early White' and 'Early Purple Sprouting' will be ready for gathering in March/April, 'Late White' and 'Late Purple Sprouting' about a fortnight later.

White Sprouting Broccoli.

Green Broccoli

See under 'Calabrese', p. 74.

Cabbages

Getting early Cabbage is a lot simpler nowadays than it used to be. With the modern F1 hybrids like 'Hispi' you can sow in January, grow on, harden off and be cutting by the middle of May. Years ago you sowed spring Cabbage, perhaps an old variety like 'Flower of Spring', during July and August, protected it, planted it out, kept it clean and safe from pests such as pigeons and pheasants and it was ready for cutting about Whitsun weekend. However, I've known many cottagers who never cut their spring Cabbage until August, by which time it was blue, tough as old leather and as full of caterpillars as hell is of devils!

Having said that, I always think it advisable for a gardener to grow a few of the older varieties of most vegetables. The reason for this is that modern hybrids are bred to be ready for cutting or picking at a certain time but older varieties (like 'Flower of Spring' Cabbage) often give you the option of letting them stay put for several weeks until you need them.

Spring Cabbage (Old Sort)

In the gardens where I've worked spring Cabbage was always the earliest brassica sowing. We used to sow it on 12 August, usually in short rows in a border, in drills 12in (30cm) apart. To avoid dog-legged seedlings which made final plants difficult, the drills were drawn with a flat bottom. The seedlings were kept free of weeds and were ready for planting out in the first week in September, usually into an onion patch which had been cleared. Most varieties of spring Cabbage need only 12 × 12in (30 × 30cm) spacing, but I always felt that 'Flower of Spring' needed 15 × 15 (38 × 38cm).

GENERAL CULTIVATION

Spring Cabbage planted in September often needs one or two hoeings before winter sets in: this stops the weeds outgrowing the plants in March. As soon as possible in March hoe again, and in late March/early April top dress with 2oz per sq yd (50g per sq m) of nitrate of soda.

Spoil yourself and cut some of your spring Cabbages before they have formed a hard head – there's really no other brassica like them!

When the bed is cleared, usually by mid- to late June, it can be used for Lettuce, Beet or Carrots.

MODERN EARLY CABBAGES

Today modern cultivars like 'Hispi' and 'Hornspi' have made the older style of spring Cabbage almost redundant. You can sow these modern early Cabbages under glass, a pinch of seed to a 5in (13cm) pot in January/early February. Prick them off into standard seed trays, plant in a coldframe, under cloches or polythene tunnels and be clear of them by late May. Any intended for planting out of doors should first be stood out so that they can acclimatise, then planted in March, 1½ft (45cm) apart. These should head in June.

Summer Cabbage

Early ball-headed varieties of summer Cabbage like 'Derby Day' can be sown in a coldframe in late February/early March in the same way as Brussels Sprouts (see p. 72). Plant out in mid-May, allowing 14in (35cm) and they should be ready for cutting in June.

Winter Cabbage

For winter Cabbage prepare the ground and sow as for a main sowing of Brussels Sprouts (see p. 72). Plant out in June into land which has received some compost in the spring. Plant firmly 20in (50cm) apart in rows 2ft (60cm) apart. They will be ready for cutting throughout the winter.

Left to right: Savoy Cabbages, Couve Tronchuda, Calabrese and early summer Cauliflower.

Savoys

Treat Savoys in the same way as winter Cabbage (see p. 73).

Coleworts

I'm including Coleworts for old time's sake because, although I doubt whether you'd find any seed, they deserve a mention. Known to some as 'Collards', these were much sought after by cooks during the autumn for serving to the mansion dining room. They were small, compact Cabbages. The variety I used to grow when I was at Stansted Park was very handsome: dark-coloured with leaves forming a pattern and an unmistakable flattish head.

Couve Tronchuda

Also known as the Portuguese Cabbage, this is an unusual old brassica that few have heard of today. My head gardener uncle, Fred Norris, grew it at Blackmoor and I've grown it from time to time either for show work or for the kitchen. It looks like a pale-leaved Cabbage and has two unusual attributes: when it's cooked it's not supposed to

smell cabbagy; and, while the leaves can be cooked like those of ordinary Cabbage, the large, white ribs in them can be cut out, boiled and served separately as a mock form of Seakale. You can get Couve Tronchuda seed from Chiltern Seeds, Bortree Stile, Ulverston, Cumbria LA12 7PB.

CULTIVATION

Sow a pinch when you sow the main brassica bed. Plant out in June, the rows 2ft (60cm) apart with the plants spaced 1½ft (45cm) apart in the rows. They should be ready for cutting in September/October.

Calabrese

Calabrese is a modern brassica which is very popular today but very expensive to grow. I feel that it's best left to the market growers. However, if you're prepared to have a go, sow it where you intend it to grow, because box-sown and -grown seedlings can be temperamental: the least little check causes them to 'head in', that is, make a tiny head, before they've made a plant. When this happens the crop is wasted. Drop a few seeds at 1½ft (45cm) intervals into a drill where you intend them to grow and thin to one seedling per station.

Cauliflowers

EARLIEST SOWING

Cauliflowers can be sown on a spent hotbed in a coldframe in late February/early March (follow the procedure described on p. 72 for sowing Brussels Sprouts in a coldframe). Plant out in early May, the rows 2ft (60cm) apart and the plants 20in (50cm) apart in the rows. They should be ready for cutting in July/August.

Early Summer Cauliflowers

Sow under glass about 10–20 October. This is a very important sowing, because if the resultant plants are put into different places in the garden you can get a good succession of heads over several weeks, all from this one sowing.

When the seedlings are large enough to handle, prick off into 3 or 3½in (7.5 or 9cm) pots and keep in cold glass throughout the winter. When there's no frost make sure that the pots aren't too dry, but during bad frosty periods don't water. Give air in all mild spells.

The plants should be ready for planting out in March in coldframes, under cloches, in polythene tunnels or in a cold greenhouse. Any left over can be planted in favourable places out of doors in late March/early April. In my young days a really early crop was got by putting two plants into a 10in (25cm) pot and placing it in a mild glasshouse. The earliest cutting I make now is about the third week in April from Cauliflowers in a coldframe.

If you're growing Cauliflowers under glass they must have adequate water supplies at all times. They must also never be allowed to get too warm and stuffy, so pay very careful attention to airing. If you're growing them under cloches gradually move the cloches wider and wider apart until, by approximately the second week in May (weather permitting), they can be taken off altogether.

SOWING IN SITU

One other way of growing Cauliflowers is to sow them very thinly in early April in a good bit of land. Don't thin them, but keep them clean and watered and they will head where they're sown. Of course, you'll get only small heads, but they're quite good and useful. Varieties like 'All The Year Round' and 'Early London' suit this method.

Autumn Cauliflowers

Sow around 14 May in the usual manner (see the method for main sowings of Brussels Sprouts on p. 72).

Keep clear of weeds, and water if dry. The plants should be ready for planting out in late June, 2 × 2ft (60 × 60cm). Many gardeners like to put them on empty Strawberry or Potato grounds. They will head from September onwards. Today there are varieties that didn't exist before the Second World War which are especially good for this crop.

Winter Cauliflowers

Formerly known as spring-heading Broccoli, winter Cauliflowers should be sown in late May/early June and planted out 2 × 2ft (60 × 60cm). I find that an old, finished Strawberry bed suits this crop.

Breeders have given us some excellent strains of winter Cauliflower to choose from, a far cry from the old 'May Queen' variety, but care has to be taken in growing this crop because frost damage can be great and a Cauliflower which has lost its head to frost doesn't compensate by producing green shoots like Kale or Cabbage stumps. I don't think winter Cauliflower is worth the risk in a small garden; it's better to be satisfied with early summer Cauliflowers from an autumn sowing and autumn Cauliflowers from a May sowing.

STORING

When they're ready for cutting, cauliflowers can be kept for several days. Instead of cutting them, you lift them by the roots. Tie two or three together and hang them upside down in a cool place. No other brassica keeps many days once it's cut, apart from the 'January King' type of winter Cabbage.

Kales

The curly Kales, 'Tall Scotch' and 'Dwarf Scotch' are the quality varieties, whose foliage is nice and sweet like Brussels Sprout greens. It's best to grow 'Dwarf Scotch' in small gardens. If you're looking for hardiness it's difficult to beat 'Cottager's Kale' and old 'Ragged Jack': with them you're assured of a crop of greens in March and April.

Sow Kale mid-March to mid-April, depending on the area and the weather. For preparation of the seed bed and sowing follow the method described for main sowings of Brussels Sprouts on p. 72. The plants will be ready for planting out in June. Don't plant them on land which is too strong or they'll become soft and unable to withstand a lot of hard frost. Kales need a planting distance of approximately 2ft (60cm) each way.

Young curly Kale.

Spinach · Florence · Fennel and · Globe · Artichokes

*Roundleaf or Prickly Spinach – Perpetual or Winter Spinach –
New Zealand Spinach – Seakale Beet – Rhubarb Chard –
Good King Henry – Florence Fennel – Globe Artichokes*

CHAPTER SIX

Spinach, Florence Fennel and Globe Artichokes

Spinach

Spinach, especially the Perpetual kind, must have been grown in 90 per cent of old estate gardens. It was a terrible job gathering it on a cold, wet or frosty morning, particularly at the end of winter when the rows had been heavily picked and there were only small leaves left. The cook always wanted a lot and it used to take ages to get enough. Thinking back, it was those cold, miserable hours which almost put me off eating Spinach.

Roundleaf or Prickly Spinach

Roundleaf or Prickly Spinach can be sown from March until August. In March it's the first of the Spinaches to be sown. I used to sow a row as an intercrop between each row of Peas or Brussels Sprouts.

Draw drills 1–1½in (2.5–4cm) deep and in these sow the seed thinly, which will help if you haven't got time to thin the seedlings. If you do have time, thin them to 6in (15cm) apart. At 9–10in (23–25cm) high, Spinach is ready for cutting. A second cut is possible but it's often better to make a successional sowing. I used to do this on ground cleared of early Potatoes and Runner Beans or anywhere a gap presented itself.

If the ground is good and the plants are well looked after – which includes being kept watered in dry weather – they'll continue producing a good supply of dark green, succulent leaves.

Perpetual or Winter Spinach

Sow Perpetual or Winter Spinach between March and July. It needs good land and a good sowing surface. Draw drills 18–20in (45–50cm) apart and 1–1½in (2.5–4cm) deep and sow the seed thinly.

Above: Perpetual Spinach. Facing page: Rhubarb Chard, an ornamental addition to the vegetable border.

Hoe as soon as the seedlings appear and water if conditions become dry and hot in June and July. Liquid farmyard manure is excellent for Perpetual Spinach. If you want to keep up supplies, make another sowing in July. Cleared Potato ground is an ideal spot for this later sowing, which should give you a good-sized leaf a long way into winter.

The crop needs to be kept clear of weeds because it's a nuisance on a frosty winter morning gathering Spinach which is smothered with weeds, and it certainly doesn't please the cook if these are inadvertently picked too! In the spring, as soon as it shows signs of new life, give the crop a booster with a complete fertiliser at the rate of 3–4oz per sq yd (75–100g per sq m) of bed. However, as the days lengthen and the temperature warms up it will quickly run to seed. It's finished as a crop when this happens, so dig it in or dig it up and put it on the compost heap.

New Zealand Spinach

If your area is really hot and dry, New Zealand Spinach will provide you an excellent crop in late July, August and September. The first real frost will kill it, however.

I always sow under glass in late April or early May, one or two seeds to a 3 or 3½in (7.5 or 9cm) pot filled with ordinary sowing compost. Push the seed into the surface, water, then stand in a temperature of 55–60°F (12.7–15.5°C). When the seedlings are 1–2in (2.5–5cm) high, put the pots into a light, airy position and gradually harden off ready for planting out in late May/early June, depending on the frost record of your area.

New Zealand Spinach appreciates a good, well-manured piece of land, trodden down and raked level before planting. Plant 1 yd (1m) apart either way. Keep clear of weeds. About a month after planting it will benefit from an application of 2–3oz per sq yd (50–75g per sq m) of complete fertiliser.

From late June onwards you should be able to enjoy masses of nice, dark green, very succulent

tips. Pick off the complete shoot, about 3in (7.5cm) in length. The shoot and leaf should be cooked together. This is a jolly good Spinach and a wonderful stand-by in a dry season.

Seakale Beet (Swiss Chard)

Seakale Beet is a dual-purpose Spinach, for in addition to the large leaf which is cooked like ordinary Spinach, the fine white stems beneath the leaf can also be eaten. The plant will withstand the winter and produce a good, early pick of Spinach leaves in March and April. I think it's very useful and should be grown more than it is. It also makes a fine plant in an exhibition of vegetables.

Sow in June on good land which has had farmyard manure dug into it. Prepare for sowing by treading the ground and raking to provide a

Above: Seakale Beet. Facing page: New Zealand Spinach.

tilth. Draw drills 1–2in (2.5–5cm) deep and 1½ft (45cm) apart. Try to make a bed of several rows together rather than a long single row: this will help to block out the light and whiten the stems. Sow the seed thinly and, to get good plants, thin to 4in (10cm) apart.

The white stems are particularly good to eat in August and September. Break off the whole stem at the base and cut into 3–4in (7.5–10cm) lengths. These can be boiled and served with butter or white sauce. Strip the green from the mid rib of the leaf with your finger and thumb and cook this like ordinary Spinach.

In March an application of 2–3oz per sq yd (50–75g per sq m) of complete fertiliser helps quickly to produce good leaves for eating.

Rhubarb Chard

Rhubarb Chard has thick, red stems below its leaf. The French and Swiss eat it, but I think it's best used as ornamentation in the kitchen garden or even in the flower borders. It makes a good exhibition vegetable too, either at a vegetable show or in floral art. It's also a showy vegetable to have if you've entered your garden in a competition and, last but not least, it looks attractive in harvest festival decorations.

Good King Henry

The Latin name for Good King Henry is *Chenopodium bonus-henricus* (*Chenopodium* is based on Latin words meaning goose and foot, the plant's leaf being shaped like a goose's foot). I've also known it by a simpler name: Farmyard Spinach. In the past many kitchen gardens afforded it a corner of its own where it looked after itself for years, but in all the gardens where I've worked I've never actually known it to be taken to the house. However, this is not to say that the plant doesn't have its uses, for it can be cooked and eaten like Spinach, put raw into the salad bowl or the young shoots blanched as a substitute for Asparagus.

My stock of Good King Henry came from a neglected patch which was taking over a flower border and a corner of the kitchen garden at Chilton. I grow it in a short, neat row which for the past four years has looked after itself. The leaves are dark green and juicy, smaller in summer than in winter, but quite attractive. Despite the fact that I've never had the desire to taste it, I intend keeping the colony going for interest's sake.

Above: Good King Henry. Facing page: Florence Fennel.

CULTIVATION

Sow in April or May, either in a corner or at the end of your herb garden. Another suitable place is where farmyard manure or compost heaps are kept – the plant loves such a position. Make shallow drills in short rows and sow the seed thinly. Cover it by hand or with the back of a rake. The plant looks weed-like in the young stages so, after covering the seed drill, I'd mark it with a line of sand to help avoid mistaking the seedlings for weeds.

Thin the seedlings to 6–9in (15–23cm) apart. The pulled-out ones can be transplanted with ease, especially in a rainy spell.

There's little else required for the production of your Good King Henry apart from keeping it clean and keeping it in check. By June, with us, it's 2–3ft (60cm–1m) high and flowering. But if you intend to use it, don't allow it to flower and seed itself; instead take the flowers off to encourage young, usable shoots.

Florence Fennel

Florence Fennel is an Italian-bred annual which produces a large, white bulb above the ground at the base of the leaf stalks. It looks attractive if it's well grown, and has a sweet, aniseed-like flavour.

Florence Fennel can be grown in an open, sunny spot on a good bit of land which contains moisture-holding compost. Sow the seeds in July in shallow drills, making the rows 12in (30cm) apart. After sowing, cover carefully. Thin the seedlings to 12in (30cm) apart and keep clear of weeds.

I like to grow my Fennel in a garden frame which contains a hotbed used for an early spring crop. When the spent crop and weeds have been cleared out, the soil should be trodden moderately firm and shallow drills drawn 12in (30cm) apart. The drills should be watered before sowing if the soil is dry and the seed sown thinly, or two or three seeds should be dropped at 9–12in (23 or 30cm) intervals. I replace the frame lights until the seed

has germinated. When this occurs the seedlings should be aired for a few days in preparation for removing the lights as soon as possible. The seedlings are thinned to 9–12in (23–30cm) and, if the weather's dry, kept well watered. One or two feeds of liquid farmyard manure always prove beneficial.

Fennel should be eaten when the bulbs are about the size of a tennis ball, or a bit smaller. After that they lose their shape and the segments of the bulb open up.

Globe Artichokes

I don't think I can remember any old estate garden without its Globe Artichokes, but I do recall there always seemed to be more left uncut than were used! However, these things had to be available then, for you never knew when Cook or the lady of the house would call for such things, and gardeners without were not all that popular. It's a vegetable that I've never tasted and have never wanted to; old gardeners used to say that it's the

83

only vegetable with which you end up with more on your plate when you've finished than you had when you started!

CULTIVATION

I'm used to bought-in plants that are planted on a piece of land which has had ample supplies of farmyard manure or compost dug well into it. The sets (as we call the plants) are planted out 2ft (60cm) apart in rows 3ft (1m) apart. They're kept watered and freely hoed, and often support stakes are put in because the leaf and stalks are otherwise easily damaged by the wind. Very few heads can be expected in the first year, but when they do appear they need cutting when they're no larger than a tennis ball and certainly before they show signs of the head beginning to make a thistle-like flower.

WINTER TREATMENT

Globe artichokes aren't hardy and I've found that, even in the warm counties of Hampshire, Sussex, Dorset and Somerset, it's as well in winter to cover the crowns with dry bracken or straw. An old piece of wire netting or ordinary netting put over the top and pegged to the ground will hold the covering in place and keep it from blowing away. The site

Globe Artichokes.

should be cleared of weeds, pricked over lightly with a fork and generally kept tidy.

Here in Berkshire I've always found that, even if they are protected, you can't rely on Globe Artichokes coming through the winter. To be really safe, in late September I always dig up some of the biggest clumps, split them and pot them in a mixture of good loam and leaf soil. By mid-October they look as though they're growing again. I stand the pots in a fruit house, often under the Peaches, and then move them to a colder house for the winter, but not cold enough to let frost in. The Artichokes are kept on the dry side at the roots from November until they start into growth naturally in March. At this time they're watered and moved to a light, airy position. In late March they're put outside in the shelter of a wall, but not too protected. In April, they're planted on good land 2ft (60cm) apart in rows 3ft (1m) apart, watered well, kept clean and, after they have settled down, mulched with farmyard manure in May.

It all sounds a lot of bother, but Globe Artichokes are fascinating to grow. The best cultivar is a French one called 'Vert de Laon'.

GLOBE ARTICHOKES FROM SEED

There is a strain of Globe Artichoke called 'Green Globe' which can be grown from seed. This should be sown in January in a heated glasshouse. As soon as the seedlings are large enough to handle, prick them off into 3 or 3½in (7.5 or 9cm) pots filled with loam and leaf soil (or peat) mixed in roughly equal parts. Grow on in a temperature of 55–60°F (12.7–15.5°C) and air on all possible days. Gradually harden the plants off ready for planting out of doors in April. Allow 2ft (60cm) between each plant and 3ft (1m) between each row.

In my opinion the head you get from this strain is not so good as the 'Vert de Laon', and for all the trouble you have to go to when growing Globe Artichokes I feel that you might as well start with the best.

Peas·Beans·and Sweetcorn

Garden Peas – Purple-podded Peas – Sugar Peas –
Asparagus or Winged Peas – Broad Beans – Runner Beans –
French Beans – Haricot Beans – Butter Beans –
Ornamental Beans and odd Peas – Sweetcorn

CHAPTER SEVEN
Peas, Beans and Sweetcorn

Garden Peas

You can't get better Peas than the ones grown in your own garden. In late July and August years ago Peas also made a sight to see, for they were the old, tall, stately varieties. In those days you could easily get hold of cheap sticks to support them, but as time's gone on, peasticks have become scarce and expensive and so now gardeners prefer dwarf Peas. Although I generally stopped growing tall Peas in 1965, I still grow a few varieties like 'Gradus' and 'Ne Plus Ultra', because there's nothing to beat the flavour of old Marrowfat Peas. 'Ne Plus Ultra' has another benefit, useful for gardens large and small: it produces its crop over a long period. I grow it on the previous year's Celery trench or on a well-manured piece of land where it reaches a height of 7ft (2.2m) with no problem. It starts to crop when it's about 3½ft (1.1m) from the ground.

PREPARING THE GROUND

Peas need well-prepared ground, especially the mid-season and main-crop varieties as these might be the tall sorts which take at least ninety days to grow. They need deeply tilled land with farmyard manure or compost worked well into it.

Left: The attractive Purple-podded Pea. Right: Peas ready for picking.

GROWING AN EARLY CROP

There are several ways of getting a crop of Peas in April:

(a) Sow in November in a sheltered border or under cloches. I used to sow 'Meteor' in mid-November under cloches and kept them under the cloches. I could pick the first Peas in late April but found that they had to be picked when they were quite small because they quickly became hard.

(b) Grow in pots. First I'll describe how this used to be done, then how best to do it today.

In the days when there was a large staff in private gardens, 5in (13cm) pots were sown in January, ten to twelve seeds per pot. Old soil from Chrysanthemum pots or Tomato beds was used and the pots filled to sowing depth, so that the top of the soil was approximately 2in (5cm) from the top. The pots were watered and allowed to stand for a few hours to drain before the seeds were sown and covered with about 1in (2.5cm) of soil. The pots were then covered with newspaper, which excluded light and encouraged germination. It also kept moisture in the pot, which meant that the Peas didn't have to be watered until they'd germinated. This was useful, for watering could have the effect of a sudden thunder shower on an outside border which checks germination. The pots were kept at 50°F (10°C) until the seed germinated, after which they were put into a cool greenhouse and gradually hardened off before being planted out. If the plants were going under cloches or into coldframes, they didn't need to be hardened off but did need brushwood to hold them up and sticks when the cloches were removed. I had frames set aside especially for Peas and raised the lights on them as the crop grew. Once picking was ready to start in late April, the lights were taken off altogether.

To grow early Peas in pots today choose dwarf varieties, such as 'Feltham First', 'Kelvedon Wonder' or 'Little Marvel'. Put a handful of old farmyard manure or compost in the bottom of a 6in (15cm) pot and top up with old potting soil (as above). Put six to eight seeds in each pot. Keep at 50°F (10°C) until germinated, then grow in a well-ventilated greenhouse. They will need brushwood placed around. The height of the brushwood will depend on the variety of pea. A tall-growing variety will need tall brushwood and a small growing variety just a few feet. When the pods have set, water with liquid farmyard manure. The crop will be ready in early May.

SECOND EARLIES

Sow out of doors from mid-March to early April, but be guided by the weather: when the soil is wet and cold, Peas won't germinate.

Make the rows 3ft (1m) apart. The seed should be sown in a flat-bottomed drill 3–4in (7.5–10cm) wide and 1–2in (2.5–5cm) deep. Half a pint (300ml) of Pea seed will sow 30ft (9.1m) of drill. If the ground is dry, water the drill and leave it for an hour before sowing. If you water it after sowing it will lie wet and can rot the seed, especially if germination has already started.

With later sowings you'll need to protect against birds, mice and slugs. Weed between the young plants at an early stage. If the peas are the tall sort, support them when they get to about 4–6in (10–15cm). If you don't and they get blown over the crop suffers, and sticking takes much longer.

As a rule dwarf varieties take seventy to seventy-five days from their sowing date to crop. 'Kelvedon Wonder' and 'Feltham First' will be ready for picking in late June, but the bulk of other varieties will be ready in the first fortnight of July.

Ground cleared of early Peas is excellent for sowings of Carrot, Lettuce and Beetroot, or, if it's cleared by mid-June, for autumn Cauliflowers and autumn Cabbages.

MID-SEASON CROP

Sow in late April/early May, following the method described above for second earlies. If sowing a dwarf variety, make the rows 4ft (1.2m) apart; if a tall one, 6ft (1.8m) apart. You can intercrop the 6ft (1.8m) with Lettuce, Beet, Round-leaf Spinach or even Cauliflower.

MAIN CROP

Sow from mid-April to the end of June unless you're using a tall variety, in which case sow no later than early June because this will need ninety days to produce its full height of haulm and make full-size Peas. Don't sow in a humid, thundery spell. Heavy storms compact the ground, and the earth's subsequent steamy temperature, combined with the heat generated by germination, will rot the seed.

If it's hot and dry in July and August, a good mulch of farmyard manure or compost placed around the plants and watered well helps to hold moisture. In dry conditions the pods should be gone over twice a week at least, otherwise many will pass their best before you get round to picking them.

Purple-podded Peas

Like Purple-podded Beans, a row of Purple-podded Peas makes an attractive addition to a vegetable garden. They need picking when they're young and, perhaps disappointingly, when cooked they lose their purple colour!

Sugar Peas

Sugar Peas show no outward sign of Peas in the pod, which is cooked whole. For cultivation they need the same attention as other types of Peas. There are several dwarf varieties available which are very good.

Asparagus or Winged Peas

Asparagus or Winged Peas are simple to grow and always attract interest. Their drawback is that picking the pods is a miserable time-consuming job. The plants are about 1½–2ft (45–60cm) in height and the seeds very small. They require a moderately rich plot. Sow the seeds thinly in May in a flat-bottomed drill, cover with approximately 1in (2.5cm) of soil and protect from mice. Short

Asparagus Peas.

brushwood supports will be needed to keep the plants upright.

The flowers are very small with a purple blotch, something like those of Vetch. The square pods should be picked when they are only 2in (5cm) long. Picked frequently, one sowing will crop for weeks. The pods are cooked whole and they were greatly appreciated by my employers in the 1950s and 1960s.

Broad Beans

In the gardens of large houses, Broad Beans were always picked young – in fact, when they were no bigger than Peas. After that stage they became a staff vegetable. In the villages around Blackmoor Broad Beans were a very important crop and large patches were sown, mostly from February to April. This sowing turned in Beans in late June and July. Often the Bean plants produced a young crop of shoots at the base and where this happened the haulm was cut down. By late August or early September the plants gave a second crop of beans! Many cottagers usually reckoned on this event coinciding with the hop picking in the estate's fields about an hour's walk from the village. I've never been able to copy their method here on the Berkshire/Wiltshire border, but that's gardening wherever you go: always something different to see and learn.

PREPARING THE GROUND

Broad Beans will grow on any piece of land that's had an application of farmyard manure or compost in the previous year. They appreciate both,

but not in too heavy a dressing for that makes them grow tall and out of character.

EARLY SOWINGS

The best early variety is 'Aquadulce', and there are three methods of sowing:

(a) Sow in November in a cold greenhouse into either pots or seed trays, allowing one seed to a 3–3½in (7.5–9cm) pot or thirty seeds to a tray. Plant

Picking a good crop of 'Aquadulce' Broad Beans in early June.

90

out during a mild spell in February or leave until early March. Choose a sunny spot and stake out a garden line. Place each plant 2–3in (5–7.5cm) away from the line and 4–5in (10–13cm) apart. Do this on either side of the line and you'll get a nice double row which you should be able to pick from late May/early June.

(b) Sow in December into a deepish coldframe. Water the young plants during February, March and April. When they reach the glass, take their tops out. Air will be needed daily from March onwards. You should be picking nice Beans by early May.

(c) In December and January sow under cloches. If you have Grower's Barn cloches (see p. 40), you can sow as a double row. Make the rows 2½ft (75cm) apart from one another and sow about twelve seeds under each cloche, allowing 4–5in (10–13cm) between them. Once the Beans are 6in (15cm) high move the cloches apart to give a 2–3in (6–7cm) gap between each. In a week to ten days widen the gap, and repeat a few days later. In April remove the cloches altogether. Their removal will neatly dovetail with the time to sow a few Dwarf Beans beneath them. If you're going to do this, sow a single row. Make a 2in (5cm) deep drill and sow at 6in (15cm) intervals. Thin out to every other one, leaving a stand of plants each 12in (30cm) apart. These Dwarf Beans will need the same hardening-off process as given to cloche-grown Broad Beans, with the final removal of the cloches in the last week of May.

SOWING IN OPEN GROUND

In very favourable areas Broad Beans may be sown in open ground in November, but I think it's safer to wait until late February onwards. Beware of sowing if conditions are very wet because this causes the Bean seed to rot. Work the ground down to a fine tilth and mark out drills 2–2½ft (60–75cm) apart with Beans placed every 6in (15cm) in the drills. Cover either by raking in the direction of the drill or, as our grandfathers did, by scuffing them in with your feet, at the same time treading the ground firm. This method leaves two rows of well-trodden footmarks side by side.

Keep an eye open for blackfly, which like to cluster on the top of the plant where the sap's at its best. As soon as they appear, remove the tops. If it's very dry when the Beans are flowering and forming their pods, water heavily.

Broad Beans require several weeks between sowings because later sowings often catch up with earlier ones. Make a second sowing during April to May. After mid-June sowings are doubtful ventures, certainly in my garden. If late June and July are dry, the Beans fail to make worthwhile plants, and if late July and early August are dry and the nights cool, rust sets in on the foliage and makes the plants stop growing before their time. Rust also spoils the look of the pod, although the Beans inside are OK.

Runner Beans

PREPARING THE GROUND

I don't mind double digging or trenching ground for Runner Beans, but for a very long time I've not believed in actually digging trenches for them. This is a method which used to be widely practised. A trench was taken out 18–20in (45–60cm) wide and 1ft (30cm) deep, dung was dug into the bottom and then another layer of it added. The trench was filled in without the sides being broken down. Runner Beans grown in such a trench had a pot-like existence. To my mind this was wrong, because their roots spread naturally sideways through the top soil, sometimes to a distance of 2ft (60cm). Instead of a trench they should be planted in ground which has had a good all-over spread of manure, well dug in during the winter. In my gardens we always used to reckon on approximately 60lb of farmyard manure per sq yd (27kg per sq m) – 'quite a poultice', as one of my old hands used to say!

Leave the digging rough for the winter and break it down in March or April. If you know where your Bean row is going to be on the prepared site, make a mark and either side of that mark you can easily get some Lettuce, Radish or 'Early Milan' Turnips off before they're a nuisance to the Bean crop. You need to sow them 2ft (60cm) away on either side of your Bean row.

EARLY CROPS

If you have glass your earliest Beans can be sown in late April. Put one seed to a 3–3½in (7.5–9cm) pot or thirty seeds to a seed tray. Grow on in cold glass and plant out in late May, after they've been hardened off, although it's never possible really to harden off a Runner Bean. Plant 12–15in (30–38cm) apart in the row and make the next row 12in (30cm) away, thus forming a double row.

Immediately after planting put in support stakes. They need to be 1 foot beneath the ground and 7 feet above it. I like the old villagers' method of crossed sticks, with a good straight stick down the middle about 2½–3ft (60cm–1.1m) from the ground and firmly bound with strong string. A row such as this, using good sticks, is a joy to see. If the Beans have already sent out their leader shoot, which can be anything from 12 to 18in (30–45cm) high, a tie of bass (raffia) is needed to start each bean off up its correct stick. Even at this early stage watering is important and mustn't be forgotten. If there's a cold snap in late May/early June, it's easy to fix old hessian bags or other covering on the sticks to give protection.

OPEN-GROUND SOWING

The first open-ground sowing is usually safe in my garden after 12 May. Sow by placing a garden line down where the middle of your row will be. About 3–4in (7.5–10cm) either side of this draw out a 2in (5cm) deep drill with a triangle hoe. Place each Bean 12in (30cm) apart in the drill and cover carefully. It's a good idea then to plant a few elsewhere. If any seedlings don't come up from the main sowing you can use these spare ones to replenish the gaps.

As soon as seedlings appear, give slug protection. When the shoots begin to leave the seed leaves it's time to stick them, but first make sure all weeds have been removed, as it's difficult to weed *after* sticking. Use one stick, or rod as we called them in Hampshire, to each Bean.

Keep watered in all dry spells. When the first set of Beans is 3–4in (7.5–10cm) long treat the plants to a feed of liquid farmyard manure (see p. 23) watered down to the colour of weak tea. You'll soon see the benefit.

WIGWAM OF BEANS

If space is limited for making rows, try making a wigwam on a well-prepared piece of land. When I was a journeyman at Stansted Park we used to make wigwams about 5ft (1.5m) in diameter.

Tie a piece of string on to a stick, the string to measure out 2ft 7in (78cm) from the stick. Push

Above and right: A wigwam of Beans saves space. Left: Putting up Bean support sticks using the old villager's method.

the stick into the ground where you intend the middle of the wigwam to be, pull the string out to full length and tie a stick on the loose end. Keeping the string pulled taut, walk round the central stick, at the same time scoring the ground. The circular score mark will take fifteen Bean sticks, each 8 feet high (that is one foot in the ground and seven above) and each 12in (30cm) apart, but put in only fourteen. The space left will eventually enable you to get inside the wigwam to pick any beans you can't see from outside.

French Beans

French Beans are available as dwarf and climbing varieties.

DWARF VARIETIES

Although dwarf Beans were always to be found in large gardens, where they were grown in pots in the fruit ranges, they weren't so popular in small gardens. The advent of deep freezers has changed that, added to which modern cultivars are a grand improvement on the flat-podded varieties of old.

Dwarf Beans are easy to cultivate and can be grown as an intercrop with Runner Beans or Peas. Unlike Runner Beans they don't need a lot of farmyard manure or heavy preparations. A plot which has received manure the year before will do them fine.

Picking Dwarf Beans at Chilton.

EARLY CROPS

The old way of getting very early Beans was to grow them in pots. 'The Prince' was the most favoured variety for this method; you can still get it and it equals any modern Dwarf Bean.

Make up a compost of one-quarter rotted leaves, one-quarter well-rotted farmyard manure and one-half old loam which has previously grown Tomatoes or pot Chrysanthemums. Half-fill a 10in (25cm) pot with the mixture and sow in it six to eight seeds. Cover with approximately 1in (2.5cm) of compost. Germinate the seeds in 60°F (15.5°C). When the plants are nicely above the pot rims, top dress the pot to within 1in (2.5cm) of the top.

Put four canes in around each pot and run a strand of bass round them. This will keep the plant upright and stop it toppling over. When the Beans are setting, feed with soot water (see p. 21) or liquid farmyard manure (see p. 23). Keep growing conditions humid but not too hot because that will cause soft growth. Pick the Beans when they're quite young and tender.

SOWING OUT OF DOORS

The first open-ground sowing can take place up to ten days earlier than that of Runner Beans. Prepare the ground as for all seed sowing and draw out drills 2in (5cm) deep and 2–2½ft (60–75cm) apart. Drop two seeds every 12in (30cm). Pull out one plant while it's still in the seed-leaf stage.

Hoe to keep clean and, when the plants are 6in (15cm) or so high, draw a little soil up to the stem like a mini-Potato ridge. This will help to hold the plants secure in winds. When the pods begin to form, the plants will appreciate liquid farmyard manure (see p. 23) or 2oz per yd (50g per m) run of complete fertiliser. If the weather is dry when they are carrying their crop, watering will help to keep the plants going, but I find that dwarf Beans are not so reliant on water as Runners.

For a succession, two to three sowings can be made over May, June and even up to mid-July in favourable areas.

Climbing Varieties

Grow climbing French Beans in a double row exactly like Runner Beans. If you sow them at the same time as the dwarf kind, you'll get a crop of Stick Beans before the ordinary Runners are ready.

Haricot Beans

In my experience growing Haricot Beans in this country doesn't meet with much success. I've tried them several times and given them up as a bad job.

Butter Beans

Butter Beans have short flat pods and you grow them like Runner Beans. I've included them once or twice in vegetable exhibits.

Ornamental Beans and odd Peas

There are several ornamental Beans which are eatable but nothing outstanding. They come into their own in large exhibits of vegetables or for decoration at Harvest Festival. I've also found that a wigwam of them in the garden makes an interesting sight and a talking point. They all require the same attention in every way as their less ornamental counterparts.

From time to time my collection of Beans has been very colourful. I've had a purple-podded variety with a dwarf pod but on a stem which grew to 7ft (2.2m); a similar tall plant that carried yellow pods splashed with red; a yellow-podded Broad Bead; a yellow-podded Dwarf Bean; a purple-podded Dwarf Bean and a green Dwarf Bean with a very flat pod.

Other oddities I keep are the 'Soldier Bean' (similar to a Dwarf Bean but the seeds have a red figure on them like a soldier in a red uniform); a black-seeded Russian Runner Bean; a blue-podded Pea; a Carlin Pea (this looks like a Vetch); and, last but not least, a Pea called 'The Niton Buckley'. This last oddity gets part if its name from

a village on the Isle of Wight where it's been grown for the last hundred years – in fact, ever since a few were found on the beach after a shipwreck. It's surprising what a garden collects in time!

Sweetcorn

It's quite simple to grow Sweetcorn but, as with many easily-grown crops, you get what you deserve, so grow it on well-cultivated land which has had its fair share of farmyard manure or compost. It needs a position in full sun and protection from wind.

Above: Sweetcorn. Top of page: Carlin Pea.

EARLY CROPS

Sow seeds under glass, one per 3–3½in (7.5–9cm) pot of any reasonable seed-sowing compost. Just push the seed into the surface and water it in. Germinate in a temperature of 55–60°F (12.7–15.5°C). Don't let the growing plants get dry at the roots.

Harden off thoroughly before planting out from the end of May. Choose a mild spell and plant in blocks, not in single rows, as the former method helps pollination. Pollen is carried by the terminal shoot of each plant and the wind transfers it to the silks on top of the forming cob. After planting, water in and be prepared to protect the plants from frost: cloches are useful for this. Protect from slugs too and (if they are in your area) from game birds.

SOWING OUT OF DOORS

For mid-season and late crops sow from late May through to late June. Sow on prepared ground in drills 1–2in (2.5–5in) deep, but if the weather's dry make the drills a little deeper to stop them becoming too shallow when you water them before sowing.

GENERAL CULTIVATION

Once established, Sweetcorn will ask for very little apart from sunshine. Keep hoed at all times and water if there's a dry spell in June. Some cultivars will throw up side shoots: take these off, because it's just the main shoot you require. It's important to water when the cobs are growing and swelling and also at this time you should feed the plants with liquid farmyard manure (see p. 23). Remove any small cobs – two good cobs per plant is the norm.

The cobs are ready for use when the silks or whiskers have turned brown and it's obvious that they're no longer alive. Split the outer case of green leaves round the cob with your finger and thumb to see if the corn is of a size you like. Some people prefer very young Sweetcorn but others like the cob to get a bit more mature.

MAKING SPENT SWEETCORN PLANTS INTO COMPOST

I learned how to turn spent Sweetcorn into compost in 1937 when I was garden boy at Wode House gardens. My employer was a South African gentleman and we grew lots of Sweetcorn for him. After the cobs had been picked the spent plants were cleared and their roots cut off. We then pushed what remained through a chaff cutter which reduced it to lengths of between 1½ and 2in (4 and 5cm). Sweetcorn stems are made up of little channels, and when these chopped-up bits were dug into the ground they held moisture for a long time because it took up to two years for them to rot away completely.

Onions·and·Leeks

Onions – Welsh Onions – Egyptian Onions – Shallots –
Cocktail Onions – Leeks

CHAPTER EIGHT
Onions and Leeks

Onions

When I was a lad the Onion beds were always quite something in old estate gardens. It was on one of these beds that I was first taught the correct way to use a Dutch hoe. I'd been put to work on a bed and thought that I was getting on fine until the foreman smartly knocked the hoe out of my hand, saying, 'No, do it like this.' He showed me how to push the hoe in front of myself, quite far, but not so far that I couldn't comfortably keep the blade flat on the ground.

What I'd been doing was dodging about, hoeing where I'd seen weeds, but the secret was, he told me, to hoe *all* the ground because that not only got rid of the weeds but also created a dust mulch which helped to retain moisture.

Work on the beds began in autumn when they were dug or trenched for the following year's Onions. Compost or farmyard manure wasn't spared; it was dug in, trenched in and, where land was heavy, put in by double spit ridging. There aren't many crops which will grow on the same piece of ground, year in, year out, for several years at a stretch, but Onions will, provided that the land is well manured every year. In fact some exhibitors stick to the same plot for years.

SOWING SEED FOR AN EARLY CROP

Sow in August. Select a good piece of land, tread it and then rake it to a fine tilth. Make shallow drills 12–15 in (30–38cm) apart and sow thinly. Rake carefully to cover the seed. Hoe and weed as soon as the seedlings are visible. Leave to over-winter where sown. Give a complete feed in early spring and keep clean. You should get bulb Onions by late June/early July depending on your area.

The list of Onions you can grow from seed is endless. However, both 'James' Long Keeping' and 'Bedfordshire Champion' usually give good results.

Above: James' Long Keeping Onions. Facing page: Making up a rope of Onions.

SOWING AND PLANTING A MAIN CROP

There are two ways in which this can be done.

■ The old method

In January sow thinly under glass in seed trays and germinate at 60°F (15.5°C). Cover the trays with a pane of glass and a sheet of newspaper on top. Turn the glass each day to stop too much moisture collecting on the underside and dripping on to the seedlings. Remove the glass and paper when the seedlings are ½–1in (1–2.5cm) high. Grow on as cool as possible and as near the glass as possible to avoid the seedlings being drawn.

In March, when it's dry enough to crumble, fork the earth down level on the planting plot. Tread it and rake it on a day when it won't stick to your boots.

To plant the first row, pull a garden line very tight and place the young onions (we used to call them 'sets' at this stage) 4in (10cm) apart. Use a dibber to do this: push it in about 1in (2.5cm) from the line and it should just touch the line when it's fully driven in. Make your rows 12–15in (30–38cm) apart. Water the onions in and, if the weather is dry, hoe on the following day to form a dust mulch. You'll need to hand-weed after a few weeks to keep the bed clean and ship-shape.

Some old gardeners used to sow a row or two of Parsley alongside the bed and at the end of the rows – they said that it kept Onion fly away. Soot applied in May and June was also supposed to ward off the fly. It was thrown on in the morning so that it would stick to the dewy plants. It also acted as a fertiliser, though liquid manure was the main fertiliser.

■ The modern way

Sow seed under heated glass in February at a temperature of 55–60°F (12.7–15.5°C) using one of the following methods:

(a) Sow into a seed box in the normal way and prick off the resultant seedlings into 3½in (9cm) pots filled with bought-in compost or your own mixture. (I like to use compost which has grown Cucumbers or Tomatoes under glass the previous year and was originally made up from loam, well-rotted farmyard manure, leaf soil and a handful of bone meal per bushel (36 litres), all passed through a ½in (1cm) sieve.) You need to prick off five seedlings to each pot, putting four around the edge and one in the middle.

(b) Sow approximately eight seeds to a 3½in (9cm) pot and pull out the weakest ones, leaving five.

In April or May knock the compost out of the pots but try to keep each group of seedlings intact and plant them, still together, 15in (38cm) apart either way. They need a good piece of well-prepared ground where they'll give excellent results, ending up like large clumps of Shallots.

I've used this method for three years now and produced five onions per clump, all at least 8oz (225g) apiece.

GROWING ONIONS FROM SETS

During the 1950s an onion called 'Rijnsburger' became very popular. It was liked because you didn't have to go through the time-consuming and costly process of growing it from seed. Instead you grew it from small Onions which had all the hallmarks, except size, of the full-grown ones. These small embryo Onions, known as sets, could be bought in garden shops from February onwards. Over the years 'Rijnsburger' has been joined by several other cultivars which can also be grown from sets. If you're producing Onions on only a small scale, sets are a good way to do so.

Sets need well-prepared ground. Begin preparation in winter by deep digging, trenching or ridging. Dig in plenty of farmyard manure or compost and leave the surface rough so that the frost will help to break it down and enable you to get a fine tilth in the Spring.

In March on a day when the ground is dry enough not to stick to your boots, break the ground down, tread it firmly and rake it down to a nice tilth. Plant the Onions with a dibber, setting them out 4–5in (10–13cm) apart and making the rows 12–15in (30–38cm) apart. The top of each Onion should show above the ground. Knowing exactly where the Onions are enables you to hoe at an early date: this is an advantage over ones grown from seed which at first are thin and difficult to see.

A lot of show competitors enter jolly good Onions that they've grown from sets, and they store well too.

LIFTING

By August Onions will show signs of having reached the end of their growing life, so bend the tops over to hasten maturity. When the tops are almost dried down, lift the Onions and place them in a dry, airy shed. Alternatively leave them on open ground, or on a made-up frame of wire supported on four posts, and cover them at night and on wet days. Leave them until the outer loose skin parts easily from the bulb. They can then be put into a dry, airy place ready for use. Either spread them out or tie them on to a rope (see below and right) which can be hung up. A little frost does them no harm, but I always prefer a storage place that's reasonably frost-free.

Drying Onions after lifting.

MAKING ONION ROPES

Old-time gardeners made a lovely job of tying Onions, a different size to each 1½ft (45cm) rope. When they'd finished tying them, all was order and readiness, so that any cultivar which didn't keep long could be used first and any size that Cook required could be seen at a glance. Here's how to make a rope:

1 Use string 2–2½ft (60–75cm) long, and strong enough to hold 20lb (9kg) of onions.

2 Tie an Onion to one end of the string, then tie the other end of the string on to a hook so that it hangs in front of you at a comfortable height for you to reach.

3 Join two Onions by twisting the top of one around the top of the other.

4 Hold the joined ends of the two Onions against the string and pass one Onion around the other. A couple of twists should lock them on to the string. Push them down on to the bottom Onion.

5 Carry on in the same way – that is, twisting two joined Onions around the rope and sliding them down to meet ones you've already tied on. To make a complete rounded ropeful put two on one side of the string and two against them on the other side.

101

WHEN STORED ONIONS SHOOT
Sometimes in February/early March a few stored Onions start to produce green shoots. This makes them pretty useless for cooking. However, don't throw them away; instead, plant them on the end of a plot in rows 12in (30cm) apart, each Onion 6in (15cm) apart in the row. They'll get away quite quickly and each will produce growth something like the small root end of a Leek. These are excellent in stews and casseroles, or cooked with game, or even in salads, and all at a time (usually May and June) when you won't have bulb Onions.

Spring Onions

See p. 50.

Welsh Onions

Welsh Onions have got many a gardener out of trouble in the past. They can always be relied on when the ordinary sort aren't available (as sometimes happens in March and April). Also, if they're picked when small, they can provide a useful stand-in for Spring Onions. They never make a bulb but instead form a swollen, white bottom, something like a small Leek with 6in (15cm) of white stem. After a year or two a clump will reach a couple of feet in height.

Welsh Onions are quite hardy and are usually grown at the end of the herb garden or in an odd corner. If you intend to make a planting of them, remember that you'll be looking at them in the same spot for several years. Before planting or sowing they appreciate farmyard manure dug into the soil. After that they somehow never seem to show signs of asking for more. In fact, they're mostly trouble-free, requiring nothing; they're there if you want them and there if you don't.

You can form a patch of Welsh Onions by splitting pieces off a large clump already in existence and planting these 2ft (60cm) apart either way. Alternatively you can sow seed in clumps 2ft (60cm) apart. The seed should germinate freely and you'll have sizeable clumps by the end of the first year.

Egyptian Onions

Like Welsh Onions, Egyptian Onions are an odd-corner type which again were both useful and made old estate gardens so interesting. They're often called the Upstairs Onions because they throw up a stem which has small Onions on the top. These are good in salads and excellent pickled.

Egyptian Onions ask very little: an odd sunny corner or end of plot. A clump will generally last for several years. Increase them by simply planting the small Onions in March to April. Put six in a clump (say, a ring of five with one in the centre), each approximately 6in (15cm) apart. They should form a good, productive clump in two years.

Egyptian Onions.

Shallots

Cottagers reckoned to plant Shallots on the shortest day of the year and lift them on the longest. I've never been able to see the gains in this! They were always grown on a large scale in gardens big and small, were nearly always a reliable crop and much used for pickling. Often a few were pulled very early when they were similar to Spring Onions, and cooks like Shallots in winter because in stews and casseroles they keep whole.

Shallots will grow on any reasonably good piece of land which has been manured for a previous crop, although the better treated they are, the better they respond. The ground needs to be firm and raked down before planting. Plant in rows 12in (30cm) either way, using a trowel or a dibber, and cover each Shallot by approximately two-thirds of its depth. Keep the bed clear of weeds. Bend over the tops as for Onions (see p. 101) when growth has ended and, after a week or so, lift and dry as for Onions.

I don't think any garden, large or small, should be without Shallots – they're such an easy crop and useful for the kitchen and the village show.

'Aristocrate' and 'Hâtive de Niort' are good croppers and excellent exhibition Shallots. However, they are a bit expensive. They're sold so much apiece whereas other Shallots like 'Dutch Yellow' and 'Dutch Red' are sold by the pound.

Cocktail Onions

As their name indicates, these are the Onions put on to sticks for cocktail-party fare, though they're useful for pickling. They're easy to grow but need a clean piece of ground because, being so small, in growth they can quickly be smothered by weeds and are then an awful job to get clean.

Sow between late April and May (though I have sown them as late as the end of June). Make the rows 12in (30cm) apart on ground which has been manured in the last two years. A sunny border suits them well. Harvest in August/September.

Leeks

The first sowing of Leeks can be made between mid-February and mid-March. You can sow under cloches or under a mobile coldframe placed on ground which has been manured in the last two years. If you're going to use an immovable frame, fill it with very old compost or leaf soil or one of the bag composts. (I use a frame which has soil left in it from a late Lettuce crop.)

Firm the soil by treading, then rake it down to a nice fine tilth.

Suggested varieties: Early Market; Musselburgh; Giant Winter and Walton Mammoth.

SOWING UNDER GROWER'S BARN CLOCHES (see p. 40)

Sow in three shallow drills, the central one directly under the ridge of the cloche and the others 6in (15cm) either side of it. Cloche back up and in April, when the seedlings have grown away, make a gap of 3in (7.5cm) between each cloche. In a week or so's time widen the gap and eventually remove the cloches altogether. The plants will be ready for planting out in mid- to late June.

Leeks.

SOWING IN A COLDFRAME

Sow the seed thinly in drills 1in (2.5cm) deep and 9in (23cm) apart. Make the drills flat-bottomed to give the seedlings more space to develop. I like to cover the seed by hand or with the back of an old iron rake. You need shortened tools if you're working in the confined space of a frame, although I think your hand is as good a tool as any. Keep the frame lights closed (except for watering) until the seedlings are 2–3in (5–7.5cm) high. From this point they'll need air and water on all fine days and, because at first they're thin and weak, weeds need to be kept under control. After weeding, water the seedlings to settle them. With this treatment you'll get sturdy plants for planting out in June.

Leeks started off in cloches or coldframes make a useful crop to fill land after an early potato crop.

SECOND SOWING

In late March make a second sowing in open ground, again in flat-bottomed drills, but this time make the drills 12in (30cm) apart. Seedlings from this sowing will form the main-crop planting which should be carried out from the third week in June to mid-July, depending on the area.

PLANTING OUT FROM THE FIRST SOWING

Clear the ground of weeds and any spent crop. If the ground has been previously manured, a dressing of complete fertiliser should be sufficient; if it hasn't, dig or rotavate compost into it. Mark out rows 12in (30cm) apart. Place a garden line in position and prepare to plant each plant 12in (30cm) apart in a hole 6–8in (15–20cm) deep. If the ground is firm, I make holes with a crowbar. Lift the plants from their seed bed with a small fork and, after shaking soil from the roots, cut off at least half the roots and at least half the tops. This makes a tidy plant to drop into the hole. Once you have dropped them in don't place any soil around them: they'll grow into the space.

Then water, taking care not to knock any soil into the hole. The young plants quickly recover from being moved. If the weather is dry, keep them watered. Leeks don't smother the ground like some crops, so weeds have to be kept in check. You can start using the Leeks from mid-October.

PLANTING OUT FROM THE SECOND SOWING

Leeks are gross feeders, so to get sizeable ones from late November onwards, I prepare the ground for planting out the second sowing by working in good farmyard manure or compost. Once that's done, firm the ground by treading and rake down level. I allow 15in (38cm) between rows but keep to 12in (30cm) between the plants.

Draw a 3in (7.5cm) drill with a triangle hoe, make the holes, prepare the plants as described above for the earlier plants, drop them into the holes and water in. When the plants have grown up above the drill, hoe the drill down level to give each plant an extra 3in (7.5cm) of blanch.

This main bed should give you leeks from mid/late November through to March/April.

GENERAL CULTIVATION

Leeks appreciate waterings in July and August, plus a good summer feed such as liquid farmyard manure (see p. 23), dried blood or a complete fertiliser like Growmore.

Any seedlings left in the seed rows can stop where they are and have a little soil earthed up around them. They might not end up any thicker than a pencil but in August and September they taste very good. Try it.

LIFTING

When lifting take care to get right to the bottom of the plant, press down the fork with one hand and give a gentle pull on the Leek with the other hand. If it doesn't yield, put in the fork on the other side and try again. After lifting trim off a few inches above the blanch in a neat arrowhead shape and trim the root close to the point where it joins the blanch.

Vegetables · for · Forcing and · Blanching

Dandelions – Chicory – Asparagus – Endives – Rhubarb – Seakale – Celery – Cardoons – Mushrooms

CHAPTER NINE
Vegetables for Forcing and Blanching

Forcing and blanching can be used to grow certain vegetables out of their normal season and to make others sweet instead of bitter. Old kitchen gardens always had a forcing house, a windowless and hence dark place heated by thick rows of water pipes. At Stansted Park the forcing house was underground and was reached through a trap door in the floor of a laundry drying room. In the light of your lantern it looked as if you were climbing down into an underground railway passage, but instead of a track running down the centre it had a pathway, and instead of platforms on either side there were beds of soil kept in place by 7in (18cm) boards. In November dormant crowns of Rhubarb, Asparagus and Seakale, roots of Chicory and plants of Endive were all brought down through the trap door and placed in the soil. The darkness blanched and sweetened the Chicory and Endive and the heat from the pipes encouraged the other vegetables to produce succulent shoots.

The problem with forcing houses was that they were always a haven for cockroaches. The best way to get rid of these insects was to surprise them with a lantern and a rolled up newspaper. Looking back, it's funny to think that, without being asked and without question, we garden boys would go out at night, leaving the warmth of the bothy and our book or wireless, to do battle with the pests!

Left: Forced Rhubarb.

Dandelions

The last garden I knew to blanch dandelions regularly was at Hungerford Park estate. That was in the mid-1950s. You can still buy packets of Dandelion seed, so if you want to try them in a salad, some methods of preparation are described below.

Dandelions need a good piece of land which has been manured in the last year (not freshly manured). Sow in spring in moist ground. Make the drills 1in (2.5cm) deep and 12in (30cm) apart and thin the seedlings to make a space 6–9in (15–23cm) between each. Alternatively plant out plants from a sowing made the previous year. Place them 6–7in (15–20cm) apart and make the rows 12in (30cm) apart so that you can get between them easily.

During the summer months cut the green leaves off and cover the plant with a flower pot, putting a crock or stone over the drainage hole to block out the light. This will blanch any new growth and make it less bitter than if left uncovered. Another method is to cover the plant with sand, but I find this more troublesome.

To get a winter supply of blanched leaves, lift the spring-sown plants in the autumn and allow them to chill by leaving them on top of the ground for a couple of weeks before putting them into warmth and darkness. When Dandelions were put into forcing houses they were planted 6–8in (15–20cm) apart in a bed, watered and the atmosphere kept humid. After ten to fourteen days of warmth and darkness they started into growth and produced white leaves for the salad bowl.

Chicory

Depending on the variety, Chicory can be grown and cut like Lettuce or forced and blanched for winter salads.

NON-FORCING TYPES

'Sugar Loaf' and Radicchio are the most well known types. 'Sugar Loaf' looks like a blowsy Cos lettuce; Radicchio has looser leaves which turn red as the year goes on and the weather grows colder. Both require exactly the same cultivation.

Sow from the middle of April until the end of May. Make shallow drills 15in (38cm) apart and sow thinly. Thin to 12in (30cm) apart. Alternatively, if you prefer a more economic way, sow two or three seeds every 12in (30cm) and then thin those out to the best seedlings.

Hoe and keep clean, and water in a dry spell. 'Sugar Loaf' will be ready for cutting in September and Radicchio from August onwards.

FORCING CHICORY

Although there are newer forcing types available I've always grown 'Witloof'. Select a piece of ground well manured in the previous year. Sow from mid-May until mid-June like Lettuce, thinly in shallow drills 12in (30cm) apart. When the seedlings are large enough to handle, thin to 6–9in (15–23cm) apart. The plants seldom need any further attention other than being kept free from weeds until it's time to lift them for blanching.

Lift in October/early November. Allow the plants to lie where dug for a few days. This will retard the growth, and a little frost won't harm them. The next stage is to cut off the green leaves about 1in (2.5cm) above the crown, then take the roots into a cool, dry shed and store them upright. Fill any spaces between them with sand or ash.

In late November/early December you can begin forcing. Small batches can be forced in a large flower pot. Plant so that the crown of each is ½–1in (1–2.5cm) above the soil and water in. A 10in (25cm) pot will take five to six roots. Place another pot over the top and cover its drainage hole to exclude the light. Keep at 50–55°F (10–12.7°C). Boxes are also useful for forcing small quantities: exclude the light from them too and keep them warm. A good place for boxes used to

Left: Radicchio. Above: Forced 'Witloof' Chicory.
Right: An old, mounded Asparagus bed.

be in glasshouses by the hot-water pipes beneath the plant benches. Either the pot or the box method should give you Chicory for Christmas.

Large kitchen gardens used to have to supply huge amounts of forced Chicory. The roots were taken to the forcing house and planted in beds, 3–4in (7.5–10cm) between each root. When the beds were cleared they were planted again to keep up a succession.

Asparagus

It used to be the practice to grow Asparagus on a mounded bed 9–12in (23–30cm) high. The bed would contain three rows of crowns 12in (30cm) apart. The problem with this method was that, with the roots being all over the mound, you couldn't hoe out weeds for fear of damaging the Asparagus. Instead, handfuls of coarse salt were sprinkled on when the weeds were just beginning and their growth was soft. Experience since the Second World War has proved that making a bed is a waste of time because Asparagus will grow just as well on level ground. This discovery has, of course, done away with the use of salt: on a flat bed you can safely hoe round Asparagus since all its roots are below the hoeing surface.

GROWING FROM SEED

You can grow Asparagus from seed, though I'd never resort to this because it's easier to use crowns. However, for anyone wanting to try seed, here's the method.

Have ready a very clean piece of well-manured ground. In the first year the Asparagus blades will be as thin as needles and you'd never be able to weed without damaging them. Sow the seed in April/early May. Make the rows 2ft (60cm) apart and sow either in a very thin continuous line or put two or three seeds per station 12in (30cm) apart and then thin to one plant. It will be two or three years, depending on the variety, before you'll be able to cut any Asparagus. The variety 'Martha Washington' is worth a try from seed.

GROWING FROM CROWNS

Prepare the bed the autumn before, digging in large quantities of well-rotted farmyard manure. It's best to plant one-year-old rather than two-year-old crowns: the latter produce little gain because they have had more roots disturbed. Plant the crowns in March/April. Years ago reputable suppliers wouldn't send out Asparagus crowns until this time, when they were beginning to start into growth. Plant in single rows, placing the crowns 12in (30cm) apart in the rows and, so that there's room to hoe and harvest, making the rows 2ft (60cm) apart. Keep free of weeds. Depending on the variety you should be able to cut a few spears in the year following planting, but as a rule you'll have to wait three years for a decent crop. 'Connover's Colossal' is a good old variety.

May and early June is the peak period for cutting asparagus. You shouldn't cut it at all after 17 June. Instead, let the feathery foliage which is known as the bower grow freely from June until September so that it will build up the crowns for the following year.

FORCING ASPARAGUS

Forcing Asparagus is expensive because it takes three years to get a good forcing crown and after forcing that crown is useless. Despite this, it used to be done in large gardens. There's a little shed behind the kitchen garden wall here at Chilton which was specifically used for the purpose. It had two beds and an ample run of hot-water pipes to heat it. In November, when the foliage had completely died down, three-year-old crowns were carefully lifted, with as little damage to their roots as possible, and then were left to lie on the ground for a few days to get really chilled. Meanwhile the beds in the shed were filled with fermenting farmyard manure. In December, seven to ten days before the crowns were due to be planted, a few inches of old potting soil was placed on top of the manure. The manure by this time would be giving nice continuous warmth. The crowns were put on to this soil and covered with a 2in (5cm) layer of ordinary garden soil. They were then watered but, because of the moisture from the fermenting manure, seldom needed another watering. However, a watch did have to be kept that they didn't get too dry, for they didn't have a mass of active root to support them. The shed was kept at 55–60°F (12.7–15.5°C) and the fermenting manure gave off the right feeling of humidity. If that nice feeling dropped, water was sprayed through a rose can on to the hot-water pipes a couple of times a day. The Asparagus was cut when the spears reached 6–8in (15–20cm).

Endives

There are two sorts of endives, the curly-headed and the broad-leaved. If you keep them clean and watered, Endives will grow on any piece of ground which will grow Lettuce.

CURLY-HEADED
'Moss Curled' is the best to grow for ease and for succession. Sow in October, April and July. The rows, depending on the size of your garden can be 12–15 (30–38cm) apart. Thin to 9in (23cm) between each plant.

BROAD-LEAVED
I grow 'Batavian Green'. It's sown in July and thinned or planted out to 12in (30cm) apart in rows 15in (38cm) apart.

Above: Broad-leaved Endive 'Batavian Green'.
Right: Curly-headed Endive.

BLANCHING

To make it less bitter, Endive needs blanching. To blanch curly-headed Endive put a slate, a tile, or a pot over each head when it's reached the stage where it looks like Lettuce fit for cutting.

Below are a couple of ways of blanching the broad-leaved type:

(a) On a dry day when the head is nearly full-grown, pull the leaves together and tie them with raffia. This blanches the hearts.

(b) Lift in October a few heads at a time, making sure that each has a good ball of soil. Place in a dark shed, a darkened frame or a blacked-out area beneath your greenhouse bench. Water in and ensure that the temperature does not rise above 60°F (15.5°C), otherwise too much rotting will set in.

When blanched Endive has a lovely, nutty taste, very good with salad or cold meat in November to January. The flavour makes up for the waste, for when you've stripped off the decayed outer leaves you end up with an Endive a third of the size of the one you put in!

Rhubarb

Unforced Rhubarb seldom made an appearance in the dining rooms of large houses, but almost the year round it was available as a dessert for the house staff. I remember staff grumbling that they'd had Dodson's Rhubarb from March until August and then they'd travelled up to Scotland to be with the Family there and were just in time for the start of the Scottish Rhubarb season!

CULTIVATION

Rhubarb can be raised in several ways. You can buy in planting sets from a reputable nursery, break off nice pieces of old clumps you've got already or grow it from seed. If you're breaking pieces off an existing clump, do it in March because the growth will get away better than if it's done in the autumn, and take pieces from the outside of the clump as that's the youngest part.

Above: Rhubarb. Left: Deciding which pot might cover the best blanched Endive.

If you're raising Rhubarb from seed, sow any time between January and March. Rhubarb seed is like Parsnip seed but more stout. Sow it in a seed box, 100 seeds to a standard-sized box. As soon as the seedlings are large enough to handle, pot them off into 3–3½in (7.5–9cm) pots filled with a reasonably rich mixture (old compost, leaf soil and loam). They should be ready for planting out in June.

PREPARING THE GROUND

Manure the ground well the winter before planting. Rhubarb is a gross feeder and the better the site, the longer the beds will go on cropping. Allow a space of 2ft (60cm) either way between each plant.

WHEN TO PICK

From big sets you can pull a few sticks the following year, but from most seed you won't be able to pull until after the second year. There is, however, a variety called 'Glaskins Perpetual' from which it's possible to harvest in the same year you've sown it. Sow this variety in January in 60°F (15.5°C), pot off into 3–3½in (7.5–9cm) pots and keep it growing on in 55°F (12.7°C). Harden the plants off from the middle to the end of May and plant out in well-prepared ground, allowing 2 ft (60cm) either way. If it's had no check you can pull a stick or two in August.

FORCING *IN SITU*

You can force rhubarb without lifting it by simply placing a cover over the best clumps in January. There are special terracotta Rhubarb-forcing pots with lids or (if you take the bottom out of it first) you can use a box or even an old bucket. (It's necessary to take the bottom of whichever of these two you use because when you start pulling the sticks you'll reach into the container. If you took the container off to pick you'd have a job getting it back on and you'd also damage the sticks not ready for pulling.) If you've got fermenting manure, so much the better, as the heat from it will speed forcing. Place it all round the outside of the pot up to the lid (or round the box or bucket). Cover their tops with something which will keep out the light. This method of forcing will give you a crop at least a month before open-ground pullings. Once you've taken off half the sticks, remove the pots altogether.

Another way to force *in situ* is to cover the crowns in February/early March with very strawy manure. The sticks will lift their way through this in May, the natural season of use, but will give you the same lovely, tender sticks that you would get from under pots. Once it's pushed through the manure, the rhubarb will grow on naturally and you should be able to go on pulling until some time in August.

LIFTING TO FORCE

This is a method I've followed to get Rhubarb for Christmas and to keep up a succession. Only really good crowns are used – ones which have been grown and allowed to build up because nothing has been pulled off them for two years. The crowns are lifted in early November and allowed to lie on the open ground for two to three weeks. Those intended to produce at Christmas are put into a forcing shed about three weeks beforehand. They're placed close together on a nice level surface and with enough soil around them to keep them closely packed and upright. After watering they're kept completely in darkness at a temperature of 50–55°F (10–12.7°C).

Rhubarb crowns forced in a shed are worthless afterwards, because it will be two or three years before you'll get another stick off them. However, forced under pots or strawy manure they'll go on to give you a crop another year.

Seakale

Seakale has fallen out of favour over the years. I gave up growing it in the mid-1960s because there wasn't the labour to tend it. I suppose that's why commercial crops have disappeared. The last nurseryman I knew to grow it on any scale was Ed Secret down in the West Country. It's a pity that this vegetable's become a bit forgotten because its grey-green foliage is attractive in the garden during summer. When this dies down the crown is forced so that it produces tender, pinkish-white stalks which make a welcome change from the usual garden fare.

GROWING FROM SEED

Raising Seakale from seed is, I think, a last resort when you've failed to get crowns (or thongs, as they're called). The problem with seed-raised plants is that they tend to flower freely and go to seed, whereas you need their strength to be concentrated in the crowns to prepare them for forcing. If you do have to raise a stock from seed, sow under glass in January/February and prick off ready to plant out in May or early June. I prefer this to sowing in an open border in April/early May. Whichever method you choose, you want to end up with the plants 12in (30cm) apart either way in three rows. Three rows make a bed; leave a 2ft (60cm) gap between each bed so that you can manipulate the forcing pots easily.

STARTING OFF WITH THONGS

You can buy thongs or get your own off crowns you already have and are lifting for forcing. To get your own thongs, lift a crown in November and break off the roots at the bottom of the main stem *(a)*. Cut the top of the roots off level *(b)* and break them into 6in (15cm) lengths. Cut the bottom of each length off at a slant *(c)*, which will give bigger root formation. Bundle up about twenty-five lengths *(d)* and stand each bundle upright in a plunge bed of ashes completely covering them to a depth of 2–3in (5–7.5cm). In spring there will be a complete ring of little shoots around the top of each length (thong). Rub off all but one shoot and plant the thongs out with a dibber. They should be 12in (30cm) apart either way in three rows with an alleyway between the beds so that you can move forcing pots.

a

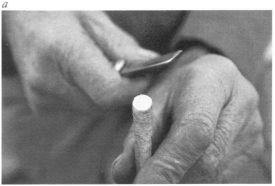

b

c

d   *Making Seakale thongs.*

Above: In summer, Seakale displays attractive grey-blue foliage. Below right: Forced Seakale.

FORCING SEAKALE

There are several ways to force Seakale. Perhaps the easiest is by using specially made lidded forcing pots. These are like Rhubarb forcing pots but squatter. In January/February when the leaves have died away, place a pot over each crown and put fermenting manure around the pot. Place the lid on the pot to keep out the light. Encouraged by the warmth from the manure and the darkness, tender white stalks should be ready for cutting in March/April, but it will depend on the winter: a very cold winter will slow down the growth.

A second way of forcing Seakale is to lift the roots in November when all the foliage has died down or been killed off by frost. Leave them on the ground for a few days to chill – a little frost doesn't hurt; in fact it makes forcing easier. You'll see that the roots have made several crowns and you want the largest of these for forcing. Cut it off with about 6in (15cm) of root below the crown. The smaller crowns can be used for forcing if good

ones are in short supply but they will throw a smaller head. (Even if good crowns are plentiful, you can still use the smaller ones. Cut them off in exactly the same way and use them to make a new bed in March. They'll make good crowns for the following year.) Put four crowns to a 10in (25cm) pot and cover with another pot or anything else which will effectively exclude the light. Keep the pot in a temperature of 50–60°F (12.7–15.5°C) – a lower temperature than this will make the growth slower.

In the days of garden forcing houses, crowns were planted in them 4in (10cm) apart either way, in beds. Kept at 55–60°F (12.6–15.5°C), they produced a crop for the Christmas season.

One final method of blanching is simply to cover any crowns left in the ground with leaf soil or clean, dry sawdust. When cutting, remove the covering carefully, because the shoots which are pushing up through it are tender and they'll break easily. They'll taste as good as shoots forced by other methods.

Celery

During the winter, and particularly at Christmas, Celery is a sought-after vegetable. It's costly to grow and not one of the easiest of crops because it has to be blanched before it's ready for use. There are self-blanching varieties which don't require earthing up, but traditional Celery needs growing in a trench and takes up to eight weeks to blanch. The husbandry of Celery trenches during all their stages was quite something to see when I was a lad. I loved it best when the Celery was about 12in (30cm) high and the top of the trenches decked with crops of Lettuce, Radish, Turnip and dwarf French Beans.

Self-blanching Celery is ready for eating during the summer and autumn; the more conventional trench type will see you through until late winter.

Suggested varieties of trench Celery: 'Solid White', 'Giant Pink' and 'Martine'. Self-blanching Celery: 'Lathom Blanching'; 'Ivory Tower' and 'Golden Self-Blanching'.

Celery.

SOWING

During February to March sow seed under glass and germinate in a temperature of 60°F (15.5°C). The seed box needs to be kept moist, so cover it with a pane of glass and a sheet of newspaper to keep off the sun. As soon as the seed leaves are big enough to handle, prick the seedlings off into a standard seed tray, thirty to a tray, or alternatively one seedling to a 3–3½in (7.5–9cm) pot. Keep at 60–65°F (15.5–18.3°C) until one or two true leaves appear, then gradually cool down and harden off.

PLANTING OUT

In early June, when the plants are at least 6in (15cm) high, plant out. Plant self-blanching Celery in a coldframe or in open ground, 9in (23cm) apart either way. If you put the Celery in open ground it's good to have a substantial crop such as Parsnips or white-stemmed Spinach on either side because these will block out light and help to blanch the outside Celery plants.

Ordinary varieties of Celery have to be planted in a prepared trench as described below.

PREPARATION OF A TRENCH

Make the trench 2ft (60cm) wide and roughly 12in (30cm) deep. Dig manure into the bottom – preferably cow manure because Celery seems to like it. A trench this size will take two rows of Celery planted side by side, 12in (30cm) apart in the rows. There is some advantage to be had from planting dog-legged: it gives you more room to put paper on and earth up.

Plant out with a trowel. It will take ten days to a fortnight for the young plants to get over their move. Celery is a maritime plant which has to have bags of moisture, so water and feed at all times.

BLANCHING

By August trench-grown Celery will need a light tie. The best way is to put a strand of bass (raffia) just under the foliage. Do this by placing both hands around the plant at soil level. Keep your hands together and gently draw them up the stems. This will bring the stems together. If you can get someone to help you, so much the better, because while you're holding the stems in your helper can place the tie around them between the top of your hands and just below the foliage. Take care that it isn't tied too tightly; there must be room for the stems to grow and expand.

Having made the plant *look* like a stick of Celery, you now need to enclose the stems to begin blanching them. I find that there's nothing better than newspaper for this. Wrap the paper from ground level up to the leaf. Don't enclose the leaf or it will rot and probably set up rot in the stick.

The next stage is to dress the bottom of the trench with slug pellets. In my young days it was heavily dusted with soot. This was also supposed to deter leaf miner because it made the leaves bitter. It's an odd thing but I find that today's soot isn't the same as it used to be years ago; it's less black and less effective!

Next comes the hard work. Fill the trench level. If the celery has gone above the level of the trench add a bit more soil until it comes up to the base of the foliage. Slant this extra soil on either side so that it looks like the roof of a house and pat it down with the back of a spade. This is called earthing-up and it helps throw off heavy rain.

As the Celery grows it will probably need two or three earthings. Another band of paper around the stick helps to keep the soil out of its centre and deters slugs. Make a good job of the final earthing-up. Pat the soil firm but not solid. The Celery will be ready for eating from November.

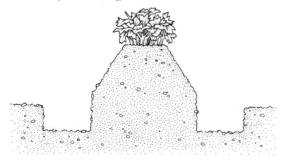

In days gone by I used to grow Celery intended for exhibition in a coldframe. It wasn't in a trench but on the level, and I blanched it by wrapping the stems first in newspaper, then in stout brown paper. From time to time I took off this double jacket to check that the stems were blanching nicely and keeping free from blemishes.

PROTECTION AGAINST FROST
Self-blanching Celery isn't hardy, so eat it before the first frosts. With trench Celery, if it looks as if the weather's going to be very frosty, it's best to cover any unused sticks. A thatching of straw or bracken makes a good cover. Anchor it down with a net to stop it blowing away.

Cardoons

A Cardoon looks like a cross between a giant Celery and an Artichoke. It's a vegetable more favoured on the continent than in Britain. You eat the first two feet up from the root, anything above gets too pithy. The first and last place I ever knew to grow Cardoons on any scale was Stansted Park. They were popular because Lady Bessborough was French. Cardoons, like Celery, have to have their stems blanched before they're ready for use.

SOWING
Sow the seed under glass during late April/early May, one or two seeds to a 3–3½in (7.5–9cm) pot. Germinate in a temperature of 60°F (15.5°C). If two seeds were sown, single out to one plant. Stand in a cool house and grow as cool as possible. The young plants should be ready for planting out in the first fortnight of June. Plant out into a deep coldframe or on to very well-manured open ground. Plant on the flat, not into a trench as with celery. Place the plants 2ft (60cm) apart either way. Water and feed regularly with liquid farmyard manure (see p. 23) or any general fertiliser of a nitrogenous nature.

Cardoons tend to branch out, and by the end of July each will need a tie around it to keep it together. Because they grow at a tremendous rate, the tie could cut through the stem after a week or two, so it's best to take it off and replace it with another. Depending on the rate of growth, you may need to do this several times.

BLANCHING

From the middle of August onwards prepare to blanch by wrapping the stems in hay or straw bands. These are made with a tool called a wimble. If you haven't got one, a piece of metal bent to the shape of the brace part of a brace and bit will do. Put a hook on the end of it. It you can get hay cut in long strands, say 2–2½ft (60–75cm), it will make a good band. Tease the hay out into a pile and fix your first piece on to the hook. You need two people, for as one turns the handle and twists the hay, walking away from the pile as the band

Wrapping straw bands around Cardoons grown in a coldframe.

grows, the other stays beside the pile and keeps up a feed of hay as evenly as possible. Aim for a band about 4ft (1.2m) in length. If hay bands defeat you, you can use newspaper instead. At the same time as covering the stems, stake each Cardoon as it will be getting heavy and could blow over.

Add more covering as the Cardoons continue to grow. By the third week in September covering should be complete: it will probably cover 3ft (1m) of the stems of each plant.

The Cardoon will be ready for use from the middle of October. They aren't frost hardy, so use them before severe frosts come along. As a short-term frost protection you can lift and pot them and put them into a cold greenhouse, though they will deteriorate within two or three weeks.

Mushrooms

Mushrooms grow from spawn, which is white threads of mycelium. Given the right conditions, these threads run through the growing bed and produce 'flowers' in the form of mushrooms.

Up until the 1950s I regularly grew mushrooms in Chilton's Mushroom house. It's a house which must have seen many a crop because it's clearly marked on a nineteenth-century map I have of the garden. It stands in a row of buildings which flank the back wall of the kitchen garden, but it differs from its neighbours in that it's the only one to have tongue-and-groove boarding on the inside of the roof. This insulation helped to keep the interior at a good Mushroom-growing temperature.

GROWING THE EASY WAY

Buy from a horticultural sundries firm a container filled with compost which has been impregnated with Mushroom spawn. Dampen the surface of the compost, put the container into the dark and keep it at 60°F (15.5°C). After a week or ten days cover the surface with the top dressing supplied. You should get Mushrooms after a month.

Facing page: The old Mushroom house, Chilton.

GROWING THE TRADITIONAL WAY

This is the method I used to grow Mushrooms in the Mushroom house, but it can be followed for growing them in boxes placed in sheds or cellars.

You will need fresh horse stable manure. If it comes from race horses, so much the better, as their food is rich and their manure ideal for Mushroom forcing. Have it put into an open-fronted shed or somewhere where you can work easily, because it has to be turned every three to four days to make it ferment and break down. Turn it from the outside to the inside. It'll become very hot and will probably take up to three weeks before the temperature drops as the straw breaks down. When the heap looks a light nut-brown colour, that's a pretty good sign that it's cool enough to be put into boxes or beds. Place it at a depth of 9–12in (23–30cm), reasonably firm and even, not in wads (that is, making hard and soft spots) or it will give you a poor crop. Moving the manure usually causes its temperature to rise again to over 60°F (15.5°C), so test it with a thermometer and wait until it's back to a steady 60°F (15.5°C) when you can spawn the bed.

Years ago gardeners got spawn from old hotbeds or the edges of manure heaps where it occurred naturally; now it's bought in blocks or in grain form. The grain form is wheat impregnated with spawn and you just spread it over the surface of the box or bed and it finds its own level. If you've got the block sort, break it into pieces each roughly the size of a walnut – it'll be flaky and easy to break. Insert the pieces into the box or bed 12in (30cm) apart either way. Put each piece roughly 1in (2.5cm) below the surface of the manure, no deeper. The box or bed then has to be kept at no more than 60–65°F (15.5°–18.3°C). Cover the top with black polythene to keep the moisture in. In the Mushroom house the beds were left open, but I used to damp them and the floor down once or twice a day to get a nice humid feel to the atmosphere. If the beds looked as though they were drying, I lightly syringed them over with a fine spray.

After about three weeks, depending on how good the conditions have been, you can pull back the manure or compost and see the mycelium beginning to run. It'll look like white, hair-like roots through the surface of the manure. At this point it's time to case (cover) the top of the box or bed with either soil from molehills or chalk (in

Collecting molehill earth.

the old days gardeners might use good loam which had been stacked for some time). I like to use molehill earth, which is nice, crumbly, maiden soil. Spread it to a depth of 1–1½ (2.5–4cm) over the surface of the manure. It'll help to keep in the heat and, when the mycelium runs into it, it'll give the same conditions as Mushrooms have in a field. Pat the casing down lightly and keep it damp but not wet. Continue to maintain a temperature of 60–65°F (15.5–18.3°C). After a month or six weeks, depending on the time of year and management, Mushrooms will start to appear.

PICKING

When you pick the Mushrooms, pull them out with the little root boss on the end, then cut off the root. Fill up the holes they've left with the same material you've used for casing and lightly damp the bed down again. This will keep the bed clear for more Mushrooms.

Depending on the time of year, a bed can last for a month to six weeks. I've had a succession of Mushrooms from October until the middle of January, but as the days warmed up I used to find it difficult to keep the Mushroom house down to 60°(15.5°C) and to keep the Mushroom fly out. This pest lays eggs that turn into maggots which burrow into Mushrooms.

A TRAP FOR WOODLICE
If Mushroom beds or boxes are troubled by woodlice, cut a potato in half, scoop out the flesh and put the 'shells' on to the bed. The woodlice will crawl into them and so be easy to remove.

Marrows, · Courgettes, Squashes · and · Pumpkins

CHAPTER TEN
Marrows, Courgettes, Squashes and Pumpkins

Marrows, Courgettes, Squashes and Pumpkins belong to the Curbita family and nearly all need the same treatment. They like a very well-manured piece of ground. For example, if you are planting or sowing them onto a plot of land which the previous year carried, say, a crop of spring Broccoli, Kales or a late-cleared crop of Parsnips, the soil won't be over-stocked with manure and you will need to supplement it. In such a case dig out a hole 2 ft (60cm) × 2ft (60cm) and work in a couple of forkfuls of manure. This will give them the right conditions.

An exception to this liking for manure is the Custard Marrow which seems to thrive on ordinary ground.

A few suggested varieties:

Marrows (Bush)
'F₁ Tiger Cross'; 'Tender and True'; 'Green Bush Improved'.
(Trailing)
'Long Green'; 'Long White'; 'Table Dainty'.
Courgettes
'Zucchini'; 'F₁ Green Bush'.
Pumpkins
'The Mammoth'.
Custard Marrow
'White'; 'Yellow'.

Left: Marrows and Pumpkins among the Onion crop.
Right: 'Green Bush' Marrow.

123

SOWING UNDER GLASS

Sow under glass in April, one seed per 3½in (9cm) pot, and keep at 55–60°F (12.6–15.5°C). These will be ready for planting out 3ft (1m) apart at the end of May/beginning of June. At this time the weather should be reasonably frost-free, but have some form of frost protection at the ready until mid-June.

SOWING OUT OF DOORS

Sow outside from the end of May, no closer than 3ft (1m) apart.

CULTIVATION

Never let them go short of water as they need plenty of moisture during their quick growing season. Insects do a good job of pollinating the flowers. You can tell them apart quite easily as the female has an obvious swelling behind the flower. Once the fruit has formed give the plants liquid farmyard manure (see p. 23) or any other nitrogenous feed. Keep free of weeds. You may need to protect the fruit from rotting as they reach a good size. Lift them off the soil and lay them on something like an old piece of slate or some wood. From a late May sowing, marrows and courgettes will be ready in early July and Squashes and Pumpkins will be ready in September/October.

HOW TO SLOW DOWN A MARROW
If you want to make Marrows keep pace with one another in size, cut a V-shape into the stem of any that are growing too fast for you.

Above: Male and female flowers. Right: Courgette 'Zucchini'.

Aubergines and·Capsicums

CHAPTER ELEVEN
Aubergines and Capsicums

Aubergines

Aubergines need the warmth and shelter of a greenhouse. They're not successful under cloches, although I did grow them in a deep brick frame in the days when there was labour to put air on when needed and take it off when not. 'Rima' is a good variety. 'Moneymaker' gives you early fruit.

Aubergine seed looks like Tomato seed. Sow it in March/April into a small pot or a seed pan containing the usual seed-sowing compost. Stand this in a propagating case or a greenhouse at 60°F (15.5°C).

When the seedlings have reached the leaf stage, prick them off into a 3in (7.5cm) pot filled with any compost that will grow Tomatoes. Keep growing on in a temperature of 60°F (15.5°C) with a bit of humidity. From the early stages check for whitefly, a pest which makes the leaves sticky and black. At the end of April/beginning of May, when each plant has three or four leaves, plant them into beds under glass, allowing 2ft (60cm) apart either way. Alternatively plant one to a 10in (25cm) pot. When the plants reach 12in (30cm) high, support each with a stake which reaches 3ft (1m) above the soil's surface.

The plants will go up on a single stem, but if they start to make a lot of side shoots pick these out when they're at the one- or two-leaf stage. If you like you can leave one or two side shoots, but

Above: Aubergines. Facing page: Red Pepper.

127

take their tops out: the plant will fruit on these as well as on the main stem. When the fruit is set water regularly and give the plants liquid farmyard manure (see p. 23) or a bag fertiliser such as Tomerite. They'll be ready for use from the end of June through to the end of August. Cut the fruit when the skins are shiny. They tend to taste bitter when they lose their shine.

Capsicums

Capsicums need the same treatment as Aubergines. They're not really successful under cloches but do fairly well in a frame which can give 2–2½ft (60–75cm) of headroom. The best way to grow them is in a bed in a greenhouse. 'Bell Boy' is a good variety.

They don't require stopping but if side shoots are too plentiful cut them off completely or pinch them back to a couple of leaves. The plant becoming too blowsy and not much fruit setting are also signs that some shoots need removing.

The fruit, depending on the variety, can be round or box-shaped. It starts off green but, again depending on the variety, becomes red or yellow.

Hot peppers or chili peppers can be laid out and dried in the sun. You can then store them in airtight glass jars and use them during the winter months.

Capsicums growing in a roomy coldframe at Chilton, but they do better in a greenhouse.

Herbs

*Angelica – Balm – Basil – Borage – Caraway – Chervil –
Dill – Fennel – Garlic – Hamburg Parsley – Horseradish –
Marjoram – Mint – Oregano – Parsley – Rosemary – Rue –
Sage – Savory – Sorrel – Tarragon – Thyme*

CHAPTER TWELVE
Herbs

Having been a cook, my mother knew how to flavour food with herbs, and when I was a lad I enjoyed her cooking, but that's as far as my interest in herbs used to go! We didn't have a great selection in our cottage garden: Parsley, Sage and Mint which, like Rhubarb, seemed to be everywhere.

My interest in herbs wasn't sparked even when I started work as a garden boy. I had to pick them when I was told and dreaded being put to work near their bed where I'd be tormented by the gnats and flies which hovered over it all day. However, whichever garden I went to work at, I unwittingly learned about herbs for they'd be growing in ordered rows, as path edging or as various oddities doing well in corners. It was useful knowledge because, when I became head gardener at Chilton, herbs in variety were always needed. Even when my employers went to their London house, the vegetable hampers which were dispatched to them every week were often topped with Parsley, Mint and French Tarragon, and always with Sage and Thyme.

Herbs were a regular part of spring sowing in the kitchen garden. Also in spring you'd always find pots of Dill in the glasshouses and in summer, under cool glass, pots of Basil. In the autumn, when the outside herb border was cleaned up,

Left: Blue Borage flowers.

Mint was lifted and potted and during the winter it flourished in the Peach house together with a few 10in (25cm) pots of Parsley. Parsley was also important enough to be given a four-light set of coldframes all to itself. These were sown up in July and provided a supply all winter.

The garden staff always paid attention to such crops, especially the man who gathered vegetables and herbs for the kitchen. It was a crime to take to the house any herb which had a flower on it. If a gardener was hard pressed, he carefully picked the flower off before the produce left the garden!

In herb cultivation soil's not too important because most herbs are weeds which have become garden crops as a result of kitchen needs. In fact trenching and manuring would be harmful to many of them, which would become fat and rich and tasteless as a result. Spartan diet and the sun's heat gives them flavour. That's not to say that they should be neglected, especially when it comes to weeds, which will compete with them. Bindweed, underground ivy, and couch grass love the haven offered by patches of Thyme, Mint, Sage and Tarragon.

This chapter is about how to grow the most well-know herbs, but before I begin on details of their cultivation I think it's only right to state that if you want only a few herbs – say, Thyme, Sage, Mint, Tarragon and Chives – don't bother with growing them from seed. Instead buy a pot or two from your local garden centre, and by their second year these will supply more than you require. This is much better than purchasing a packet of seeds which will produce a huge number of seedlings that will need hours of weeding in their early stages.

Angelica

First of all, it should be said that it's much cheaper to purchase ready-preserved angelica from your local stores. However, it's an attractive plant in the

Angelica.

herb garden, so if you want to grow it you can raise it from seed. Sow in April in a standard-sized seed box filled with poor, gritty soil. Moisten the soil before sowing and cover the seed with approximately ½in (3mm) of soil. Cover the box with a pane of glass and, when the seeds have germinated, prick off the seedlings, one to a 3½in (9cm) pot. Grow on cool and in full light.

Plant out on to a piece of reasonable ground (not too heavily manured), allowing 2ft (60cm) apart either way. Keep watered and mulch if the weather's very dry. In winter protect with cloches or dry litter. Be patient and wait until the plant has made good-sized stems before crystallising them, otherwise you'll go to a lot of trouble for little return.

Balm

Balm is a perennial plant which looks after itself. It can be raised from seed or propagated by division. Sow the seed under glass from late February to March, two or three seeds per 3in (7.5cm) pot. Open-ground sowing can take place in March/April. If you're propagating by division, lift an old clump in the autumn or spring and, using a spade, chop a bit off the outside of the clump. Plant the piece where you want it to remain.

CULTIVATION
Balm will be trouble-free for years but it's very invasive, so keep it strictly within bounds and hoe off immediately all unwanted seedlings that appear. It will grow to 2½–3½ft (75cm–1.1m) in height.

Basil

At my present garden I've never grown Basil successfully out of doors. I grow it instead in 6in (15cm) pots. In April each pot is filled to within 1in (2.5cm) of the rim with old potting soil (that is, from another pot crop). Six seeds are sown per pot and lightly covered with sandy soil. These are germinated in a temperature of 50–60°F (10–15.5°C). The plants are grown on in a temperate house and the pots are given light or shade as the day requires.

Borage

When I was a lad it was my job to take a bunch of Borage up to the butler's pantry so that he could float the blue flowers on the claret cup served mid-morning. Borage likes a good, open, sunny site. It's fairly hardy and, once sown, comes up year after year. Sow the seed in March/early April under glass and plant out in early May. Alternatively sow in a shallow drill in open ground in March or April.

Caraway

Caraway is another herb which seems to look after itself. My patch was sown four years ago and is still going strong.

It's unlikely that you'll get Caraway in the same year that you sow it. Sow under glass in January, two or three seeds to a 3in (7.5cm) pot, and plant out in April/early May.

In March broadcast seed in a coldframe or in drills on open ground. Make the drills 12in (30cm) apart. A June or early July sowing will build up nice plants for cropping the following year.

When you have some well-established plants, allow a few to set and drop seed where they will. Apart from keeping the seedlings free from weeds, this should take care of your Caraway's requirements.

Top: Caraway in flower. Above: Shaking seeds out of dried Caraway heads.

KEEP SOWING-SEED FOR SOWING
Don't be tempted to cook with Caraway or Coriander seed bought for sowing. It might have been treated against rot or disease. Wait until you can produce your own!

Chervil

Chervil is best grown in a corner. Sow a little seed in spring under an Apple tree or in a similar out-of-the-way position where there are few weeds. It will need very little attention. We've got a few odd corners of Chervil here at Chilton although I can't remember when I last sowed it because there's been no need: it grows, it flowers, it seeds and reproduces itself. It's not invasive or a nuisance in any way.

Chives

See p. 50.

Dill

On and off I've had to keep up a supply of Dill and found, after a few failures, that the best way to grow it is to sow little and often.

For early work it should be sown in pots. Use 6–7in (15–18cm) pots filled to sowing depth with soil from another pot crop. Sow ten to twelve seeds per pot and lightly cover the seed with porous soil. Cover over with paper and keep at 55°F (12.6°C) until the seed has germinated, then put the seedlings into as light and airy a position as possible. Dill plants are frail, spindly things which don't last long, hence the need to keep sowing.

SOWING UNDER A CLOCHE
From April onwards you can sow under a cloche: the old lantern type is ideal for Dill. Place the cloche on ordinary kitchen garden soil, anywhere in the sun. Make the ground under the cloche level and water it if dry. Broadcast seed on the surface and lightly cover with ordinary garden soil. It usually germinates freely and will need water in the cloches. Dill is a herb suited to odd corners, or you might like to grow a pot or two on spare glasshouse benches. I think it's a waste of a row if it's spread across good growing ground.

Fennel

Fennel is a perennial but it can be treated as an annual and sown each spring. It's aniseed taste is used for flavouring fish and vegetable dishes. There is a bronze-leaved cultivar which, if left alone, grows up to 7ft (2.2m) in height. It looks attractive in either the herb or flower garden as it produces yellow flower heads which last for a very long time. However, once it goes to flower, the plant loses its usefulness for flavouring and becomes pretty much an ornament only.

Sow in April on land which was manured the year before. Rake and tread the land down to a fine tilth and draw out a shallow drill. It's rare that anyone would want more than one drill, but if several are required make them 1½ft (45cm) apart. Thin the seedlings to 6in (15cm) apart and keep free of weeds. If it's important to have a continuous supply, feed with liquid farmyard manure (see p. 23). In the autumn/winter, cut the plant down to ground level and clean up. Top dress with some very old farmyard manure. Fennel seems not to be troubled by aphids or other pests. If you're treating Fennel as an annual, sow and cultivate as

Above: Fennel both bronze and green. Right: Hamburg Parsley.

outlined above but in the autumn chop it up and dig it in. However, I'd recommend leaving a plant or two to grow as a perennial, perhaps in a flower border, because they'll provide an earlier picking than the next seed-sown crop.

Garlic

Garlic isn't easily grown in Britain. I find that what usually happens is that the top dies off before the bulb has made much size. If you get a 2in (5cm) bulb, you're doing pretty well.

For growing it needs lightish soil and a sunny, well-drained spot. Plant in February/March. Split up a big bulb and place the sections (cloves) 12in (30cm) apart with 1in (2.5cm) or so of soil over

each. Keep clear of weeds. I've never known Garlic to be watered. The crop will be ready from the end of July onwards, when it should be dug up and dried like an Onion. Store in a dry, airy, frost-free shed.

Hamburg Parsley

Hamburg Parsley has a root which looks like a Parsnip but is much smaller, more the size of a Carrot. I believe that some people cook the root like a Parsnip, but all the cooks I've known have just grated it and used it as a garnish.

The foliage looks like that of plain-leaved parsley, but is a lighter green. It can be used like ordinary Parsley but the latter has a better flavour.

Horseradish

Horseradish takes up a lot of room, so if your garden is very small I'd advise that instead of growing it, you buy it from your grocery store. If you do want to grow it, it can be raised from seed or by propagation. Sow the seed in March/April in a corner, an old orchard or any place out of the way. From seed it will take two and a half years before you get a really good root which you'll be able to grate. The plants will look after themselves.

If you're propagating by roots, take them off the parent plant in winter. Make each about 6in (15cm) long and ensure that it has a crown on the top. Put the roots into damp soil and cover to protect from frost. Plant them out in March, 12in (30cm) apart either way, on land where they won't be disturbed.

Horseradish.

Marjoram

Both Sweet Marjoram and Knotted Marjoram should be sown on an open site in April to May. They don't need rich land. Make shallow drills 12in (30cm) apart and sow the seed thinly. Don't bother to thin the seedlings. All they'll ask is to be kept free of weeds.

Mint

Although Mint can be sown from seed, it's much simpler to go along to a garden centre and buy a pot of it or to scrounge a cutting.

HOW TO TAKE CUTTINGS

Take cuttings any time between May and August. Select a shoot and cut it cleanly below a joint. The shoot should be about 3in (7.5cm) long: if it's longer, it'll flop over. Put five cuttings to a 4in (10cm) pot filled with light, sandy, peaty compost and water in. Place the pot in a polythene bag and tie the top. The cuttings should root within three weeks. When they have rooted, plant them out where required. In August/September, when your main bed is looking tired, these young plants will provide nice, fresh shoots for your Mint sauce!

Oregano

Oregano needs poorish soil and full sun. Sow during April and May in shallow drills 12in (30cm) apart. There's no need to thin the seedlings but keep them free of weeds.

Parsley

Parsley is probably one of the most used herbs. It likes a plot of land which has had some compost or farmyard manure dug into it the previous year.

FIRST SOWING

You can make your first sowing under glass in January. Use 3–3½in (7.5–9cm) pots, filled to

within 1in (2.5cm) of the rim with a light seed-sowing compost. Water the compost, allow to drain and sow approximately half a dozen seeds per pot. Cover the seed with ⅛in (3mm) of soil, put a pane of glass over the pots and keep at approximately 60°F (15.5°C). Germination will be slow. As soon as the seedlings appear, place them in full light as near the glass as possible. This method will produce nice plants for planting out at the end of March or for potting on for a window box herb collection.

OPEN-GROUND SOWING

Sowing in open ground can take place as soon as the soil can be worked without clinging to your boots. Sow as handy to your kitchen as possible and near a path, so that when you pick in wet weather you won't have to tread on sticky soil. Rake the ground down to a fine tilth, draw a shallow drill and sow the seed thinly. Weed as soon as the seedlings show a clear row. Thin the seedlings to 3–4in (7.5–10cm) apart to help the

remaining plants develop good stems of Parsley. Water in very dry weather.

If space permits, a few plants can be allowed to seed and these will reproduce the bed, but usually self-seeded plants give a smaller stem of Parsley than hand-sown ones.

Above: Pots of plain-leaved Parsley.
Top of page: A frame sown with Moss Curled Parsley in early June provides a crop through the winter.

137

Rosemary

Plant Rosemary in the open or against a wall or fence. It also looks well in a flower garden.

GROWING FROM SEED

Sow in a standard seed box under warm glass in January/February. Make up an open compost from 1 bushel (36 litres) of sifted loam, ½ bushel (18 litres) of peat or leaf soil, a shovelful of grit and a couple of handfuls of bone meal. Prick the seedlings off into this compost, one seedling per 3in (7.5cm) pot. Plant out 2ft (60cm) apart in April/May.

GROWING FROM CUTTINGS

There are two ways:
(1) Follow the method given for taking a summer cutting of Mint (see p. 136).

(2) Cut some semi-ripened shoots in August, treat in the same manner as summer cuttings, then over-winter in a coldframe or under any cold glass. Plant them out in March and April of the following year.

Rue

I doubt that you'd need more than one plant of Rue. Buy it from a garden centre in April or May and plant it in a sunny spot. It doesn't become rampant and can stay in the same position for several years. If it does begin to show signs of deterioration, take some nice, fresh cuttings of semi-ripened wood during August. Put two or three of them round the edge of a pot and keep the pot under a cloche or cold glass through the first winter. Plant out where required in the following April.

Above: Rosemary. Right: Rue. Left: A bunch of Parsley surrounded by (clockwise from centre top) Purple Sage, Sorrel, Apple Mint, Rue, Balm, Chives, Bronze Fennel, Thyme, Sage and Rosemary.

Sage

Grow Sage from seed or from a cutting, following the methods given for Rosemary (see p. 139).

Savory

Summer Savory and Winter Savory both require the same treatment as Oregano (see p. 136).

Sorrel

Sow Sorrel in March in shallow drills in open ground. Thin the seedlings, allowing 2–3in (5–7.5cm) between each to give them a chance to

Sorrel.

make good plants. Keep hoed. This herb is pretty trouble-free and goes on for years. It does tend to run to seed quite early in April/May, however, so if you want to keep up a good supply of leaves cut off the seed stems. Should you miss doing this, cut the whole lot off to within 1in (2.5cm) of the ground and it will quickly reproduce a nice crop of succulent leaves.

Increase by division (splitting a piece off the root) in March/April.

Tarragon

After a year or two Tarragon spreads, so it needs a corner away from open ground. However, because it requires to see the sun, you should ensure that it is a sunny corner. Sow as for Rosemary (see p. 139) but prick off three to five seedlings to a pot. Alternatively sow in a favourable outdoor spot in April.

Thyme

Thyme seed is very tiny and the seedlings are also small, so it pays to sow it in a pot. Sow in March under warm glass and use the same compost described for pricking out Rosemary (see p. 139). When large enough prick off to three to five seedlings to a pot. Plant out in May/June. Thyme is mat-forming and you'll quickly get a useable leaf by August, but don't be too hard on young plants.

Introduction·to·Fruit

*Forms of tree – How to wire a wall – How to erect a
fence to support espaliers or cordons – Heeling-in –
General instructions on planting and pruning*

CHAPTER THIRTEEN
Introduction to Fruit

I first became interested in fruit growing in the late 1920s. It was then that the Blackmoor estate was building up its stock of fruit trees. On winter afternoons when I went to the farm to collect our daily supply of milk, I saw the fruit hands using their knives to trim root stocks which would be planted when conditions were right. The stool bed, in which the stocks were grown, looked an odd sight: like a great big row of earthed-up Potatoes. When the stocks were planted out they took up large areas of the estate and, standing at the back of Church Cottages, I used to watch men budding them. These budders worked from early morning until late evening and so fast that some had a man working behind to tie the bud in.

My early fascination with the work that went into fruit trees grew and grew when I began to see the wonderful collections and varieties of fruit in large private estate gardens. The Gages my head gardener uncle grew under glass at Blackmoor were a sight to see, and when I was put to do menial tasks under glass at Stansted Park gardens I loved the smell of the Peach house and the way the Figs were stood neatly in pots along the border. As well as the Peach house and vineries, Stansted had an orchard house. It was a small orchard under glass, about ¹⁄₁₆ acre (0.02 hectare). There were three beds in the middle of the house

containing Peach trees as big as Apple trees. Where the roof space lessened, pots of Cherry and Plum trees stood in rows. A hive of bees used to be put in to pollinate the blossom. It looked lovely then and later when the fruit ripened.

I've seen outside fruit grown in many shapes and forms, a lot of it spread, a picture of neatness, against the garden walls.

Soft fruit grew in rows in the kitchen gardens or in a fruit cage. When I worked as a foreman at Nuneham Park near Oxford, I was told that the fruit cage there was the second largest in the country. It consisted of a framework of metal closed in wire, so high that it could accommodate a standard Cherry tree. The gardeners used to grow crops of vegetables between its fruit bushes.

I think that it was these early insights into fruit which drew me into life in the walled garden and I was encouraged along the way because, like all true horticulturalists, fruit growers are friendly and helpful to beginners. Experience has taught me that fruit is a year-round job, for as soon as the last crops are gathered it's time to start all over again. But it's hard to find an occupation which gives so much pleasure and can be profitable too!

Fruit, like vegetables, has its basics. You need to know the different forms of fruit trees and the best situations for them. For example, a wall is the ideal location for a fan-trained tree; a post and wire fence can support an espalier or cordon and open

Left: Inside Chilton's unique storehouse.

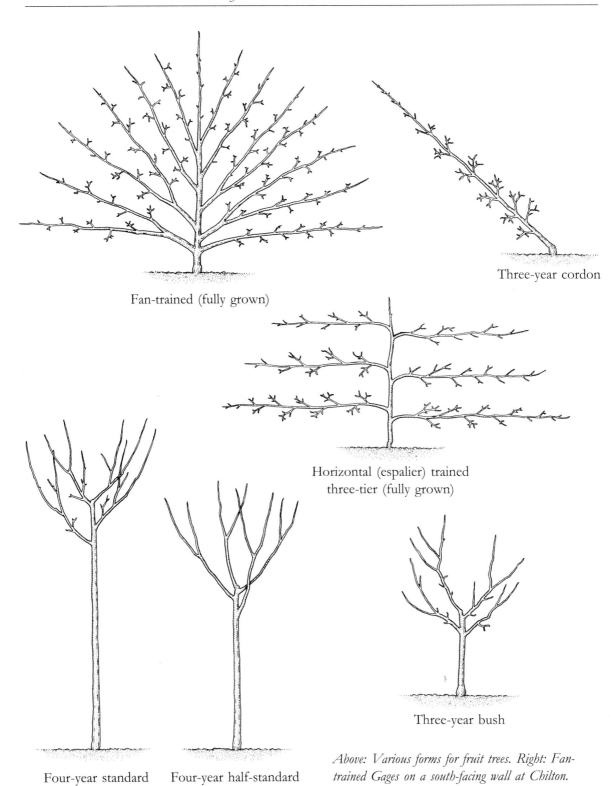

Fan-trained (fully grown)

Three-year cordon

Horizontal (espalier) trained
three-tier (fully grown)

Three-year bush

Four-year standard

Four-year half-standard

Above: Various forms for fruit trees. Right: Fan-trained Gages on a south-facing wall at Chilton.

ground is best for bush and standard trees. Tree planting has its basic dos and don'ts and it is important to know why pruning is done.

How to Wire a Wall
for a Fan-trained Tree

To wire a wall for a fan-trained fruit tree you'll need vine eyes and strainers to pull the wire really tight, both available from garden centres. If you're planting only one tree you'll require strainers at just one side with the vine eyes on either side. Each eye should be driven into the wall so that it ends up sticking out approximately 2½–3in (6–7.5cm). This will allow a current of air between the wall and the tree. Make the first line of wire 2ft (60cm) from the ground and further rows every 12in (30cm) above. For one tree the span of wire should be about 12ft (3.6m).

145

How to Erect a Post-and-wire Fence to support Espalier or Cordon Trees

Put good, strong posts where you intend each end of the fence to be. Strut the posts or sink them in concrete for extra strength, then put other posts between at intervals of 10ft (3m). These posts should stand 6ft (1.8m) out of the ground. Fix strand wire to the posts and straining bolts to the end posts. Three or four wires should be enough, the first line 2ft (60cm) from the ground and further rows every 12in (30cm) above.

Right: Post-and-wire fence.
Below: An espalier-trained Apple.

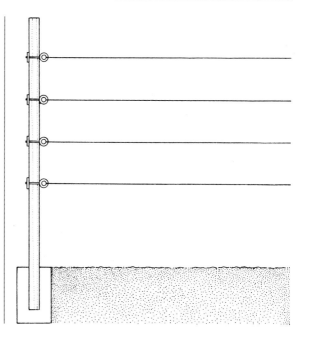

Heeling-in

If, for any reason, fruit trees or bushes can't be planted straight away – for example, the ground might be too frosty – they can be safely kept 'heeled' into a trench. If the ground is too hard even to allow a trench to be dug, leave them in their packing and put them into a shed. They'll be safe enough for a few days, but as soon as the frost eases dig a trench large enough to take their roots. Throw the soil into a heap just clear of the trench and pile it up like a Potato ridge. Then, putting their roots into the trench, lay the trees against the ridge of soil. Cover the roots over by digging along, just as if you were digging a piece of ground. Being inclined like this, trees won't blow over and possibly break as they might if they're temporarily planted upright.

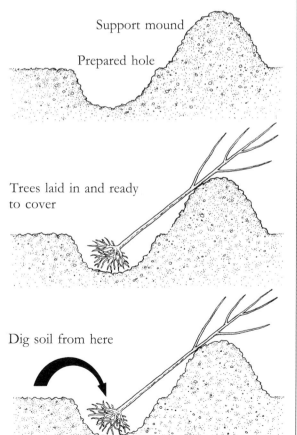

Support mound

Prepared hole

Trees laid in and ready to cover

Dig soil from here

Planting Fruit Trees

PREPARING THE GROUND

If you're going to plant a new fruit tree in a spot which has grown a similar tree, it's best to start afresh and replace the soil in the planting area. Do this by digging out a hole 1½ft (45cm) deep, 4–5ft (1.2–1.5m) long and 2ft (60cm) wide. If new topsoil isn't available to replace the old, the next best thing is to take some from another part of the garden which hasn't been used for growing fruit trees.

PLANTING

Plant no deeper than the mark from the nursery's planting which should be easy to see, for that's the point at which the tree has found its natural root run.

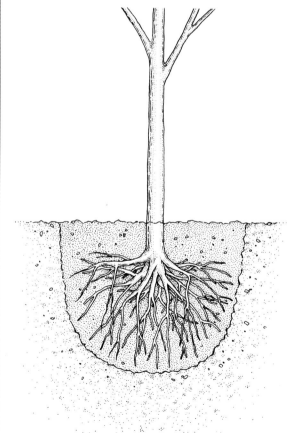

Bare-rooted trees

Plant bare-rooted trees any time between October and late February. Make the hole so that it's large enough to take the roots without any being bent. Place the tree in the hole and spread out its roots, trimming off any broken ones. Work some fine soil into the roots and shake the tree to settle the soil. Tread the soil down firmly. Fill in some more, tread, and continue in this way until the hole is level with the existing site. Then tread it firm as this helps the tree to recover from its move.

Container-grown trees

Although container-grown trees can be planted at any time, bearing in mind the dry summers we've had it's sensible to plant them in the autumn. Water the tree well before taking it out of its container. When you do take it out, don't break up the ball of soil. Tease a bit of bottom root out and, with a pointed stick, gently break up a little of the soil on the ball's surface to tease out root from there too. When it's in the planting hole, surround the ball with ordinary soil.

SECURING

After planting a tree against a wall or fence, make a few *loose* ties to secure it just enough to prevent wind damage. The reason for this temporary tying is to allow the tree to settle down. It will sink in quite a marked way and, if tied to tightly, will have a 'hung' look by the time spring comes. In spring add soil to relevel the ground around the base and secure the tree well.

Free-standing trees will need staking after planting and those on dwarfing root stocks will need staking through their entire life. This is because they tend to have poor roots.

Pruning Fruit Trees

YOUNG TREES

Pruning a young tree helps to form its framework: that is, the removal of one bit stops the growth in that direction and sends sap to other parts which are stronger or in a better position for training into shape.

FOUR-TO-FIVE-YEAR-OLD TREES

A standard tree of this age usually has the branches thinned out only to let light in.

A fancy trained tree such as a fan or espalier will have reached its allocated wall space, so pruning is carried out to keep it within that. It's also done to encourage young wood because fruit will eventually come from the fruit spurs formed on young wood.

OLD TREES

Pruning old trees involves removing decayed wood and thinning out unfruitful spurs so that young spurs will come in their place.

GLOSSARY OF PRUNING TERMS

Central leader The trunk.

Leading shoot The youngest end of each branch consisting of wood made during the previous growing season. Leading (leader) shoots are pruned in winter.

Lateral A side shoot on a leading shoot.

Sub-lateral A side shoot on a lateral.

Fruiting spur A stumpy branch which produces leaf shoots as well as fruit buds. The leaf shoots are pruned in summer to let in light to the fruit. The stumpy branch builds up the future supply of fruit buds.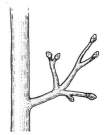

Fruit buds Rounder and plumper than a leaf bud, its rounded top looks something like a half Pea seed. A leaf bud is much smaller and closer to the stem. When pruning, the cut should be angled away from the bud, about ¼in (0.6cm) above it.

 right   wrong

Tree·Fruit

Apples – Pears – Cherries – Plums and Gages –
Peaches and Nectarines – Figs

CHAPTER FOURTEEN
Tree Fruit

Apples

Apples can be trained in all sorts of shapes. A favourite method in kitchen gardens was to have them as cordons and espaliers beside the pathways. This had two benefits: they were handy to attend to and they obscured the vegetable plots which many gentry didn't want to see!

Bush specimens were also grown around the outside of vegetable plots, about 10 or 12ft (3–3.6m) from the paths. The border between trees and path formed a useful site for raising brassica seedlings and catchcrop Lettuce, Radish and Turnips.

Kitchen garden foremen were masters at rejuvenating old trees. They used to top graft so that trees ended up with a young head on old branches.

CHOOSING VARIETIES

If you're planting only a few Apples, ask your nurseryman if they will pollinate one another. This has been something I've not had to bother about, because whichever garden I've been at, there have always been plenty of different varieties of this fruit. However, I know that commercial growers who grow a lot of only one variety – say, 'Cox's Orange Pippin' – have to plant so many pollinators to so many 'Cox's'.

Any of the following varieties will pollinate a 'Cox' – in fact they'll all help one another: 'James

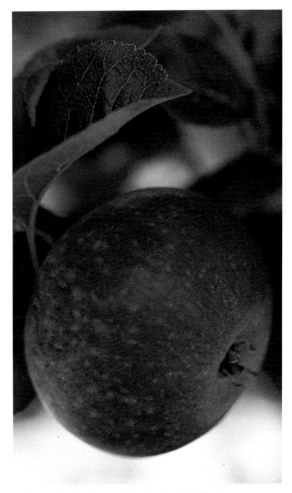

Above: Cox's Orange Pippin Apple. Facing page: Doyenné du Comice Pears.

Grieve', 'Charles Ross', 'Ellison's Orange', 'Merton Beauty', 'Worcester Pearmain', 'Howgate Wonder', 'Grenadier' and 'Golden Delicious'. I wouldn't recommend a 'Cox' for an amateur, though, because it's difficult and needs skill. Instead I'd suggest, by way of dessert Apples, 'James Grieve' (crops in August/September), 'Worcester Pearmain' (early September), 'Sunset' (September) and 'Lord Lambourne' (October). Culinary apples I'd recommend are 'Peasgood's Nonesuch' (crops September/early October), 'Bramley's Seedling' (October), 'Warner's King' (October/November) and 'Lord Derby' (November). In fact the list is endless, and the more varieties you have, the less you have to worry about pollination difficulties.

FORM

Apples can be grown as bush trees (on dwarf stock), cordons, espaliers and standards. However, if I have the choice, I never plant standard or half-standard trees because I think that they take too long to come into cropping (some ten to twelve years usually) and they are step and ladder work right from the word go. Another point against them is that for years they'll need staking, and stakes are expensive to buy and a labour to drive into the ground.

Another form of Apple tree I wouldn't bother with is the 'step-over' used for edging a path. This is pushed by nurserymen today, but nothing's new: it's been about many years. To tell the truth, I've always felt that they get in the way, and it's better to grow a decent crop on an espalier or cordon.

SOIL

Plant Apple trees in autumn. They will grow in any good garden soil or on land which has had its fair share of compost or farmyard manure. If the spot chosen has previously grown Apples, replace the soil. If it hasn't, just dig a hole large enough to receive the tree. A few handfuls of bone meal spread over the filling-in soil are useful, but too much compost or farmyard manure at this stage will cause rank growth.

BUSH TREES

A bush tree is easy to grow and, if it's on semi-dwarf stock, is suitable for a small garden. Plant trees on dwarf stock approximately 10ft (3m) apart and those on stronger root stocks 18ft (5.5m) apart. The trees will need staking.

Ideally purchase a two-year-old tree. Three years is the limit, because above that age the branch formation will be too advanced. Don't allow more branches than those already begun by the nurseryman. After planting prune the leader shoots to about half their length. This will help to keep sturdy branches and well-balanced fruit buds. You should aim to retain an open middle to the tree, so take the leaders back to a bottom *side* bud. That is more likely to send out a shoot which will spread than a top bud, which will send up a shoot that will close the middle of the tree.

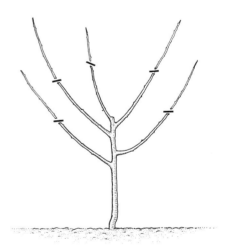

After planting, prune back leaders to about half their length.

In summer, if the tree has made good growth on the laterals which form on the branches, cut each lateral back to four leaves (not counting the cluster of leaves usually found at the bottom of the summer's growth). This will save a lot of winter pruning. However, if a shoot appears on this pruned stub, it should be cut back in winter to one or two buds.

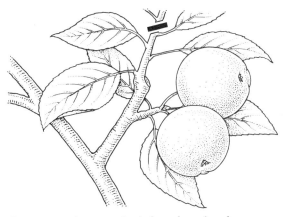

Summer pruning – cut back laterals to four leaves.

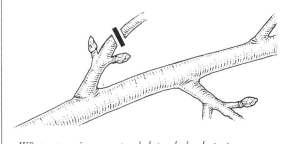

Winter pruning – cut sub-laterals back to two or three buds.

In the following and subsequent winters prune the branches by 6–12in (15–30cm). The weaker the branch, the harder you should prune it. Also prune the sub-laterals (the side shoots on the laterals) back to two or three buds. These in due course will produce fruit buds. Don't touch fruit buds that appear on the stem of the young branches.

CORDONS

Gardeners of the past considered planting cordon Apples against a wall a waste of wall space, but if you need a supply of this fruit over a long period and you live in a frost pocket, a few cordons of choice varieties on a wall will pay off.

Below: Winter reveals the shape of cordons.

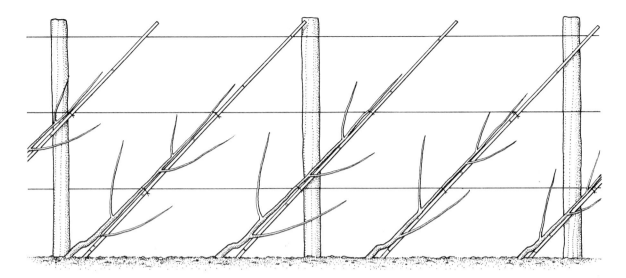

Cordons are excellent on wires beside a path. Space them 2½ft (75cm) apart. They're also productive planted in a block. Make the rows in the block 6ft (1.8m) apart for ease of working and plant the trees 2ft (60cm) apart in the rows.

Train cordons to grow at an angle of 45 degrees, pointing north. This helps to check their growth; instead of racing away they'll settle down and you'll get fruit instead of growth. A few years after planting you can give a bit of extra length by pulling them down to 60 degrees.

How to start

Buy a two-year-old cordon. It will probably have a leader shoot about 2ft (60cm) long. You'll see the mark where the second year's growth has started. Cut the shoot back to leave 6in (15cm) of the second year's growth. Make the cut just above a nice *side* bud, because the shoot from this will grow sideways to start your cordon growing at an angle instead of straight up.

The laterals made on the first year's growth will have been cut back by the nurseryman and they will have the beginnings of two or three fruit spurs (fruit buds won't appear until the second or third year). Laterals from these spurs should be cut back to two or at most three buds. Any laterals made on the second year's growth will probably have

Above: Begin by training cordons at an angle of 45°. A cane positioned at this angle will help guide young trees. Previous page: Picking Apples on a misty morning.

been pruned off by the nurseryman to avoid damage in transit. If they haven't, prune them back to two or three buds from where they join the leading shoot. Do this before planting or by early March.

From this point on take care to keep the leader shoot safely tied to the wires. Don't neglect to water in April and May if conditions turn dry.

If the tree has made good growth by August – say, 12in (30cm) or more – on the laterals and they are quite woody, cut each one back to four leaves (not counting the cluster of leaves usually found at the bottom of the summer's growth). This will save a lot of winter pruning. However, if a shoot appears on this pruned stub, cut it back in winter to one or two buds.

This summer and winter pruning should be carried out every year. Also each winter cut the leading shoot back to about half of its length. Cut it back to a side shoot so that the tree can continue to be trained at an angle. Another winter job is to remove completely any thin, weak growth. Later some weak fruit spurs may need thinning out.

ESPALIERS

I like espaliers. They are excellent on wires, cropping well and giving good-quality fruit which is easy to get at. They also make a nice finish to many areas in a large kitchen garden. In such a garden they're usually planted at intervals of 18–20ft (5.5–6m). I've seen wider planting, but what happens then is that the trees lose spurs at the beginning of their branches and this makes the middle of the trees fruitless. Where space is limited you can plant espaliers as close as 12ft (3.6m) apart.

How to start

Buy a two-year-old tree. Don't cut back any of the growth. Take the central leader (or the nearest shoot to the centre) and fix it upright against the wall or fence. The tree will also probably have one or two shoots about 2–3ft (60cm–1m) in length. Tie these out horizontally on to the wire nearest the ground.

In its first year the leader should reach two wires above the wire where the two horizontal branches are tied. In winter prune the leader back to one wire above them: it's along this wire that you want to train your second pair of horizontal branches.

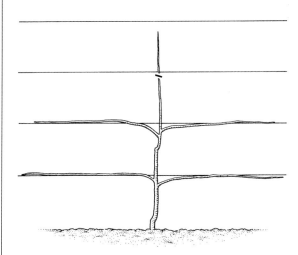

In the next winter, repeat the operation, pruning back to the wire above the second pair of horizontal branches.

Do the same each year, carefully tying the shoot of the new season's growth as soon as it's practicable, because if you lose it you'll cause a gap in the tiers of arms.

Also in winter cut each leading shoot on the wires back by about half its length. Cut to an *underside* bud – the resultant shoot will be easier to pull down to the wire than a shoot from a top bud. Doing this will make a good, strong arm which will fill nicely with fruit spurs. In the years to come these fruit spurs will need some thinning.

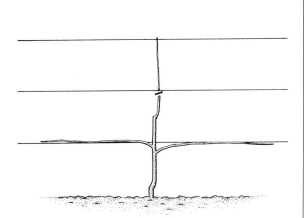

In winter of the first year, prune the leader back to one wire above the horizontal branches.

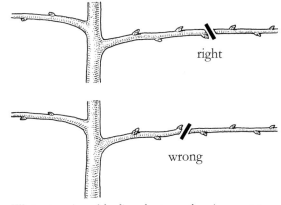

Winter pruning of leading shoots on the wire – cut to an underside bud.

In summer, if growth has been good, cut the laterals which have formed on the horizontal branches back to four leaves (not counting the cluster of leaves usually found at the bottom of the summer's growth). If shoots appear on these pruned stubs, cut them back in winter to one or two buds. When the central leader and horizontal branches eventually reach the length you require, stop them by taking out the tips. Do it in summer when the cuts will quickly seal over.

END FRUIT BUDS

Some trees may develop fruit buds on the end of the year's growth. If the tree is a tip bearer (for example, 'Irish Peach'), you obviously have to leave these, but if it isn't, prune them off, because if fruit is allowed to grow it's likely to swing in the wind and become damaged.

GENERAL CARE

Don't dig fresh manure in among the roots of Apple trees as it will cause them to make rank growth at the expense of fruit. Instead feed in spring with a general fertiliser such as 3 of sulphate of ammonia, 2 of superphosphate, 1 of potash. Applied at 2oz per sq yd (50g per sq m), this will give a tree good, dark green leaves and colour and size to the fruit. In later years it will also help the tree to carry large crops.

In dry seasons mulch Apple trees with compost or strawy manure but clear it away each year to stop the tree rooting into it and becoming rank.

Pears

Pear trees grown on stocks raised from Pear pips used to take so long to grow that someone once wrote of them:

But slowly comes the tree which thou hast sown
A canopy for grandsons of thine own.

However, once nurserymen started to grow Pear trees on Quince stock they began to fruit a lot quicker. The stocks generally used today are Quince A and Quince C. Quince A is a good, semi-vigorous all-rounder which produces bushes 12–15ft (3.6–4.6m) high. Quince C is a moderately dwarfing stock suitable for strong land and strong-growing cultivars like 'Pitmaston Duchess', 'Beurre Hardy' and 'Bellissime d'Hiver'. There are, however, some varieties of Pear (for example, 'Bristol Cross', 'Marie Louise' and 'Packham's Triumph')

Above: Cordon Pear trees. Right: Apples (top line) James Grieve, Cox's Orange Pippin, Pitmaston Pineapple. Apples (middle line) Egremont Russet, Lord Lambourne, American Mother. Pears (bottom line) Williams' Bon Chrétien, Bristol Cross, President Roosevelt, Beurre Hardy.

which, if budded on to Quince, won't take: they blow out the union. This means that they have to be double worked in that first a variety like 'Beurre Hardy' is budded on to the Quince stock and in the following year the variety really wanted is budded on to the 'Beurre Hardy' maiden.

Tradition once had it that you couldn't raise a good crop of Pears on anything but a wall, though that was disproved. In fact, some of the best Pears I've seen were on espaliers grown on wires around vegetable plots. As to other growing places, one oddity I once came across was a small glasshouse devoted solely to Pears. It had had its day by the time I saw it and was over-planted and neglected. In my early days I used to grow a few pots of 'Beurre Easter' under glass but costs got the better of them and they ended up being planted outside where to this day they crop well.

CHOOSING VARIETIES

Most varieties need a pollinator, so choose ones which help each other, for example: 'Beurre Hardy' and 'Doyenné du Comice'; 'Williams' Bon Chrétien' and 'Conference'; 'Pitmaston Duchess' and 'Beurre Hardy'; 'Merton Pride' and 'Conference' or 'Joséphine de Malines'. 'Improved Fertility' is self-fertile and will pollinate many others. If you're unsure about what will pollinate what, a reputable nurseryman will always help.

Durondeau Pear.

SOIL

A good crop of Pears depends largely on good beginnings. A Pear doesn't like heavy clay or very thin, sandy land; it also needs good drainage.

If your soil is clay remove it, especially if you're going to put the tree by a wall, because if you're giving it a good, sunny position it's also worth giving it good soil. Take the existing soil down to a depth of 2ft (60cm), break up the bottom of the hole and put in a layer of brick rubble to a depth of 4–6in (10–15cm). Cover that with turfy loam turned upside down. Use as your planting soil a mixture of chopped-up turf, ⅛in (3mm) aggregate (ask your local builder for a supplier of this), old mortar rubble, charcoal, bone meal and, if it's available, leaf soil. This will result in a nice, balanced tree which will produce strong growth without being rank. The tree should also give a good crop year in, year out. The planting mixture will allow you to water the tree thoroughly in a dry summer too without the fear of its becoming waterlogged.

If your ground is very sandy, give the planting soil some extra body by adding turfy loam.

PRUNING AND TRAINING

Prune Pears much as described for Apples (pages 152–158), one slight difference being that you can prune Pears harder without causing a lot of rank growth. Pears can also be grown in all the forms given for Apples. An additional form which can look attractive is a fan shape trained against a wall.

HOW TO TRAIN A FAN

If the wall isn't ready wired to support a fan, follow the instructions for wiring on p. 145.

A fan tree needs a central leader and an even number of shoots on either side of it. These shoots should be approximately 12–15in (30–38cm) apart and, in due course, be sufficient in number to make the size fan you'd like. Unfortunately, people nowadays, including nurserymen, often don't bother to train a fan correctly. To save time and trouble

Above: The modern method of fan training a fruit tree.
Below: The more attractive result obtained by using the old ways.

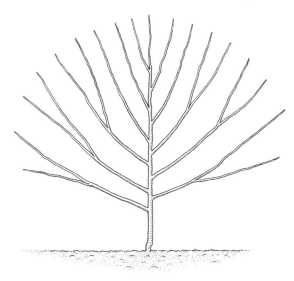

they simply pull branches out into a fan shape from the base. The correct way, and the way I was taught, is to train the tree so that all the fan arms radiate out from a straight central 'spine'. It looks lovely.

You should start with a two-year-old tree which hasn't had its central shoot removed. In fact, the tree itself will look like a long, whippy stem. Leave that shoot intact and let it grow unchecked until it reaches the top of the wall or wires. Then take the top out. You can do this at any time of year, but I like to do it in summer because then the cut heals over and I prefer that to leaving an open cut in winter.

On its way up the leader shoot will produce laterals (side shoots). Train these out to the shape of the fan. If these laterals make more than 3ft (1m) of growth in a year, in winter cut at least a third of that off. If you don't do so you could end up with gaps in the fruiting spurs. Cut back to an *underside* bud because the shoot from this will grow up and it'll be easier to pull down on to the wire than a shoot from a top bud.

The sub-laterals coming from these formation branches should be pruned back in the spring when they're 3–4in (7.5–10cm) long but still soft enough to be easily pinched out with finger and thumb. Take off a third of their length.

The laterals or 'arms' of the fan should be secured when the growth reaches a wire. When they reach the full length you want them to be, stop them by taking the tops out of each one.

As the years go by the only attention the fan needs is for you to make sure that the ties aren't cutting and choking a branch and that no growth gets longer or stiffer than that which can be pinched out with your finger and thumb. It's all quite simple but very effective.

GENERAL CARE

A mulching of farmyard manure or compost in the first year of planting, and certainly in any dry summer, is an advantage. However, I always like to remove what's left of this mulch in the autumn so that the roots don't get into it and upset the tree's balance of growth.

As Pear trees grow older you should make room for fresh fruit spurs by removing those which show few fruit buds and a lot of little dead ends and dead twiglets. Do this spur pruning when the tree is dormant. Bush and standard trees will also need to be thinned to keep their centres open.

Cherries

When you consider buying a Cherry tree, find out whether or not it's self-pollinating. If it's not, enquire as to what variety is needed to pollinate it and, if that variety isn't already in your garden, buy it as well and plant one next to the other.

The variety 'Stella', the first self-fertile Cherry to be introduced, is a good self-pollinator. So is 'Sunburst'. Of the older varieties that need pollinating one of the best is 'Early Rivers'. This needs to be pollinated by either 'Merton Bigarreau', 'Merton Bounty' or 'Merton Heart'.

Above: Stella, the pioneer self-pollinating Cherry.
Left: Keeping a Cherry tree tidy.

FORM

You can grow a Cherry tree as a bush or as a fan trained against a wall or trellis. If you have the space on a suitable site I'd go for the fan every time, both for yield and appearance. Buy a two-year-old fan which hasn't had its central leader removed, then you'll be able to train it in the traditional way.

The planting position isn't very important. I've seen sweet Cherries facing, variously, south, west and north-east. Naturally it's helpful to have an early cultivar on a warm, south-facing wall and I've seen a late dessert on a west-facing wall hang on, though ripe, well into August. (It was well netted against birds!)

PLANTING

Any ordinary, well-looked-after garden soil will suit a Cherry, as long as the tree is watered in dry seasons and fed at appropriate times. If the soil is heavy clay, break it up with the aid of coarse sand or fire ash. Both bushes and fans can be planted at any time between October and early March. I think October is ideal. If you're planting a fan against a wall, your tree stem should be 3–4in (7.5–10cm) away from the wall.

GROWING A BUSH CHERRY

When you get your bush from the nursery it will look something like a bush Apple. In the first year select nice shoots and cut the rest off. It pays to start off with stout shoots because weak ones could flop over with the weight of the fruit. Let these leaders grow on up until they're the height you want: it'll take some time, but when they reach that height take the tops out. I always think it's best to do this in summer when the cuts will seal over quickly.

As the leaders are growing up they'll produce side shoots. Pinch these side shoots back to three or at most four leaves from the point at which they join the leader. This can be done in the summer or as the growth requires. These pruned side shoots will produce fruiting spurs.

GROWING A FAN CHERRY

Follow the instructions for growing a fan-trained Pear (see p. 160), with one exception. This concerns the laterals which form the 'arms' of the fan. On a Pear, to avoid gaps in the fruiting spurs, you should prune these back by a third each year. However, because a Cherry is less vigorous in its growth, there's no need to prune the laterals. Instead let them grow without check until they've reached their full fan shape. At that point stop them by taking the top out of each one. Do this in summer when the cuts seal over quickly.

GENERAL CARE OF BUSH AND FAN CHERRIES

Make sure that Cherries are watered in dry seasons. Feed them when the fruit has set and again after it has been cleared. Feeding after you have picked the fruit will aid the build-up of buds for further crops.

GROWING POTS OF CHERRIES UNDER GLASS TO GET THEM TO CROP EARLY

This method can be applied to pots of Peaches, Nectarines and Figs too. I've also known it to be used by nurserymen anxious to exhibit at important shows pot-grown Apple and Pear trees in fruit. Be warned that pot-grown fruit entails a lot of work and needs skill; however, it's worth it when the early fruits come along.

Buy small bush trees and pot them between October and early November. Use pots no less than 10in (25cm) in diameter and ensure that drainage is adequate by placing crocks, covered with turf fibre, in the bottom. Prepare the potting mixture by adding the following to one barrowful of chopped-down loam: some well-rotted farmyard manure, a double handful of bone meal, a shovelful of charcoal and a couple of shovelfuls of coarse sand.

I've found that the best way to pot a tree is to spread its roots evenly in the pot, then with one hand hold it firmly just above the rim of the pot and with the other hand use a small household fire shovel to drop a fine mix of potting compost gently on to the roots, at the same time gently lifting the tree to allow the soil to settle nicely between the roots. When the roots are covered, put a little more compost in and ram it down with a rammer made from a stick 1½–2in (4–5cm) in diameter. Continue to add more compost and firm it with the rammer until it is 1in (2.5cm) below the rim of the pot.

Now stand the pot out of doors or plunge it up to its rim in ashes. The latter will help to cut down on watering and to build up the roots. In the following spring move the pot into a cool glasshouse. Don't attempt to force it in heat at all, because the first year should be given over to getting the tree established in the pot. In June stand it out again. In October/November remove the top 2–2½in (5–6cm) of original soil and top dress with sweet, fresh compost.

In late autumn place the pot under glass and in January apply a little heat, building it up so that by the end of February it's a steady 55–60°F (12.7–15.5°C).

When the tree comes into blossom, pollinate the flower with a camel-hair brush or a rabbit's tail tied to the end of a small bamboo cane. Keep the heat steady because unlike, say, Peaches or vines under glass, it mustn't be unduly forced at any time.

After blossom fall, be very careful with watering. Without letting the tree suffer, water only when it's needed. The little Cherries will swell away quite freely, but then you'll notice that they've stopped. This is because they're forming stones. You must continue to be very careful with watering and also at this stage with airing. From time to time take a berry and see if, with your knife, you can cut it in half. If you can, it's still stoning. As soon as you can't, it's finished. Give the tree a feed every seven days until the fruits begin to change colour. As the colour increases, the feeding should stop. Never let the tree get dry at the roots, but don't over-water either. Give air freely on all fine days.

As soon as the fruit has been picked, work has to start to build the tree up again. Stand it outside in late February/early March and feed once a week with liquid farmyard manure (see p. 23). Spray with clear water twice a day during June, July and August and keep free of aphids. In October top dress and in late autumn move again under glass to begin again the process of gentle forwarding.

Morello Cherries

The dark fruit of Morellos isn't sweet to taste; it's grown for preserving, especially in brandy. The trees are weaker in growth than sweet Cherries, so new shoots need a lot of tying-in on fan-trained trees. Apart from tying, however, the Morello is usually much less trouble than the sweet Cherry. It's self-pollinating, mostly escapes the frost, doesn't seem to attract a lot of aphids, and the fruit splits less.

You can grow a Morello as a bush, but it's traditional to grow it as a fan on a north-facing wall. Allow the central leader and side shoots to grow as if you were training a fan-shaped sweet Cherry. However, unlike in the case of sweet Cherry, you don't pinch off sub-laterals, because Morellos fruit on the previous year's wood. In winter, therefore, when the leaf has fallen and you can see what you're doing, remove all the wood which has carried a crop of fruit and tie in the new unfruited wood. Tie it to the wires or against the existing laterals so the tree keeps its fan shape. If it's been a good season the new wood will be anything from 1 to 2ft (30 to 60cm) in length, although as the tree gets older you'll find that this growth will become shorter and thinner.

The tying-in will probably take a little time. I can vividly remember what a monumental task it was to tie in a wall of Morellos where each tree was 18ft (5.5m) wide and 7ft (2.2m) high. The wood to be tied in was often not more than 1in (2.5cm) apart, but when the trees fruited they were an unforgettable sight!

A time-consuming job – Morello Cherries need a lot of tying in.

165

Plums and Gages

Plums and Gages cannot be relied on to crop well every year because they blossom at a chancy time. Wall-trained ones are more reliable as you can protect them easily from frost. Trees grown under glass are perhaps the most reliable. However, few people will bother with that method today though it was done successfully years ago, especially in the case of early Plums and late Gages. The finest Gages under glass I've ever seen were grown by my Uncle Fred in the Blackmoor gardens. They were in a lean-to fruit house together with Peaches, Nectarines, a Fig tree and, a bit of a rarity then, a climbing gold-petalled Rose called 'Lady Hillingdon'. To this day I can remember the scent of that house. At that time large numbers of Plums and Gages were also grown out of doors, the best trained as espaliers or fans on the kitchen garden walls. The fruit from these was used as dessert. It wasn't picked until it reached its peak because that was when the flavour was best. I used to hold the basket for Uncle Fred as he picked, only a short time before dinner. The fruit was then taken immediately to the house.

Looking back, I can't remember any bush or standard Plums or Gages being grown within the kitchen garden. They were usually in an orchard close by and supplied fruit for tarts and jam and for bottling. These orchard trees cropped well, though they had very little pruning. There wasn't a lot of hard pruning done on the walled trees either, but they were well trained and tended.

FORM

Owing to their size, standard trees are best planted in a large garden or an orchard where they'll need 20ft (6m) between them. I'd never advise standards for another reason: it's time-consuming step-and-ladder work when it comes to pruning them and picking their crops. Bush Plums might find a place in village gardens but, in the main, I'd advise anyone to grow their Plums and Gages as espaliers, fans or cordons.

CHOOSING A VARIETY

Although many varieties are self-fertile, some will need pollinators. The following are self-fertile: 'Oullins Golden Gage', 'Cherry Plum', 'Denniston's Superb', 'Victoria', 'Marjorie's Seedling', 'The Czar', 'Severn Cross', 'Warwickshire Drooper'. These will also act as pollinators for a beautiful Gage called 'Coe's Golden Drop'.

If you are choosing only a couple, I'd recommend any two of the following: 'Victoria', 'Oullins Golden Gage', 'The Czar', 'Kirke's Blue'. The first three are self-fertile and 'Kirke's Blue' is pollinated by 'Oullins Golden Gage'.

Above: Oullins Golden Gage. Right: Coe's Golden Drop Plum.

PLANTING

Plant in autumn. If you're planting against a wall, the tree should be 6in (15cm) away from it. Plums and Gages will grow in almost any good garden soil which hasn't grown them previously. However, if you select a spot which has grown such trees before, it will pay you to dig a planting hole 4–5ft (1.2–1.5m) long, 2ft (60cm) wide and 1½ft (45cm) deep. Break up the bottom of the hole and work into it some very well-rotted farmyard manure or your own compost. If new topsoil isn't available, take some soil for placing round the tree from a part of the garden which hasn't grown a fruit tree and work a little compost into it.

PRUNING STANDARDS

The head of the standard should have been formed by the nurseryman, but it's usual to prune it for a few years after planting to make it produce good branches. Each year, in winter, cut the leading shoots by at least a third of their growth; and during the growing season, when wounds heal over quickly, stop the centre becoming congested by removing unwanted growth. Once its head has a good outline, a standard is usually allowed to go unchecked.

PRUNING BUSHES

Purchase a two-to-three-year-old bush. Its shape will be already formed, but it will need some pruning to strengthen the branches. To give good, stout ones cut off a third to a half of the leader growth in August. Each May pinch the laterals off the branches back to three or four buds from where they join the branches. These pruned laterals will form fruit spurs. Keep the middle of the bush uncluttered by removing small growth.

ESPALIERS, FANS AND CORDONS

These forms produce high-quality fruit which can easily be protected from birds. Their shape also makes it easy to protect their blossom from late frosts. For fixing support wires follow the instructions given on p. 145. Espaliers and fans need a planting distance of 24ft (7.3m); cordons need 2ft (60cm).

TRAINING AN ESPALIER

Don't cut back any of your young tree's growth. Take the central leader, or the nearest shoot to the centre, up to its middle position and secure it to the wall or fence. The tree will also probably have one or two shoots about 2–3ft (60cm–1m) in length: tie these out horizontally on to the wires.

In its first year, with any luck, the leader will reach two wires above the one where the two horizontal branches are tied. In winter prune the leader back to one wire above them, because it's along this wire that you want to train your second pair of horizontal branches. Do that every year, your aim each time being to obtain two shoots to add another tier to your espalier. If you don't you'll be wasting wall space and suffer a loss of fruit in due course. I like espaliers but you can get into a right old 'two-and-eight' if you're an amateur. Should you have problems, prune a bud off just above a wire and that gives you a chance of three to four shoots, one of which will be near enough to be pulled on to the wire.

Once you've secured a shoot to a wire don't prune off the tip until it's reached the end of the space allocated for it. Each year the only pruning needed will be to pinch out all the laterals growing from these side branches. Do this with your finger and thumb when the growth of each lateral is 3–4in (7.5–10cm) long. This will make fruit buds form along all the side branches as the tree grows. You may have to go over the tree two or three times a year in the early stages, but the older a tree gets, the less it'll need this treatment. When the side branches are as long as you want them to be, stop them by taking the tips off. Do this in summer so that the cuts seal over quickly and there is less risk of disease entering.

TRAINING A FAN

Follow the instructions given for training a fan Pear on page 160.

TRAINING A CORDON

Cordon Plums or Gages can be grown against a wall on wires, against the supports of fruit cages or, as I saw them before the Second World War, against the pillars which support a greenhouse.

To start off a cordon, purchase a maiden tree. It will look like a whippy stick but might have a few side shoots on it. These side shoots are called feathers, though many gardeners know them as 'whiskers'. If any of the whiskers are more than 6in (15cm) long, cut them back. They will then start to form fruit spurs. Each winter cut the leading shoot on the main stem back by half. This will ensure a good foundation and the production of side shoots which will form fruit spurs. In summer, when these are no more than 5–6in (13–15cm) long and the job can still be done with your finger and thumb, pinch their tips out to leave stubs of about 3–4in (7.5–10cm). There will be no winter pruning except to remove approximately half the leader.

GENERAL CARE

In May and June espaliers and fans are often attacked by aphids. Any good insecticide will usually take care of them, especially it it's sprayed on before they get a real hold.

In June both espaliers and fans will benefit from a mulch of farmyard manure or compost, well watered in.

> ### PLUMS THAT GROW ON THEIR OWN ROOT STOCK
> Cultivated Plums don't normally grow on their own root stock, they have to be grafted, usually on to the root stock St Julien A. However, there are some strains of Plum, both blue and golden, which do grow on their own root stocks. They can be grown from cuttings and will grow and fruit from suckers. I have a golden strain in the garden which I hope to see fruit soon.

Peaches and Nectarines

When you buy a Peach or Nectarine tree, choose a fan-trained two-to-three-year-old. By that age it should have a foundation of branches.

Peaches

PREPARATION FOR PLANTING

A Peach will grow out of doors in any well-looked-after garden soil provided that the drainage is right and that the site has a warm aspect.

Suggested varieties of Peaches:
Out of doors: 'Hales Early', 'Rochester', 'Duke of York', 'Princess of Wales'.
Under glass: Any variety you can get, but worth-while are: 'Peregrine', 'Alexander Noblesse', 'Duke of York', 'Barrington', 'Royal George'.

If you opt for growing a Peach under glass, dig out a fair-sized hole, especially if the spot has had a Peach or Nectarine tree in it for some years previously. Make the hole at least 3ft (1m) square and approximately 1½ft (45cm) deep. Break up the bottom, incorporating a little farmyard manure and, if you can, because it'll help drainage, some good, fibrous turf. A possible source of the latter is where contractors are clearing land for a housing site. This will bring the hole up to approximately the right depth for planting.

The actual planting soil should be good loam compost. In large gardens years ago this would be mixed to the head gardener's specification. The loam used would come from a yard on the estate where it had been stacked as turves for at least a year. To every barrow of chopped-down loam was added: a shovelful of old mortar rubble, a shovelful of coarse grit, half a shovelful of charcoal and two handfuls of hoof and horn. This was mixed and left for a few days before use.

PLANTING

Plant bare-root trees from a nursery from October to late February. If you're planting out of doors, make a few ties to keep the tree rigid until spring.

TRANSFERRING A TREE FROM OUTDOORS TO INDOORS

Mid-October, before the leaf has fallen, is the best time to move a young tree growing out of doors into a glasshouse. Dig it up carefully, getting as large a ball of soil as possible. You will need a helper to slip a polythene sheet under the root ball when you lift the tree, then each take two corners of the sheet and carry the tree to its new planting spot. Make sure that the prepared hole is large enough to take the ball of soil and roots before putting the tree in. When it's in, one person should lift the tree slightly and the other should pull the sheet out.

Fill the hole with good, loamy soil or chopped-up turfy soil. If you have to plant with your ordinary soil, add a few handfuls of coarse bone meal. Fill in the hole gradually, treading firm all the time.

If the tree still has green leaves, water well after planting, and in sunny weather shade it and spray it with clear water once a day.

Above: Nectarine 'Elruge'. Top: A good crop of 'Rochester' Peaches. Left: Peach Blossom, flowering Schizanthus and pots of Peas in the Peach house.

171

PRUNING

Gardeners used to prune newly planted trees back to a few buds, but I always think that this is a wasteful practice because I've often planted bare-rooted trees and taken a few Peaches off them in the first year. In fact, letting them crop controls rank growth which often doesn't have any fruit buds anyway, so if you prune them back when they're first planted you could end up losing two years instead of one! A newly planted unpruned Peach (or Nectarine) will romp away if it's in a house being generously treated because its neighbours are mature fruiting trees.

Pruning from the second year onwards

New growth will begin just before the blossom falls. Usually a growth bud comes from every leaf joint. As soon as the growth starts rub off all the buds except for:
(a) one or two buds as near the base of last year's growth as possible;
(b) the top shoot, because that's needed to draw the sap. (Your crop of fruit will be between the bottom two shoots and the top shoot.)

If the leaders which form the 'arms' of the fan are to the length you require, pinch the end of each leader out after it's made five to six leaves. If you want the leaders to go on growing, tie each one in and, as they grow, keep them tied in, in the direction you want them to take.

The shoots from the base of last year's growth will need tying in two or three times during the summer. Tie them in the direction they are meant to fill the following year. Very often other shoots come from latent buds. If these aren't required, rub them off, because it's pointless to tie in more than you require.

THINNING

Thin the fruit to one fruit per 8 × 8in (20 × 20cm) square. Select only the biggest fruit and, on trees which are trained against a wall, make it one which sticks straight out at you from the tree. Those that are facing the wall are useless because they won't get sufficient sunlight and will be cramped by the wall.

GENERAL CARE
Out of doors

If they are carrying good crops, mulch the trees with farmyard manure in June and give them a good soak. Protect the fruit against wasps and birds: some old net curtains can be used or, better still, buy the curtain material and sow widths together to get a suitable size to cover your tree properly.

Under glass

After the blossom has fallen, the fruit will begin to swell. In the early stages it will swell quickly but then seem to stop. This is a critical time for watering because the stone is beginning to form and too much water at this stage can split it. Too great a fluctuation in temperature can also play havoc with stoning. To test if stoning is over, pull off a spare fruit and see if you can cut it through. If the stone is complete it will be impossible to cut through. As soon as this happens, feed once a week with liquid farmyard manure (see p. 23).

From petal fall on all bright, warm days, forcibly spray the trees with a hosepipe. Do this once or twice a day but stop when the fruit begins to ripen otherwise the spray will mark the surface of the fruit and spoil its appearance. On warm days open the glasshouse vents. On really hot days leave them open all the time and protect the trees by applying a coat of glasshouse shading to the outside of the glass.

When the fruit shows signs of ripening – that is, it's putting on colour – stop feeding. The trees should be moist but not wet and should not have water put on to their leaves. Air freely but not so much that on dull days the temperature falls dramatically. To help fruit ripen, a useful tip is to push a label behind each fruit to 'face it up' – that is, to lift it away from the foliage. This will improve its colour and flavour.

Facing-up.

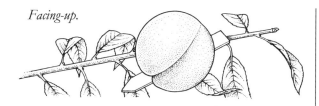

PAMPERED PEACHES OF THE PAST

Up until 1939 the amount of time taken seeing to the airing and wellbeing of fruit houses on private estates was something you had to live through to appreciate.

The nightmare months for a young journeyman were April, May and early June. In any of those months a day might start off warm, so after the morning spraying he would open the glasshouse vents. The outdoor temperature might continue to rise, so he would open the vents a little more, and perhaps a bit more after that, but then suddenly the sun would go in and, to stop the temperature in the house dropping, he would have to close the vents completely. Not long after this the sun might come out again and so he would have to reopen them, and so it went on, and he could be in and out of the house umpteen times a day!

The same care was taken with watering. Using a garden syringe, a man would forcibly spray tepid water on to the trees and their surrounds twice a day.

All this came to an end when costs and the shortage of good-class labour meant that short cuts had to be taken: for example, cold water was used instead of tepid and air was left on all day on warm days. It was then discovered that the fruit didn't come to any harm for being less pampered; in fact, you still got good peaches. So, cost notwithstanding, no one has gone back to the old methods.

Nectarines

Even when I lived in the warm counties of Hampshire and Sussex I never knew a really worthwhile crop on a Nectarine tree that was planted out of doors. The tree seems to make plenty of growth but not much fruit. Another snag is that, because the fruit is so delicate and thin-skinned, changes in the weather affect it. Rain causes it to crack, sun scalds it and cold nights bronze it. If, as it should be, the tree is against a wall, a 2ft (60cm) span of glass protruding from the wall coping might help. However, I would put the tree in cold glass – that is, in a house without artificial heating at any time – during its growing season. If you do that you'll get a good crop of Nectarines and they'll be of excellent quality. For planting and cultivating Nectarines under glass, follow the directions given for Peaches under glass on p. 169.

Suggested Nectarine varieties: Any will grow under glass but I think the best fruit comes from: 'Lord Napier', 'Pineapple', 'Humboldt' and 'Crimson Galande'.

PESTS AND DISEASES

Peach and Nectarine trees can suffer from a disease known as peach leaf curl. Outside trees are more prone to it than those under glass. The symptoms, which appear in spring, are thickening, reddening and curling of the leaves. The disease is caused by a fungus and cold, wet weather favours its development. To combat Peach leaf curl, spray outdoor trees at leaf fall with a copper fungicide and again in spring when the buds are just beginning to swell. An alternative and better preventative measure is to cover outside trees securely with polythene from early December. Leave the polythene on until bud burst or a little later.

Another problem you may face is aphids. They can often be a menace on young shoots in spring. A garden centre will fix you up with a suitable spray to combat these.

Figs

In the days when they were up to strength, most large kitchen gardens had a few Figs under glass or out of doors. I've grown them under glass at about 60°F (15.5°C) and had a first picking of fruit in late May/early June, a second crop in August and a third in late October/early November. The last crop provided Figs for the Royal Horticultural Society's Fruit and Vegetable Show in the second week in October and for the Reading Gardeners' Chrysanthemum Show in the first week in November. Talking about shows, the Fig is the only fruit you exhibit when it's split! A split down the side shows that it's at its peak and fully ripe.

At one time the list of Fig varieties available for purchase was endless. Now it's likely that most nurseries will only offer 'Brown Turkey' and 'Brunswick'. 'Brown Turkey' has an excellent flavour and is good inside or out. 'Brunswick' isn't much good inside.

WHERE TO GROW FIGS

My Uncle Fred believed that Figs did best in sight of the sea, and my journeyman days in southern Hampshire and Sussex bore this out. The finest outdoor tree I've come across was a half-standard at Goodwood Park gardens; this tree also produced the largest outdoor Figs I've ever seen. If you do grow a Fig tree outside put it against a wall, and if it's very unprotected be prepared to lose a lot of wood during the winter. It will be happiest in poor soil, not in rich. Turfy loam, leaf soil and something gritty or old mortar rubble will suit it fine.

Fig trees will also do well in an unheated sunny glasshouse or in pots which you can move out of the house on to the patio in summer. 'Brown Turkey' is a good, reliable cultivar for growing inside or outdoors.

RESTRICTING ROOTS

Wherever you grow them, Fig trees should have their roots restricted, otherwise they will make rampant growth and never produce any fruit. If its roots are restricted a tree will feel insecure, so it will fruit in order to reproduce itself. That's why there's the old saying: 'A woman, the Fig and the Walnut tree, the more you beat 'em, the better they be'!

GENERAL CARE

A Fig needs an even supply of water. It's no good not watering it and then, when you see it's carrying a crop, giving it a good soak. The shock and sudden rush of sap this causes will, in a few days, make the fruits drop off. Feed the tree with liquid farmyard manure (see p. 23) when the figlets are about half-grown. Birds and wasps love Figs, so protect your crop.

Above: A winter morning in the Fig house at Chilton.
Right: The fig 'Pingo de Mel'.

GROWING FIG TREES OUT OF DOORS

Prepare a spot beneath a wall and dig a hole about 3 × 3 × 3ft (1 × 1 × 1m) in size. Line this, sides and bottom, with concrete or bricks but leave some drainage holes at the bottom. Every year after planting dig down to look at these holes and cut off any of the tree's roots which have grown through them.

A newly purchased Fig tree will almost certainly resemble a small bush. However, don't worry, because it can easily be cut to size and within a year it will be quite shapely and happy to be trained against the wall.

Select the best shoots and tie them to support wires. Tie the shoots 6–8in (15–20cm) apart, as figs make big leaves and overcrowding is bad for the fruit. The earliest and best fruits come, as a rule, on wood of last year's growth. This doesn't have any figlets showing, just bumps on the stem.

In the early stages of a Fig's life you need to let some of the growth reach 2–3ft (60cm–1m) in length, but once the wall is covered, prune the main branches by stopping all new growth at five leaves from its starting point and prune sub-laterals back to two leaves from the point where they join the main branches. Discontinue stopping the growth after the first week in August as the growth from then onwards will be the fruiting wood for the following year. In winter tie this growth in; it will probably be 2–3ft (60cm–1m) long but will show no sign of figlets. Prune out all wood which is weak or is two to three years old

175

and has reached the full height of the wall with only a piece of short fruiting wood left on top.

Outdoor Fig trees carry only one crop a year, in August or September, depending on the area.

GROWING FIG TREES IN POTS

Being restricted in a pot, the tree will require little pruning. Just cut a bit off when it's obvious that that piece is not going to give any more fruit.

The best pots of Figs I've seen were at Stansted Park. These cropped under the early vines.

MY METHOD OF GROWING FIGS UNDER COLD GLASS

At Chilton I have a wall of Figs under cold glass, five different cultivars in all, and, in the same house, two free-standing trees. All these started off life as cuttings which I'd brought from Nuneham Park gardens in 1947. In the winter of 1947–8 the cuttings, in 5in (13cm) pots, had reached 12–15in (30–38cm) in height and I had them transferred into 10in (25cm) pots. My intention was to put them into a glasshouse which is built against the south-facing wall of the kitchen garden. However, before they went in, I had holes dug in the border at the foot of the 12ft- (3.6m)-high back wall of the house, each deep enough to hold two house bricks stood edgeways and a pot containing a Fig. When the pots had been dropped down on to the bricks, soil was filled in around them.

After a few years, in order to supply the trees with extra nourishment, a 3in- (7.5cm)-deep ring of zinc was placed inside the rim of each pot. The rings were pegged in place with four 'hairpins' of wire and filled with soil. Each year they are emptied of the previous year's soil and top dressed with new.

These Fig trees flourish without any heat except that which they get from the sun. On very sunny days they're aired freely and each year, when they start into growth, a small quantity of water is sprayed on to them. During their lifetime the trees have climbed to the top of the wall many times and have been cut back down. They're pruned in the same way that I've described earlier for pruning a Fig on an outside wall. Also, every other year I dig down to the bottom of each pot and cut off all the roots which have come through its base.

PROPAGATING FIGS

There are three ways:
- Taking a hardwood cutting.
- Taking a greenwood cutting.
- Air layering.

■ **A hardwood cutting**

Take this when the leaf falls in the autumn. Select a piece of ripened wood about 6in (15cm) in length. Pull it off so that it comes off with a heel. The heel has got a ring around it which callouses over well. Put the cutting in a bed or pot in a coldframe. This isn't a very reliable method. If you take off a dozen cuttings you'll probably end up with half that will 'take'.

■ **A greenwood cutting**

Take this at any time from July onwards. Again a 6in (15cm) piece pulled off with a heel. Put the cutting into a propagator at about 60°F (15.5°C).

■ **Air layering**

This was first perfected for propagating Camellias. On Figs do it any time during the growing season. Find a leaf over a joint, take your knife down a couple of inches from that, then at that point peel the bark off right down to the cambium layer for a couple of inches. Then take some moist sphagnum moss and wrap it completely around and tie it on with bass. Next get a piece of polythene which will overlap the moss by 2in (5cm) top and bottom and tie it tightly (so that no air gets in) top and bottom. Sometimes roots from the cut will grow quickly into the damp moss, sometimes it will take until the following year, but you'll be able to see them through the polythene. When they have grown, cut through the stem 6–9in (15–23cm) above the new roots and immediately below them and you'll have a new little rooted Fig tree.

Soft·Fruit

Raspberries – Gooseberries – Currants – Loganberries – Strawberries

CHAPTER FIFTEEN
Soft Fruit

Raspberries

One of the easiest and most trouble-free of fruits to cultivate is the Raspberry. The canes that you buy from a nurseryman will fruit a little in the first year but you'll get no fruit in the second year, so it's best to cut them down in the first year and get a fair crop in the second year.

Suggested varieties: 'Malling Jewel', 'Malling Delight', 'Glen Clova'. For autumn fruiting: 'Autumn Bliss'.

*Above: A basket of Raspberries. Left: Strawberries —
the most popular soft fruit.*

PREPARING THE GROUND

Select a piece of open ground for Raspberries, preferably a site which hasn't grown them for some time. In September/October it will pay to double dig it and work in plenty of farmyard manure or your own compost. The ground will then have time to settle down before planting.

PLANTING

Planting can take place at any time from late October to mid-March. I always aim for an October planting because the warmth still remaining in the ground will encourage fresh, new roots on the canes and when spring comes they'll grow away because they've had a good start.

Plant the canes 12–15in (30–38cm) apart in rows no less than 4ft (1.2m) apart. If the ground is good and can be spared, 5ft (1.5m) apart will be beneficial because the canes will develop better and you'll have more room to pick. Tread the canes in so that they are really firm, then rake all the tread marks out with the back of a fork so that the ground looks freshly and lightly forked.

GENERAL CARE

If it looks as though there could be a stretch of frosty weather, mulch the canes with some very strawy manure. Too much frost will cause them to lift and might damage the nice new roots gained by early planting.

In March cut the canes down to within 6–9in (115–23cm) of the ground. If wire supports aren't already in, provide some. The best way is to put good, strong posts at each end of each row. Strut the posts for extra strength, then insert other posts between them at intervals of 10ft (3m). These posts should stand 6ft (1.8m) out of the ground. Attach strand wire to the posts. If the run is over 25ft (7.6m), it's a good idea to fix straining bolts to the end posts. Three or four wires should be enough. Make the first wire 2–2½ft (60–75cm) from the ground and allow 12–15in (30–38cm) between the first and second, second and third, and third and fourth.

Spare no effort to get the canes growing strongly. They should be well watered if April and May are dry, and then in late May/early June I wouldn't hesitate to give them a 6in (15cm) mulch of farmyard manure or compost, watering the mulch well. Hoe to keep free of weeds and check from time to time that their roots are moist.

Tie your new canes to the bottom wire as soon as they are high enough to reach over it. Ordinary gardener's bass (raffia) will be strong enough for the job. As the canes grow, continue to tie them to the wires but cut off any really weak canes so that the good ones have every chance.

In the first autumn cut all your ties and retie, a tie at each wire, with soft string like fillis. Don't tie weak canes but remove them. Provided that you've looked after the canes through the growing season, you should have enough to furnish the wires. Each cane needs to be 6–8in (15–20cm) from its neighbour.

Above: Rows of Raspberries. On the right-hand side fruited canes have been removed and the best new canes tied in.

If by the following February any canes are over 6ft (1.8m) high, cut their tops off.

In May mulch again. Keep the rows free from weeds and just before the berries begin to colour up give the canes a really good soak. Net the fruit against birds if you feel that you must, but I think that in a year where there's a really good crop and you're able to pick every day or every other day, the value of the few berries the birds take will be far less than the cost of a net and the time spent fitting it.

As soon as the last berry has been picked, prune out all the canes which have fruited (that is, the ones you tied in last winter). You should have plenty of new canes, so tie in only the best of these. Place each cane 6–9in (15–23cm) from its neighbour and tie it to every wire. Clear all the old canes away and burn them. Tidy up the plot and fork very lightly or prick the surface between the rows with a fork. Dig out any canes which have sprung up away from the rows. By keeping only the ones under the wires you'll maintain a tidy plot and the neatness will aid a successful crop for years.

Gooseberries, Black Currants, Red Currants, White Currants and Loganberries

Gooseberries, the three types of Currant and Loganberries all have the same requirements as far as ground is concerned, so if you want you can plant them on the same piece of land. They'll live happily together and within reason will tolerate acid or limy soil.

PREPARING THE GROUND
If the plot has previously been growing vegetables and has been well looked after, it'll just need a good digging and some additional farmyard manure or compost. However, it it's maiden ground covered with turf, it'll need double digging. Turn the turf into the bottom and put farmyard manure or compost on top. If it's full of perennial weeds,

it'll also need major cleaning. In days gone by this constituted an important job. As many perennial weeds as possible would be forked out in late summer and early autumn and the ground would then, to use an old farming phrase, be summer tilled: that is, in the summer it would be worked over and over again by hand. It sounds like hard work but it prevented the fruit bushes being over-run with bindweed or ground elder.

Gooseberries

Gooseberries were grown on quite a scale in my young days and estate gardens had to supply the cook with them over a stretch of time. The first call on these berries was at Whitsun weekend when she wanted them for making tarts. Being young and small, they kept their shape and looked good in the tarts. (Spring cabbage was another requirement on that weekend.) The cook's next demand on gooseberries was for making jam and for bottling. Later still, certain varieties were thinned in their early stages so that only the biggest and best berries were left. These were protected by nets and, when they ripened, went up to the mansion to be served as dessert.

Good dessert gooseberries are 'Leveller' and 'Golden Drop'. Varieties like 'Invicta', 'Whinham's Industry', 'Whitesmith', 'Lancashire Lad' and 'Keepsake' are really culinary but if they're thinned out and the remaining berries left to ripen, they'll also pass as dessert.

PLANTING
Plant Gooseberries at any time from October to early March. I'd advise October when the ground is still warm enough to encourage them to make a little root. You can grow them as bushes, cordons, standards or fans. I had fan-trained ones at Chilton from 1947 until 1955. Cordons need to be planted 12–15in (30–38cm) apart against a wall or a wire trellis. Both bushes and standards need to be 3–5ft (1–1.5m) apart; the distance between fans should be 4–5ft (1.2–1.5m).

GROWING GOOSEBERRIES AS BUSHES

You should aim to make a Gooseberry bush open at the centre, so that the berries ripen easily and you can pick them without scratching your arms! An open bush also helps to ripen the wood which will bear fruit in the following year. In fact, the shape should be the same as that of a bush Apple. However, unlike an Apple, a Gooseberry doesn't make strong growth, so when you're training it choose only good, stout shoots.

To start your bush off you need to have a rough circle of shoots. To get this begin with a maiden bush and cut off the weakest shoots completely. Prune each remaining shoot by half its length. Take it back to a bud which is on the underside. This bud will grow *outwards* (the bud opposite, on top, is likely to have grown upwards). Gooseberries fruit on one-year-old wood, so in the following and subsequent winters prune the leading shoots off to about half of their growth. The side shoots which have formed on them should also be pruned back to one or two buds from where they join the leading shoots. Very often a Gooseberry will suddenly throw up a lot more growth from the base and centre. If none of the existing branches needs renewing, cut this extra growth right out. You must be firm with pruning, or the bushes will quickly become a thicket.

Gooseberries.

If your bush started life off as a well-grown container specimen, you'll probably get a few fruits in the first year.

CORDON GOOSEBERRIES

Cordon Gooseberries can be purchased from a nursery or you can train them from a hardwood cutting taken in October/November from an existing bush. Cut off a piece of the current year's growth immediately below a bud and make it 6–9in (15–23cm) long. Trim the buds off the bottom half, because if they're put into the ground they'll throw up shoots you don't want. After planting the cutting tread it in firmly or frosts will lift it. The

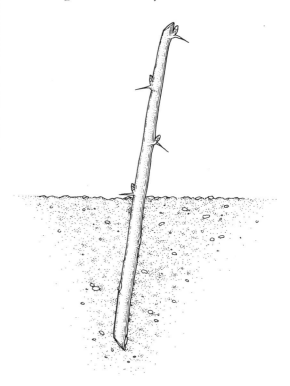

cut will callus over and roots will form in the spring. When the cutting starts to produce shoots, remove all but the one on the top, for that's the one you take on up to form your cordon. In August summer-prune the side shoots which have formed on this leading shoot. Cut them back to two or three buds from where they join the leading shoot. These will bear the fruits, though it will be two years before they build up spurs which have fruit on them. In early winter cut off a third of the length of the leading shoot.

Carry on each year until the leading shoot has reached the height you want, then take the top out. I've found that cordons seldom seem to have the ability to go much above 6 or 7ft (1.5 or 2.2m).

STANDARD GOOSEBERRIES

You can buy a standard or train one yourself. To do this take a hardwood cutting exactly as you would for starting a cordon (see above) but so that the leading shoot forms the 'leg' of the standard, keep all its side shoots rubbed off. Continue to keep the side shoots rubbed off until the leg is the height you require. At this point allow shoots to form on the top 6in (15cm): these will form the head. In the first year you'll have anything up to a dozen shoots on this top 6in (15cm), so select the best and cut a third of their growth off each, removing completely the shoots you've disregarded. Don't be disappointed if you don't get enough good shoots to give a decent head in the first year, for making a standard Gooseberry takes some time. Continue to cut a third off each leading shoot every August until you have about 3ft (1m) of fruiting wood. From that point on (to stop them getting too large) take each shoot right back to the last bud of that year's growth.

FAN-TRAINED GOOSEBERRIES

There was an excellent row of fan-trained gooseberries at Chilton when I took over. It was over 100ft (30m) long and was planted against six strands of wire beside a path. Each fan was 4–5ft (1.2–1.5m) apart and, in those happier days, beautifully trained. The Gooseberries they bore were picked mainly for jam and bottling. They were a wonderful sight.

To make a fan take the top 6–9in (15–23cm) out of a maiden bush. It should then form shoots on either side. Select the strongest of these and tie them out against wires or a wall to form a fan shape. Allow these leading shoots to grow on, but every year cut each of the side shoots which grow on them back to two or three buds, because it's new wood which makes fruit. It will probably take four to five years to make a decent fan shape. However, the fan will produce fruit before that time on the side shoots which are on the bottom half of the fan arms.

When the fan has reached its allocated space, take the top out of each leading shoot in August. In fact August is the pleasantest time to handle these thorny monsters! Also, as a general rule, I think that if Gooseberry pruning is left until the spring a lot of wasteful growth will have been allowed to develop in August and September.

GENERAL CARE

Gooseberries like a mulch in summer of farmyard manure or compost and a dressing in spring of potash. If they become over-dry at the roots they get mildew; this also occurs if there's a hot, dry spell in March and April but the nights are cold. Treat with a fungicide spray – it's important to eradicate it, because a bad outbreak will also settle on the fruit and make it useless.

In some areas in the springtime birds, particularly bullfinches, peck and spoil the swelling buds. To combat this cover the gooseberries with a net or leave the pruning until late spring. Personally, I'd rather net against them.

HOW TO GET GOOSEBERRIES FOR WHITSUN
Simply thin the fruit on a bush or cordon. Do this by picking off the smallest fruit. Alternatively, if there's a really good set of fruit, run three fingers and a thumb up a branch, starting at the bottom. Many will come off easily but a lot will stay on. The thinning will pay other dividends too: it will make room for large, choice berries to develop which can be eaten as dessert fruit.

Black Currants

Black Currants are easily propagated from hard-wood cuttings taken in autumn, but if you're growing them only on a small scale I'd advise you keep a healthy stock by purchasing plants from a nurseryman who has certified stock. In October (if possible) buy plants no older than two years. There's no gain to be had from older ones, because you're going to cut the growth off anyway to help them get a roothold.

Suggested varieties: 'Baldwin', 'Boskoop Giant', and 'Hilltop Baldwin'.

Plant Black Currants 3–4ft (1–1.2m) apart. Dig a hole large enough to allow the roots to spread out and, if possible, cover them in with fine soil. Don't plant deeper than the nurseryman's mark as that's the point at which they've found their natural root run. Place a mulch of farmyard manure or compost around them after planting.

In the spring cut them down to 3–4in (7.5–10cm) from the ground: there's nothing to be gained by leaving on the growth which they had when you bought them. In the first year April and May are important months in their growth and they shouldn't be allowed to become dry because they still have very little root to help them.

You should get a little fruit in the second year. During the second winter any wood which has fruited should be removed completely. Black Currants fruit best on one-year-old wood and this often stops coming if you allow them to carry two-to-three-year-old wood.

Black Currants appreciate 2oz per sq yd (50g per sq m) nitro chalk applied in the spring when the buds begin to move. Give them a mulching of farmyard manure or compost a bit later, when you've had time to clear the weeds. Spray as soon as you spot greenfly.

If, after four years, they have made really big bushes and you have them in a row or block, cut every other bush down to ground level. You'll get fruiting bushes again in a year which will be easier to manage and will bear better fruit.

PROPAGATING BY CUTTINGS

Currants, if they're not looked after, quickly go down with virus, so I'd always advise getting new stock from a nurseryman. However, if you want to take cuttings, do so before Christmas – say, in October/November. Take off 6–9in (15–23cm) of that year's growth as your cutting and leave the buds on it along its entire length. The reason for doing this is that the buds planted beneath the soil will throw up strong shoots which will fruit well. Plant the cuttings and tread them in firmly to stop the frost lifting them.

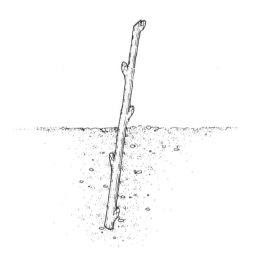

Red and White Currants

Red Currants and White Currants can be grown as bushes, standards or (my preference) as cordons.

Suggested varieties:

Red Currants

'Laxton's No. 1', 'Red Lake', 'Rondom'.

White Currants

'White Dutch', 'White Versailles'.

BUSHES

You should aim to get a bush with a fairly open middle, which will help the fruit ripen. One method I've seen in old gardens that helps to achieve this is a stiff wire ring placed over the bush and tied to a couple of stakes. Growth is tied around the ring and all the growth in the centre cut right out. (A ring can also be very effective when you're training a standard.)

Cut the leading shoots back each winter by at least half their length and in August cut the side shoots back to one or two buds from the point where they join the leading shoots.

Above: White Currants 'White Versailles'. Left: A basket of 'Baldwin' Black Currants.

CORDONS

You can buy a cordon from a nursery or you can make one from a cutting. If you take a cutting to start the cordon, remove the bottom buds before planting it. When its top buds begin to make shoots, select the strongest one near the top and remove the others. Grow this leading shoot on up and in August prune the side shoots which have grown from it back to two or three buds. This method of pruning forms fruit spurs in much the same way as they form on cordon apples. The spurs will fruit when the wood is two to three years old.

In winter cut the leading shoot back by a third of its length. Allow it to carry on growing until the leading shoot has reached the height you want, then stop it by taking the last bud out of the current year's growth.

To prune ready-bought or fully formed cordons, cut off at least half the length of the leading shoots each winter and in August prune the side shoots to two or three buds from the point where they join the leading shoot.

Cordon Currants will ask for very little maintenance and they won't even require much farmyard manure.

STANDARDS

To start off a standard take a cutting in exactly the same way described above for starting a cordon, but after the leading shoot has developed keep all the side shoots rubbed off it. When this leading shoot reaches the height that you'd like your standard to be, continue to rub the lower buds off but let them develop into shoots on the top 6in (15cm) because these will begin to form the 'head'. Allow all the top shoots to grow in their first summer until August when you should select the best and cut each back by one third of its length. Do this every year until you have about 3ft (1m) of fruiting wood. By that time you'll have a good head, so stop the branches by taking them back to the last bud of the current year's growth. Continue to do the same each year.

GENERAL CARE

The fruit on Red Currrants and White Currants must be well protected from blackbirds and later from wasps.

Red Currants can live a long time. Years ago it used to be the fashion to grow bushes on a 1½ft (45cm) stem before letting them bush out. Some of the stems I've seen were as thick as a man's wrist – goodness knows how old the bushes were, yet they fruited each year.

Loganberries

Loganberries always seemed to do well on the light land around Blackmoor. The mansion gardens had the longest row I've ever seen in any garden. People don't seem to grow Loganberries much today, perhaps the decline in popularity had something to do with so many stocks being affected with Virus after the Second World War. It's a great pity because its a lovely fruit where it does well, added to which there's a thornless strain available today.

CULTIVATION

Loganberries are simple to grow. They need a row of wires much the same as Raspberries (see p. 180). Plant at 6 inch (15 cm) intervals anytime between October and early March.

After planting cut down to 6 inches (15 cm) from the ground. When the new growth reaches the first wire secure it and keep tying as needs be. You'll get fruit the following year from growth made in the current year.

When you've picked the last berries, cut out all the fruited canes as these are now useless. Tie in the new growth made during the summer. This will fruit the following year. In fact, new growth should have a few ties during its growing season because it grows quite fast and is apt to ramble like a Blackberry.

Loganberries appreciate a good mulch of farmyard manure (see p. 23).

Be warned, birds love the berries!

Strawberries

Old-time gardeners in charge of kitchen gardens used to produce Strawberries for five months of the year. They did it by having glasshouse raised ones from March through until June, then picked from under frames and cloches until the open Strawberry beds began to crop. In fact, if you followed their cropping plan today, you'd better their achievement by two months, for there are now some varieties available which will crop well into September and even into October!

Two old varieties still worth growing are 'Cambridge Favourite' and 'Cambridge Vigour'. Some newer ones are 'Aromel' which crops over a long period; 'Pantagruella' and 'Pandora'.

PLANTING A BED OF STRAWBERRIES

Strawberries need a good piece of land which hasn't been starved for want of farmyard manure or compost. Land which has had ample supplies from a previous crop will suit them.

Plant a new bed in July. This will give the plants a long period in which to establish a good root formation that will help them build up good crowns for the next season. Years ago this wasn't such a necessary requirement, because no gardener would dream of cropping a maiden plant. Instead all the bloom was picked off in the first year and the plants weren't allowed to produce fruit until they were two years old. The cost involved in such a method makes it out of the question today!

When you plant your Strawberries put them in at intervals of 15in–2ft (38–60cm) and make the rows the same distance apart. The crowns should be just above ground level. Plant firmly.

CULTIVATION

If August is hot and dry, keep the plants watered. Feeds of liquid farmyard manure (see p. 23) will help to build them up and make them healthy. Keep the hoe going whenever weeds spring.

In March the plants will show signs of life. Hoe

the bed and generally tidy it. When flowers appear watch out for frosts, because the flowers can easily be damaged: have something handy to cover the plants during frosty nights.

When fruits begin to swell, get clean straw and carefully lift with one hand the developing berries and foliage and with the other hand tuck the straw under them. When you take your hand away, the fruit should lie on the straw. Straw the whole area down. Should dry weather set in, watering will help to keep the berries swelling. If your bed is small it will pay you to net it against the birds.

PROPAGATING

If you're thinking ahead to next year's crop you can get new Strawberry plants from the runners which spring from your existing plants. For each new Strawberry you'll need a 3in (7.5cm) pot, into the bottom of which you should put a small piece of well-rotted manure and then fill up with old potting soil. As soon as the first runners appear and are long enough, place each one on to the soil surface of a pot. Pin the runners down with either a pebble or a small piece of wire bent like a staple.

Look at the pots every day to see if they need watering. Don't sever the runners from the parent plants until roots begin to show at the bottom of the pots. When roots do appear, cut the runners by the rim of the pots.

Stand the pots in a little shade for a few days. If your new site isn't ready for the young plants, keep them potted and feed them with liquid farmyard manure (see p. 23). Endeavour to get the new bed ready before the plants become pot-bound or their growth will be checked.

GROWING UNDER CLOCHES, POLYTHENE TUNNELS AND IN COLDFRAMES

Strawberries grown with the aid of cloches, polythene tunnels and frames need ground which has had plenty of moisture-retaining compost incorporated into it. Plant in July so that they'll build up strong crowns before the autumn.

Growing under Grower's Barn-type cloches

Plant at intervals of 1½ft (45cm) in a single row. Cloche up in January and keep free of weeds at all times.

If April and early May are dry, water the plants. There's no need to take the cloches off to do this: simply water along the sides of the cloches and the moisture will seep underneath them. If the sunshine is really warm during these two months, move the cloches 1in (2.5cm) or so apart. The old type of Grower's Barn cloche (see p. 40) was useful when it came to ventilation because it had a device on the top clips which allowed the top two panes of glass to be opened 1–2in (2.5–5cm).

Put straw beneath the fruit and foliage in the usual way when the fruit sets.

Growing under polythene tunnels

Follow the same cultivation as for cloches. The walk-in type of tunnel has the advantage over frames and cloches because you can work in it during wet weather.

Growing in coldframes

This too is much the same as growing under cloches. Place the lights (covers) on the frames in January and keep them closed until growth gets under way. At that time the plant will need careful airing. Weed and water. During the ripening period throw a net over the open frame to deter birds – blackbirds love to get into frames.

RAISING STRAWBERRIES IN HEATED GLASSHOUSES

If a gardener had to produce Strawberries for the dining room as early as March, he'd raise them under heated glass. I've grown 300 plants a year in this way, sometimes 500, but never matched the pre-war totals many old estate gardens managed.

In 1960 economy dictated that I had to give up growing Strawberries under glass, but it's worth recording how it was done just to illustrate the care and work involved!

The new plants came from the same propagation method that supplied outside beds; however, the plants destined for use under glass took priority and their propagation was generally done as overtime.

During August the young plants were ready for potting on. The pot boy prepared 5 and 6in (13 and 15cm) pots by crocking them and then placing rough fibre over the crocks. The concoction destined to go over the fibre consisted of chopped loam, coarse grit, very well-rotted farmyard manure, soot, charcoal and often old ceiling mortar too. The last ingredient was favoured as potting material because in those days it contained cow and horse hair. This would all have been well mixed and left for several days before the garden journeyman used it in the crocked-up pots. The task of potting the Strawberries was so important that I've known gardens where men weren't allowed to take their holidays until after it was completed. It also had to be done in a certain way: that is, you didn't firm the plant with your hands but used a piece of wood called a rammer. One old foreman from whom I had the pleasure of learning used to say that you could pick up a well-potted Strawberry by its foliage and it wouldn't come out of the pot!

After potting the plants were given a little shade for a few days during which, if the weather was bright and warm, they were sprayed with clear water once or twice daily. When they'd become established, they were stood out in the open in the garden's frame yard, carefully watered and regularly fed with soot water (see p. 21) or liquid manure (see p. 23).

In October they were moved and the pots plunged up to the rim in ashes. This cut down on the Strawberry plants' water requirements and also protected them from frost. A batch for forcing was lifted from the ash plunge bed every three weeks, the first of these in mid-December. It was taken into a cool glasshouse where, in mid-January, the plants were knocked out of their pots. This was to make sure that the drainage was free. At the same time any loose soil was pricked away from the surface of the root ball. The plants then went back into the pots and were top dressed with a mixture similar to that used in August.

The next move was to stand them on shelves in a glasshouse heated at between 45 and 50°F (7 and 10°C). In a few weeks they were putting up new foliage and were moved on into either a vinery or Peach house, where they had special shelves waiting for them. Once a day their pots were tapped to see if they wanted water and twice a day they received a forcible jet of water from a garden syringe to deter red spider.

When flowers began to open on the plants they were kept a little drier and given slightly more air. This helped the pollen move freely as a journeyman or his foreman pollinated the flowers, dusting a rabbit's tail from one to another, a ritual that ensured a good set of fruit. As soon as the fruit began to swell it had to be thinned, leaving only the best seven to nine berries per pot. The plants were fed with liquid farmyard manure and kept sprayed with clean water until the fruits showed signs of ripeness. When they did, spraying and feeding stopped and little forked sticks were placed around the top of the pots. The fruit stems were gently rested in the forks to stop them coming into contact with the edge of the pot. Any foliage covering the fruit was removed.

The ripening process was often finished not in the fruit house but in a more airy place. A Carnation house used to be ideal, and I remember that one of these had a shelf specially constructed for the purpose. When the fruit was finally ripe it looked a wonderful sight and its scent was pretty good too!

Grapes·and·Melons

CHAPTER SIXTEEN
Grapes and Melons

Grapes

When I was fourteen my uncle's inside foreman taught me to thin a bunch of Grapes. It was a job he did as overtime to earn himself some extra holidays. His family lived away and it took a day to travel to them and a day to travel back, so the extra days were precious.

A decent bunch of Grapes still has to be thinned by hand and the vine looked after, but, as with the cultivation of Peaches, there can't be many places now where vines are managed as they were between the two World Wars. For example, here at Chilton there used to be three vineries: an early house (for an early crop), a Muscat house (the Muscats being valued for their perfumed flavour), and a late house (for a late crop). These three houses provided Grapes for the table from mid-June until the end of January. After Christmas the Alicante grapes from the late house would cause a few complaints about tough skins, but it was their tough skins which kept them!

It was tradition to close and start the early house and the first Peach house on Christmas Eve. The Muscat house had boiler heat all summer and, although the late house got its heat from the sunshine, when it was cleared in January the hot-water heating pipes were kept warm to stop them from freezing. Think of the cost of all that today! It's small wonder that by 1969 all the vines had

been pulled out. Three of the Peach houses received the same treatment. They might be gone but they're not forgotten, for old gardeners love to talk about such things between themselves.

CULTIVATION

I doubt very much that there are many parts of the British Isles warm enough to grow dessert Grapes successfully outside, so I'll concentrate on growing a 'Black Hamburg' under cold glass. A 'Black Hamburg' will produce a good crop with the minimum of attention, although the more it receives, the more it'll reward you, especially if a little warmth can be given from bud burst until the bunches are set and again during August nights to help finish ripening and keep dampness at bay.

Plant a vine at any time between October and March. It can be grown in a pot placed in the glasshouse or planted in a bed or border in the house. If you're going to put it in a bed or border, that will need some attention. According to the room you have, remove the existing soil to a depth of approximately 1½ft (45cm) from an area 2–3ft (60cm–1m) wide and 6ft (1.8m) long. Dig the bottom over, breaking it up and put in brick rubble to help drainage. If possible, cover the rubble with good fibrous turf laid upside down.

Next prepare the compost to go into the border. Chop up a barrowful of turfy soil and to it add:

two shovelfuls of coarse grit

two shovelfuls of very well-rotted compost, or farmyard manure

two shovelfuls of charcoal, plus any old bones you can get (crush them to get greater distribution), or two handfuls of hoof and horn.

Mix everything together well.

When you purchase a vine it will almost certainly be in a pot. Remove it carefully. The best way is to tease the roots out of the bottom of the pot and prick the soil on the pot's surface with a sharp-pointed stick so that, when the pot's turned upside down and knocked, soil falls out. Continue to do this until you've found some roots. The vine should then slip out with the root ball intact.

Make a hole in the prepared border to receive the vine, ensuring that the hole is deep enough to allow its root ball to be approximately 3in (7.5cm) below the surface of the bed when planting is complete. Begin planting by spreading out the roots you initially teased from the base of the pot, and then work fine soil well into them, just covering them. Tread that firm and add another layer, tread that, and so on until the hole is full and level.

If you're planting in winter, there shouldn't be any need to water the vine in. You can test for moisture by pushing a stick into the prepared bed. If, when you pull it out and touch the end, it makes your hand muddy, the soil's wet enough for the vine to start off into growth in March.

PRUNING AND TRAINING

Your object is to train the vine so that it runs directly below the roof glass – to be exact, about 12in (30cm) from the glass. In this position the leaves will get the necessary sunlight but will shade the bunches of grapes hanging beneath them. To facilitate this you will need to run lengthways support wires 12in (30cm) beneath the roof glass and 12in (30cm) apart.

A newly purchased vine is likely to be one or two years old and will be like a whippy stick 6–8ft (1.8–2.4m) long. You will probably have to cut

it to encourage the start of growth of shoots at the first roof wire. If you leave it the sap will go to the top and you'll end up with about a foot or eighteen inches with no shoots on it. How much you cut off will depend on the height between the ground and the eaves of your glasshouse. You should aim to cut it back to about a foot and half *beyond* the first roof wire. This will give you a sufficient amount for the rod to make two sets of spurs.

After you've cut the rod put vine styptic on the cut to stop the flow of watery sap known as 'bleeding'. Then rub all the buds off the length of rod which stretches from ground level to the glasshouse eaves. Beyond that the rod will probably produce something like six side shoots (laterals) to tie in to the wires. You also need a good shoot to act as the leader to carry on the growth of the rod up the wires.

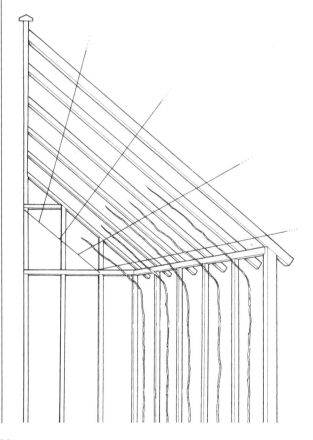

Bunches of Grapes will form on the laterals, but if your rod is only a year old you might get just one or two bunches or perhaps none at all. To have none would be ideal, because the rod will instead put its energies into forming a good roothold and making some useful buds at the bottom of the laterals. Next year these will probably give you half a dozen bunches.

Tying laterals

Each year, when the laterals get to about 6–9in (15–23cm) in length, tie them in very carefully. Don't pull them down to the wire too quickly, because you could pull them off; or you could find after tying that a sudden burst of sunshine causes them to lift and break themselves. Instead take a piece of bass (raffia) 1–1½ft (30–45cm) long and make a loop around each shoot, then, with the slightest tension between, tie the other end with a slip knot to the wire. Over several days gradually make new ties tightening the bass and easing the shoot down to the wire.

Laterals which are going to show a bunch will do so when they're about 12in (30cm) long, by which time they should be nicely tied to a wire.

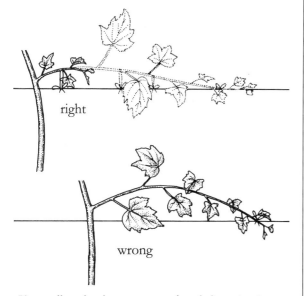

right

wrong

If you allow the shoot to get too long before tying in, you risk it snapping from the rod.

SYRINGING

In a closed-up greenhouse a vine will show signs of growth towards the end of March/early April. From that time start to syringe once a day on nice sunny days, spraying the leaf and the rod. Old hands used to reckon that this softens the bud.

POLLINATING

As soon as the bunches come into flower, aim for drier conditions than the vine has had and stop syringing. Let more air into the house too. Grape flowers are tiny, not much bigger than a pinhead, and all stamens and pollen. Pollinate them at about noon on warm sunny days either by carefully running a rabbit's tail over the flowers or clasping your hands together and, starting from the top of the bunch, lightly passing them down the bunch. I prefer the rabbit's tail method. When you've gone over all the bunches, give the rod a tap with your hand to shake a bit more pollen about them.

Very shortly you'll see the berries begin to swell and when this happens resume syringing. Do it on all warm days, once in the morning and again, after closing the house, in the late afternoon. Inspect all the bunches carefully, and if one is small remove it. Also remove bunches which have pollinated badly, because there's no point in keeping ones which have got only half a complement of berries.

GENERAL SUMMER CARE

The laterals carrying the bunches should be stopped at two leaves beyond the bunch. In due course some of these laterals will produce sub-laterals which should be stopped at one leaf from the point where they join the laterals.

Keep the border moist but not too wet. A weekly watering will probably be sufficient.

When the berries are about a third of their mature size, stoning will begin to take place. A good indication that it has started is that the berries will suddenly stop growing. When this happens, be very careful with watering; in fact, it's best to stop watering altogether until stoning has finished. You can tell when that has occurred because the berries will get slightly darker and swell away again. As soon as stoning is complete the vines will appreciate a general feed like liquid farmyard manure (see p. 23). Also at this point a mulch of strawy manure, well watered, will help to keep moisture in the bed and cut down on watering.

Recommence syringing the vines on all fine sunny days, morning and late afternoon as before. Syringing will help to control red spider, which, if it gets a foothold, will take the chlorophyll out of the vine leaves and eventually kill them. Another pest to look out for is mealy bug. This excretes a sticky substance like clear treacle which grows a black mould. The mould makes the leaves look black, and if it gets into your bunches of Grapes

Glasshouse-grown Grapes.

it'll ruin them. Mealy bug looks like little white patches of fluffy cotton wool. To deal with it dab the white fluff with methylated spirits using a camel-hair brush. Take care to keep the methylated spirits away from the berries and take care not to knock the bunches or rub the bloom off the berries with your own hair. Once gone, the bloom can't be replaced.

When the berries start to colour, stop spraying and generally keep a drier condition in the house. Give more air, including a little air all night. If August turns out to be cold and damp, still leave air on but give the house a little warmth at night as well. This sounds expensive but it will make a lot of difference to the Grapes.

Protect the bunches from birds and wasps. Once wasps have found them, they won't leave them alone. Mice will also rob the bunches at night. Net curtain material placed over the vents and the door will help to keep these pests out.

When the fruit is ripe, cut each bunch from the vine with a 'T' handle. Bunches can hang on the

rods for a week or two after ripening; however, it's best to clear them as soon as possible to avoid certain pitfalls. For example, you have to water the roots of the vine to keep it moist, but too much water could cause the berries to split, and mould might also set in.

As soon as the crop is cleared, cut all laterals back to four or five buds from the rod. Also feed the vine with liquid farmyard manure (see p. 23) to help build up buds for another year.

STORING BUNCHES OF GRAPES

Even if you're not going to eat them straight away, you can still cut bunches and store them. The best way to do this is to cut each bunch so that you leave on it a long piece of the stem which is nearest to the rod. Fill a bottle with clear water, support it on a shelf so that it's leaning at a slight angle and push the piece of stem down the bottle neck into the water, allowing the bunch to hang away from the bottle and over but not touching the shelf edge. If the bottles are in a dry, cool place, the bunches will keep safely for three to four weeks.

WINTER ROUTINE

In winter untie the vine rod. Support the top of it against one of the roof wires so that it's at an easy angle for you to work on and cut the laterals back to one or two buds from the point where they join the rod. Do this every year. After a year or two of being cut back to two buds, each lateral will get 2–3in (5–7.5cm) further away from the rod. They are then known as 'spurs'. On a twenty-year-old vine the spurs can be up to 15in (38cm) long.

Next set about scraping any loose bark off the rod. Young vines won't have much, but, rather like an Apple tree, the older it becomes, the more loose bark a vine will have. By removing loose bark, you get rid of the hiding place used by bugs and scale insects. If these pests are left undisturbed, they'll migrate into the eyes of the spurs and you'll have a job to get rid of them. Don't scrape the bark off too vigorously or you'll cause the rod to bleed. Either use an old knife or simply put both hands round it and rub. The older the vine, the more easily the rough layers will come off. Then deter further bugs with the following mixture:

½lb (225g) Flowers of Sulphur

1 tablespoonful of soft soap

approximately ½ teaspoon of paraffin

a little warm water (to dissolve the soft soap). Combine these ingredients thoroughly and, with a fairly stiff-bristled old paintbrush, paint the mixture on to the rod.

If your greenhouse is large enough for the rod to be left hanging down without it getting in the way, allow it to do so, because this will help an even distribution of new growth along it. This is how it works: sap flows quickly to the upper part, and if the rod if left tied upright you'll get laterals on the top 12in (30cm) long before the bottom ones start into growth; however, with the rod hanging down, the sap can't run so quickly and so the growth will be more even.

Sweep the border clear of all bark scrapings and bits of prunings, for bugs may be lurking in them and could soon re-infest your vine next year. Having cleared up everywhere, you can dress the border with 2–3oz per sq yd (50–75g per sq m) of coarse bone meal or hoof and horn. Then with a small fork (like a lady's border fork) lightly prick the border all over but to no more than 1–2in (2.5–5cm) in depth. The house will look nice and ship shape and ready for the go-ahead in spring.

In days gone by vineries and Peach houses looked lovely in winter. Glass had been washed down, gratings cleared of weeds, brick surrounds and back walls whitewashed and hot-water pipes stove-blacked. All that, plus the occupants pruned and tied: they were a sight to behold.

THINNING GRAPES

The outside berries on a bunch of Grapes, especially those nearest the stalk, are always better than those on the inside which are generally miserable in size. To give the best outside berries an opportunity to develop well and to improve its general look you should thin and shape the bunch. You can buy special Grape-thinning scissors with narrow, pointed blades to help you do this.

I think that the best time to thin a bunch is when the berries are no bigger than Sweetpea seeds. At this stage you can easily get the scissors into the middle of the bunch, which is where you should start thinning. Take off the smallest berries from the outside of the bunch too.

I once knew a glasshouse foreman who didn't thin until the berries were about half the size of ordinary marbles. The problem with this was that, if a bunch was good, the Grapes were packed together tightly and it used to take him ages fiddling around with the scissors and a small forked stick to part the berries.

To the uninitiated a bunch properly thinned will look as if it's been spoilt, but the remaining berries will soon swell up to make a good bunch.

Melons

The Melon is the king of fruits and at one time there used to be nothing to beat those grown in kitchen garden hothouses. Wherever a gardener was kept, whether the garden was large or small, there would be a crop, watched over and cared for at all times. The old seed catalogues carried pages of Melon varieties, named after the garden in which they'd been raised or after lords and ladies. If a gardener raised a new variety, he would guard the seed jealously. His waistcoat pocket was about the safest storage place. Kept there for several months, the seed also 'aged' very nicely, so that when it was planted it made more fruit than foliage!

I grew my first Melon before I was sixteen. It flourished in a frame on a hotbed of horse manure, leaves and a few lawn clippings.

GROWING MELONS IN A GLASSHOUSE

There can't be many people nowadays who'd go to the trouble and expense of devoting a heated glasshouse to Melons; nevertheless I'll describe how it was done, because I think it's an art worth recording.

My first insight into it was when I helped cut turf from the parklands which surrounded the mansion where I was employed. Old estate parks had wonderful turf, full of fibre and rich from the droppings of sheep and cattle which had grazed on it for years. I had to cut each piece of turf so that it was roughly a spade's width and, depending on the depth of the soil, between 6 and 9in (15 and 23cm) deep. The turves were taken back to the gardens on a cart pulled by the garden's pony. When they arrived they were carried into the Melon house, turned upside down and packed close together on the bench. This went on until there was a bed about 2ft (60cm) wide. The crumb which had fallen from the turves was also carried in and spread over the bed. Then with a rammer like a rolling pin but not as long, the bed was rammed down fairly firmly.

At this point the melon-growing compost was brought in. This was mixed in the proportions of one barrowful of chopped-up loam, one bucketful of charcoal and two handfuls of bone meal. (If the loam was of a 'close' nature, a couple of shovelfuls of ½in (3mm) grit were also added.) Mounds of this compost, each the size of a molehill, were placed 2ft (60cm) from one another along the middle of the bed. Each mound was to be the planting place for a young melon plant. The entire bed was constructed a few days before the crop was due to be planted, so that the soil had time to warm up.

The young Melon plants destined for the house had been germinated in pots of much the same mix as that described above. When they were sown the compost was just moist enough to cling together when it was squeezed in a man's palm, but no so wet that it didn't crumble apart when he touched it with his thumb. Each seed had been laid on its edge, pressed down into the compost and thinly covered with soil. The pots had then been put into a seed tray packed with damp (not wet) moss and stood on or near the hot-water pipes in a glasshouse where they could be kept at 60–65°F (15.5–18.3°C). When the seedlings started to develop the first true leaf, they were put near the roof glass to stop them becoming drawn and spindly.

When each had three to four true leaves, the seedlings were planted in the Melon house, one per molehill of compost. The compost was firmed around them and watered. A stake was placed beside each plant and the plant tied loosely to it. This support helped it reach the first overhead wire.

Each plant was allowed to grow on up until the centre stem reached between 3 and 4ft (1 and 1.2m), then the top was pinched out to encourage laterals (side shoots) to come thick and fast. After a week or ten days both male and female flowers appeared on the laterals. Up to that point there'd generally been only a few male flowers on the central stem. (If you're wondering how to tell the difference between female and male flowers, females have a tiny Melon, about the size of a pencil top, underneath the petals and male flowers just have a short stalk.)

Preparing a Melon bed in a glasshouse in the traditional way.

As soon as the female flowers appeared, the tip of the lateral which bore them was pinched back to two leaves in front of the flower. Then came the task to set as many fruit as possible. This was done at 12 noon when the sun was high, the house warm and the pollen able to run freely. Male flowers were picked off, stripped of their petals and the little boss that remained brought into contact with the centre of the female flower. Another method was to pass pollen from male to female on a camel-hair brush.

When the fruits began to swell, two of even size were chosen and the rest removed. Sub-laterals coming from the laterals were pinched out at one leaf and any surplus shoots taken off completely. As the fruit reached golf-ball size the plants were given feeds of liquid cow manure. When it was a bit bigger than a tennis ball, each fruit was given the support of a string net.

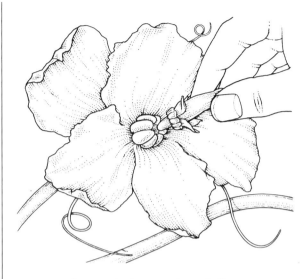

Above: Pollinating by bringing the male flower into contact with the female. Right: Testing a Melon for ripeness. Below: Melons supported in nets.

The temperature throughout the growing time was 65°F (18.3°C); if it reached 75°F (24°C) air was admitted via the vents but only through an inch or so. In fact, the gap was never allowed to be greater than 8in (20cm), because anything wider than that would have caused the humidity to disappear.

On all sunny days the plants were sprayed with tepid water in the morning and in the late afternoon. Just before the afternoon spray the vents were closed to help keep in the heat and humidity – not that heating was really a problem, for in my experience no expense was spared in producing Melons. As the crop began to ripen, the morning and afternoon spraying stopped and drier conditions were given, but sufficient water was supplied to prevent the plants from finishing (dying) before their time.

As soon as the slightest sign of cracking appeared at the point where a stalk joined a fruit, the fruit was severed from the plant. This was done by cutting the branch either side of the stalk so that it looked as though the fruit had a 'T' shape over it. The fruit was left to hang in its net for a few days and then tested to see if it was ripe enough to eat. The test consisted of holding it in both hands and gently pressing both thumbs against its base. If the base yielded slightly, the Melon was ripe.

Cantaloupes

Cantaloupes or frame Melons are popular today because they don't need to be grown in a heated glasshouse. Instead they can be raised in frames or cloches. I prefer frames because cloche cultivation needs a lot of attention and, to be satisfactory, a hot summer. Try using a frame which has been cleared of Lettuce or early Carrots.

'Ogen' is the best-flavoured Cantaloupe, 'Charentais' is quite good and 'Early Sweetheart' worth a try.

SOWING AND PLANTING
Use a good loam compost (like the one described on p. 197 for glasshouse Melons). Sow in April to May, one seed to a pot, and germinate in a temperature of 65°F (18.3°C).

Plant out from late May until early July. Each plant needs approximately 3 × 3ft (1 × 1m) of space. Plant on a small mound of the compost and water in. Close the frame for a few days but spray the plants with tepid water once a day.

GROWING
When the plants begin to grow, admit a little air on all sunny days but close the frame in the late afternoon.

When not more than five leaves have developed, 'stop' each plant by pinching the top out. This will encourage side shoots to form. Select the best three or four of these side shoots and peg them out evenly. Stop them when they reach five leaves. It's the sub-laterals from these shoots which will produce fruit. When flowers appear, pollinate at 12 noon as described on p. 198.

When the fruits are set, take off all but two per plant. If the Melon is a large-fruited variety, leave only one fruit. Once the fruits are swelling away, liquid manure will benefit them. When each fruit reaches the size of a tennis ball, rest it on an upturned flower pot, tile or brick to keep it out of the way of slugs. Regularly pinch all the side shoots back to one leaf. Ease off watering when ripening starts.

Storing · and · Saving

Making a root store and a clamp for vegetables – Picking and storing Apples and Pears – Saving and storing seed – Storing herbs

CHAPTER SEVENTEEN
Storing and Saving

Getting a crop is an achievement but, nature being what it is, in autumn you will often find yourself with a glut of fruits and vegetables and, so that they aren't wasted, they have to be stored.

This storage was vital in the kitchen gardens on country estates, for stored supplies had to last through the winter and into spring, and in winter the cook's daily produce order could be formidable. For example, the Family might be home for a month or more and then there was also Christmas to be catered for.

In the early part of the New Year the Family would have mostly forced vegetables, but the previous autumn's stored crops would be sent to the mansion for the twenty or more house staff. Stored vegetables also fed the head gardener and his three foremen, the bothy boys, the bothy caretaker and her husband and two gatekeepers. Each week a hamper of vegetables was sent to the staff at the Family's London residence too.

The coffer which supplied this huge amount of vegetables was the garden's root store. In my present garden that useful building still exists, but it now houses timber. In the root store's heyday strings of onions used to hang in the alcove outside the door. Once inside you stepped on to a chalk floor which had a central pathway wide enough to wheel a barrow. On either side of the

Apples ready for storing in the thatched fruit house.

path there were cubicles with walls 3ft (1m) high and 4ft 5in (1.34m) wide. They looked a bit like small cattle stalls and their walls, made of a single layer of bricks, had the finishing touch of a brick laid crossways where the wall met the path. Each held one type of vegetable. It could be Carrots, Beet, Turnips, Celeriac, Jerusalem Artichokes or Parsnips. They also housed crowns of Seakale and roots of Chicory before they were planted in the forcing house.

At the far end of the chalk path the cubicles gave way to a large space. This was reserved for 2 or 3 tons of maincrop Potatoes which were usually brought in by the end of September. To ward off frost they were laid on straw, hessian sacks were laid over them and covered with at least 12in (30cm) of new straw.

As much care was taken to keep frost out of the house built to store fruit, for that was, and still is, thatched from the roof right down to ground level. Beneath the fruit house's thatch there's a cavity and then a lining of match board. This insulating combination means that for every 16°F (9°C) rise or fall outside, the inside will alter only 1 or 2°F (0.5 or 1°C). In winter the temperature inside keeps at about 40°F (4.4°C), which is ideal for storing Apples and Pears. The house was built at the turn of the century and we're lucky to have it. There's only one other like it in the country and it's now a school's boat house!

Storing vegetables

MAKING A ROOT STORE
Preparation
Any dry shed that's reasonably frost-free will make a good root store. (If the weather turns really nasty, you can cover the roots with straw.) Partition off spaces, each a couple of feet long and a couple of feet wide. Have ready a bag of sand, more dry than wet.

Lifting
Some vegetables, perhaps Carrot and Beetroot, will be ready for storing in late September, but main crops are generally lifted in October/early November. Parsnips will be ready a little later (from early December until Christmas.) Lift a few Parsnips and a few Jerusalem Artichokes because,

although both keep best left in the ground, there may be times when you want them but very frosty weather or snow prevents you digging. If you don't have a lot of storage room and have to leave these two vegetables in the ground, cover a few with strawy manure to ensure a supply even when the ground's frost-bound.

After lifting
When you've lifted the roots, don't wash them; just scrape them off with the back of a knife blade. Put sand on the floor of each partition *(a)* and, right at the front, build up a wall of the particular vegetable to be stored in it *(b)*. Start to build the wall by laying a single row of the root vegetable, thick end outwards. Top that with a layer of sand, then put another row on top and cover that with a layer of sand. Carry on laying a row of vegetables

a

b

c

d

and covering it with sand until the 'wall' is high enough easily to retain a quantity of the same vegetable tipped in loosely behind *(c)*. Then put a layer of sand over the top *(d)* and throw handfuls of it into the crevices of the rows which make up

e

f

g

the front 'wall'. If space is limited or you are storing relatively few vegetables, you needn't build separate enclosures. You can position parsnips next to carrots, for example, just keep them in separate piles or they'll be difficult to sort out when you need them *(e)*. Continue to fill in with sand until the vegetables are completely covered *(f and g)*. The sand will help to keep the roots from shrivelling up.

MAKING A CLAMP

A useful way of storing Potatoes, Carrots and Beetroot, particularly if you have got more than you can store indoors, is in a clamp outside.

First clean a piece of ground either on the edge of your vegetable plot or in any odd corner of the garden. Begin forming the circular-shaped clamp by shaking out a straw base roughly 3–4ft (1–1.2m) in diameter and 12in (30cm) deep. This size will accommodate a conical heap about 3ft (1m) high.

Any Potatoes or roots you've allocated for storing in the clamp should be dug and left for an hour or two to dry. This will help to stop them rotting. When they're dry, tip them on to the straw base *(a)*. Different vegetables or different varieties of Potato can be partitioned from one another with a wad of straw. When all the roots or Potatoes are in place, cover the whole heap with 12in (30cm) of clean straw.

Next, measure approximately 12in (30cm) away from the base of the clamp, then dig out a spit of earth and pat it back on to the straw at the foot of the clamp *(b)*. Dig all round, transferring the earth on to the clamp as you go. It will probably take a width of two or three spits (working away from the clamp) before the straw is completely covered with soil to a depth of 12in (30cm).

When the soil is near to the top of the clamp, place a small land-drain pipe upright on the pinnacle *(c)* and add more soil until it's almost to the top of the pipe *(d)*. The pipe will let stale air out and stop the contents of the clamp sweating. In really bad weather place a tile or brick over the pipe's opening. The clamp will be frost-proof in

a.

b

c

d

an average winter, but if the weather's very severe add more soil or cover it with strawy manure. If you open the clamp in frosty weather, make sure that it's sealed again securely.

Picking and storing Apples and Pears

PICKING

For early varieties of Apples the best test of ripeness is simply to take a bite out of one or cut one open to see what colour the pips are. If they're dark brown or black, it's likely that the majority of the crop's ready for eating. There's no point in storing early varieties like 'James Grieve' and 'Beauty of Bath' because they have a limited shelf life. Simply keep an eye open to see which ones are ready and eat them direct from the tree.

Pretty well the only varieties of Pears I know that you can eat direct from the tree are 'Jargonelle' and 'Clapp's Favourite'. All the others come to maturity after picking.

For longer-keeping varieties of Apples and Pears one of the first signs that they're ready for picking is that a few will fall off the tree. If the fallers appear free from any infestation (which might have contributed to their fall), cut one open and check whether the pips are dark.

Dark pips are a sign that fruit is ripe and ready for picking.

When you pick an Apple or Pear, place your palm underneath it so that three fingers are outstretched towards the stalk end. Lift the fruit up to the horizontal and if it's ripe enough for picking it will come away from the tree freely. Go all over the tree and take off every fruit which comes off easily. With some Pear trees you'll find it's necessary to go over a tree two or three times before you clear the crop. For a choice variety like 'Doyenné du Comice' that's an advantage, because it means that you can use them over a longer period.

STORING

The back bedroom isn't a particularly good fruit store but it's better than nothing! If you've got a shed that's vermin-proof and fairly free from frost, it will keep Apples until Christmas or early January. Keep the shed cool; anything over 50°F (10°C) is a bit warm. Store Apples and Pears separately because the Pears will encourage the Apples to go off.

Storing Apples

There are several ways of storing Apples:
- In slatted trays which have a leg on each corner so you can stand one on top of the other without crushing the fruit. Wooden Tomato boxes are ideal if you can get them from your greengrocer.
- In polythene bags. (Pears don't seem to keep so well in these.) Don't seal the bag but put it on to a shelf with the top open just sufficiently to let air in and out. Alternatively seal the bag but make some holes in it. This is a good method for preventing shrivelling, especially with russet apples.
- Years ago gardeners used to wrap choice Apples in thin oiled paper which looked like waxy tissue paper. This kept them a month to six weeks longer than unwrapped ones. I doubt whether you can buy that oiled paper now, but you might find an equivalent which would do just as well.
- Another old tried and tested method is to wrap each Apple in newspaper and put it into a barrel.

I used to know a gardener who successfully kept 'Harbinger' Tomatoes in the same way!

Storing Pears

Put Pears on shelves where you can keep an eye on them, for apart from some culinary varieties like 'Uvedale's St Germain', 'Bellissime d'Hiver' and 'Catillac' (which all keep for months), Pears mature very quickly once they're picked. In fact, when I was at Stansted Park there was one Pear that had only one week's shelf life. Once a Pear's reached maturity there's no point in keeping it.

A tell-tale sign that a dessert Pear is mature enough for eating is that it will turn a lighter colour. You can test it further by cupping it in both hands with the stem uppermost and very gently putting pressure with your thumb just below the stalk. If the Pear is ready, your thumb will make a slight dent. This method needs practice because it's easy to ruin a Pear by squeezing too hard.

If the Pear's been kept at 40°F (4.4°C) or just below, improve its flavour by bringing it into room temperature for a few hours before it's eaten.

Testing a Pear for ripeness.

Saving and storing seed

FOR RESOWING

Many of today's vegetables are F_1 hybrid first generation. That means they're the result of crossing two pure bred closely related selections or varieties. If you save and plant the seed from an F_1 hybrid it won't come true. It will take characteristics from each of its grandparents. To overcome this professional seed raisers get their new batches of seed by going through the same cross made originally. The skill and time this involves makes F_1 hybrids more costly than ordinary seed. However, as an F_1 hybrid is usually vigorous, uniform and will crop more or less all at the same time, it's worth buying. In fact if a crop's worth growing it's worth having the best seed you can get for it.

Straight varieties are reasonably true but brassicas can be pretty dodgy unless each sort is grown in isolation. For example, if you've got Cabbages and Brussels flowering together, heaven knows what you might get. Lettuce is the same if you have different sorts near each other. Parsnips and Beetroot also need to be well separated. You can save a bit of Leek seed, but Onion seed is doubtful. In fact, the safest seeds for saving are from Peas and Beans, and if you've a good, rare variety it's worth doing. Old cottagers used to save their Broad Bean seed, but of course they didn't get much off a crop for eating because they saved all the good pods for seed!

Store seeds in bags, tins or screw-top jars. Put these in a cool, dry place: in a warm room seeds tend to lose their power to germinate and anywhere too damp makes them fusty.

FOR FLAVOURING

Celery seed gives flavour to soups. To get the seed you have to keep Celery through to the following year, protecting it during the winter.

Caraway sown the previous year will have ripe seed in late June/early July. That sown in April of the current year won't be ready until September. Watch it because it will drop. Better to pick the heads a bit early and put them in a tray or a box lined with paper where the seeds can fall out safely.

Again, store the seed in a cool, dry place.

SEED POTATOES

Save seed Potatoes only if your crop has been disease-free; and even then, after one or two years I think it's best to buy a fresh stock.

Store your own seed Potatoes somewhere airy but frost-free. Put them into boxes and stack the boxes on top of each other. Keep them cool. In March put them in a light, airy house or frame to chit (begin to sprout). If you leave them in the dark their shoots will become drawn to the light.

Storing herbs

You can dry herbs, but for Parsley, Sage, Thyme and Mint I think it's best to freeze them. Simply pick and wash them, put them on a cloth to soak up most of the moisture, then pop them into plastic bags, label the bags and put them into the freezer. Labelling is important because the bags will frost over and you won't be able to see what's inside. You can have bags holding one sort or bags of mixed herbs. When you take a bag out there's no need to chop the herbs: just give the bag a bash and the contents will break up into pieces!

A·Brief·Introduction to·Showing

Planning ahead – Preparation – At the show

CHAPTER EIGHTEEN
A Brief Introduction to Showing

I grew up knowing what good specimens of fruit and vegetables looked like because Uncle Fred, being head gardener at Blackmoor, judged at all the shows funded by the Selborne family. However, it wasn't until 1947, the year I took charge of Chilton's gardens, that I myself became involved in exhibiting. The owner of Chilton, Colonel Ward, was keen to see exhibits entered at shows and it was decided that, as vegetables were always in demand for the house, it would be sensible from time to time to stage an exhibit of them at the Royal Horticultural Society shows. I had every support and encouragement from the Colonel, which was just as well, for our exhibits used to cost a fortune. It took one man fifty-two weeks of the year to prepare, what with sowing and cultivating. Washing and getting vegetables ready alone filled a fortnight before we left for the show and, once we were there, it took two to two and a half days to stage our exhibit. That used to be 30ft (9.1m) long and 8ft (2.4m) deep (it had three tiers of staging at the back). It contained up to thirty-six different kinds of vegetables made up of a hundred varieties.

In retrospect, all the care and attention paid off, for by the late 1960s, when we finished showing, we were fortunate enough to have been awarded a Gold Medal ten times. That equalled the record set in 1934 by Mr Edwin Beckett, gardener to the Honorable Vicary Gibbs. No one has bettered it

and I doubt now that they ever will, for the days when private gardens had the capacity to stage such exhibits are gone. I do, however, have a daily reminder of those times and what we once achieved: a photograph of our last exhibit. Getting a bit faded now, it hangs, appropriately, on my dining-room wall.

Planning ahead

Decide what to grow and, because some favourites sell out, order seeds in good time to be sure of getting them. Sow and plant so that maturity date coincides with the show date. The more you do this, the better you'll become at it. Keeping a record of sowing dates helps. For example, if there's been no problem with the weather and a crop has come to fruition too early or too late the previous year, you can adjust the sowing date in the following year. With crops like Beetroot and Lettuce you can cover yourself by making a couple of sowings.

If you are going to enter a collection of vegetables, aim to make it up from ones which will get you high points: that is, Onions, Celery, Leeks, Cauliflower and Potatoes. Even if these are awarded only half the points they could be, the chances are they'll still get more points than very good Lettuce, Radish and other salading vegetables which have low maximum points.

Submit your entry form for the show by the date given in the show schedule. This will probably be two or three weeks before the show. It's seldom any earlier, because show organisers know that the nearer the show date, the more likely it is that no mishap will occur to the intended show fruits and vegetables and the entrant will turn up!

Preparation

GENERAL CARE

Keep vegetables free of weeds and watered. Keep earth drawn up over the shoulders of Carrots to stop the tops going green. Make sure that you don't spoil the tops of Beetroot by touching them with a hoe. Keep caterpillars off brassica leaves. Feed Tomatoes every week with a high potash feed or they'll get greenback.

Keep a daily eye on Peas and Beans and if any look like coming to maturity before the show date take them off. This will help to increase the size of those following on.

Tie a plastic bag over every choice fruit to stop birds pecking it. Cut off the corner of the bag to let out condensation.

Grow soft fruit in a bird-proof cage.

A FEW DAYS BEFORE THE SHOW

If you're staging a collection of vegetables or entering a lot of classes, you can spread the work load by selecting and lifting some vegetables a few days before the show. Carrots, Beetroot and Turnips will keep for several days if carefully washed and stored in cool, damp moss, peat or sand. Potatoes will keep even longer. I used to lift these in August and show them in October. Wash the vegetables with a sponge and clear water. Don't be tempted to add anything to the water: the judges will realise what you've done. Wash vegetables as soon as they're lifted, because you'll find it a dickens of a job to get little beads of soil out of their skins once it's dried. When I prepared for a show I had a chap who used to lift Potatoes and place them straight away into a bucket of clean water. After washing Potatoes put them where they'll dry quickly but not in direct sunlight because· that will turn their skins yellow. When they're dry, wrap them in tissue and store them somewhere cool and dark.

Runner Beans and Dwarf Beans can be kept for a few days after picking. Put flat pieces of wood against them and roll the Beans and wood up in a damp cloth; the wood will keep the Beans straight. Most root vegetables will also keep two or three days in a damp cloth.

Mark good Peas and Beans which aren't quite ready with a piece of raffia. This will help you go straight to them and it also stops them being picked for the pot by mistake!

At the show

ARRIVING AT THE SHOW

Allow yourself time to set your exhibit and reread the show schedule first to make sure you're going to do what is wanted – for example, putting the correct number of specimens on the dish.

SETTING YOUR EXHIBIT

'It's that first appearance, boy.' Ralph Thoday, a head gardener and a show judge, told me that over forty years ago. I've been judging since 1954 and find that his words still ring true. A dish of specimens neither too large nor too small and all of uniform size looks good immediately. This is especially true of dessert Apples, although some exhibitors spoil the effect by putting a big Apple in the middle!

Have your exhibit set and leave it before the judging starts.

JUDGING

The Horticultural Show Handbook, published by the Royal Horticultural Society, contains a useful guide as to the number of points which can be awarded to different fruits and vegetables. It also outlines the merits and defects judges take into consideration.

In my experience, if points are tight between a couple of competitors, judges count up the number of blemishes and the exhibit with least will win. The commonest blemishes on fruit are: bough marks, bruising, scab marks, hail damage, bitterpit beginning to show through the skin, capsid bug damage and the tell-tale holes where codling moth has entered. Blemishes on vegetables are usually the result of slug or fly damage or an injury sustained in cultivation or lifting. Potatoes can be blemished by scab and Carrots by having green shoulders.

Blemishes aside, below is a selection of other common faults which lose points.

Faults in vegetables

Onions Skinned too hard so that they're green and not a nice 'harvested' colour.

Unsound around the neck. This is found particularly on large prize winners that have entered a lot of shows!

Small ones not solid. They should be, because they're for keeping.

Cauliflowers Yellowing; curds have started to lift or gone ricy – that is, little knobbles are standing up about ⅛in (3mm) – as a result of leaving the leaf over for too long.

Celery Attempts to hide a seed stem in the centre. Not well blanched; and if a pink or red variety, not distinct enough in colour.

Lettuce Limp leaves and soft heads.

Leeks Shaft not well blanched or 'onion-bottomed': that is, a bulb at the bottom which indicates it's received a check.

Carrots, Parsnips and Long Beet Roots not intact and tapers uneven.

Faults in fruit

Most people realise that Apples and Pears should be shown with their stalks *intact* but some forget that so too should Cherries, Plums and Gages. If the stalks are removed from these, it lowers them to market class. Strawberries, Raspberries and even Gooseberries should also be shown with their stalks left *on*.

Picking and allowing to ripen afterwards loses points. A judge can tell if this has happened to a Peach or Nectarine, because if these are picked when they're ripe (as they should be) the fruit comes away from the stalk. The give-away on an Apple picked too soon is that there's a slight flabbiness to the skin.

Currants lose points if the berries are over- or under-ripe and if they're uneven on the strig. The strig is the term used for the bunch or raceme of berries. Another point loser has nothing to do with their quality – some shows stipulate so many *ounces* of Currants and other shows so many *strigs* on a plate. It pays, as I stated earlier, to read the show schedule carefully!

List of Suppliers

Vegetable Seeds

John Barber (Hertford) Ltd,
Old Cross, Hertford SG14 1JD.
Tel: (0992) 582304

J. W. Boyce,
Bush Pasture,
Lower Carter Street, Fordham, Ely, Cambs.
CB7 5JU.
Tel: (0638) 721158

Chase Organics (GB) Ltd,
Coombelands House, Coombelands Lane,
Addlestone, Weybridge KT15 1HY.
Tel: (0932) 820958

Chiltern Seeds,
Bortree Stile, Ulverston, Cumbria LA12 7PB.
Tel: (0229) 581137

Samuel Dobie & Son Ltd,
Broomhill Way, Torquay, Devon TQ2 7QW.
Tel: (0803) 616281

Mr Fothergill's Seeds,
Gazeley Road, Kentford, Newmarket,
Suffolk CB8 7QB.
Tel: (0638) 751161

S. E. Marshall & Co. Ltd,
Wisbech, Cambs. PE13 2RF.
Tel: (0945) 583407

W. Robinson & Sons Ltd,
Sunny Bank, Forton, Nr Preston,
Lancs. PR3 0BN.
Tel: (0524) 791210

Suffolk Herbs,
Sawyer's Farm, Little Cornard, Sudbury,
Suffolk CO10 0NY.
Tel: (0787) 227247

Suttons Seeds,
Hele Road, Torquay, Devon TQ2 7QJ.
Tel: (0803) 612011

Unwin Seeds Limited,
Histon, Cambridge CB4 4ZZ
Tel: (0945) 588522

Herbs

J. W. Boyce,
Bush Pasture, Lower Carter Street.
Fordham, Ely, Cambs. CB7 5JU.
Tel: (0638) 721158

Chase Organics (GB) Ltd,
Coombelands House, Coombelands Lane,
Addlestone, Weybridge KT15 1HY.
Tel: (0932) 820958

Chiltern Seeds,
Bortree Stile, Ulverston, Cumbria LA12 7PB.
Tel: (0229) 581137

Hollington Nurseries Ltd,
Woolton Hill, Newbury, Berks. RG15 9XT.
Tel: (0635) 253908
(Mainly plants, which have to be collected but some seeds available by mail order)

Suffolk Herbs,
Sawyer's Farm, Little Cornard, Sudbury,
Suffolk CO10 0NY.
Tel: (0787) 227247

Thornby Herbs,
Thornby Hall Gardens, Thornby,
Northampton NN6 8SW
Tel: (0604) 740090

Seakale

John Barber (Hertford) Ltd,
Old Cross, Hertford SG14 1JD.
Tel: (0992) 582304

Chiltern Seeds,
Bortree Stile, Ulverston, Cumbria LA12 7PB.
Tel: (0229) 581137

S. E. Marshall & Ltd,
Wisbech, Cambs. PE13 2RF.
Tel: (0945) 583407
(Supplies thongs)

Suffolk Herbs,
Sawyer's Farm, Little Cornard, Sudbury,
Suffolk CO10 0NY.
Tel: (0787) 227247

Mushrooms

J. W. Boyce,
Bush Pasture, Lower Carter Street,
Fordham, Ely, Cambs. CB7 5JU.
Tel: (0638) 721158
(Spawn)

Samuel Dobie & Son Ltd,
Broomhill Way, Torquay,
Devon TQ2 7QW.
Tel: (0803) 616281
(Grain spawn and pelleted spawn)

S. E. Marshall & Co. Ltd,
Wisbech, Cambs. PE13 2RF.
Tel: (0945) 583407
(Mushroom kits)

Suttons Seeds,
Hele Road, Torquay, Devon TQ2 7QJ.
Tel: (0803) 612011
(Grain spawn and pelleted spawn)

Tree Fruit and Soft Fruit

Blackmoor Wholesale Fruit Nurseries,
Blackmoor, Liss, Hampshire GU33 6BS.
Tel: (0420) 473576
(*Fruit tree cash-and-carry for amateur gardeners
November to March, Saturday mornings only*)

Chris Bowers,
Whispering Trees Nursery, Wimbotsham,
Norfolk PE34 8QB.
Tel: (0366) 388752

Deacons Nursery,
Godshill, Isle of Wight PO38 3HW.
Tel: (0983) 840750 or 522243

Everton Nurseries Ltd,
Everton, Nr Lymington,
Hampshire SO4 0JZ.
Tel: (0590) 642155

Highfield Nurseries,
Whitminster, Gloucester GL2 7PL.
Tel: (0452) 740266

RHS Enterprises Limited,
RHS Garden, Wisley,
Woking, Surrey GU23 6QB.
Tel: (0483) 211113

St Bridget Nurseries Ltd,
Old Rydon Lane, Exeter EX2 7JY.
Tel: (0392) 873672
(*Closed on Sundays*)

The above all stock Figs and Grapes but the
largest selection of these is at:
Reads Nursery,
Hales Hall, Loddon,
Norfolk NR14 6QW.
Tel: (050846) 395
(*Holds the national collection of Figs and also of
greenhouse Grapes*)

Melons

John Barber (Hertford) Ltd,
Old Cross, Hertford SG14 1JD.
Tel: (0992) 582304

J. W. Boyce,
Bush Pasture, Lower Carter Street,
Fordham, Ely, Cambs. CB7 5JU.
Tel: (0638) 721158

Chase Organics (GB) Ltd,
Coombelands House,
Coombelands Lane,
Addlestone,
Weybridge KT15 1HY.
Tel: (0932) 820958

Mr Fothergill's Seeds,
Gazeley Road, Kentford, Newmarket,
Suffolk CB8 7QB.
Tel: (0638) 751161

S. E. Marshall & Co. Ltd,
Wisbech, Cambs. PE13 2RF.
Tel: (0945) 583407

Fertilisers

Joseph Bentley Ltd,
Beck Lane, Barrow-on-Humber,
South Humberside DN19 7AQ.
Tel: (0469) 30501

Chase Organics (GB) Ltd,
Coombelands House, Coombelands Lane,
Addlestone, Weybridge KT15 1HY.
Tel: (0932) 820958
(*Green manures and organic fertilisers*)

Pelco Fertilizers Ltd,
251–253 London Road East,
Batheaston, Bath BA1 7RL.
Tel: (0225) 859962
(*Manufacturers of 'Dug' and 'Super Dug', manures which are made from composted deep litter from poultry houses*)

Suffolk Herbs,
Sawyer's Farm, Little Cornard, Sudbury,
Suffolk CO10 0NY.
Tel: (0787) 227247
(*Green manures*)

Cloches

Power Garden Products,
3 Daytona Drive, Allesley, Coventry CV5 9QG.
Tel: (0676) 23062
(*Supplies Grower's Barn-type cloches*)

Horticultural Sundries

Joseph Bentley Ltd,
Beck Lane, Barrow-on-Humber,
South Humberside DN19 7AQ.
Tel: (0469) 30501
(*Mail-order catalogue includes, among other sundries: riddles, soil sterilisers, greenhouse heaters, thermometers, insecticides, galvanised watering cans, tools*)

Index

American Land Cress, 52
  cultivation, 52
  sowing, 52
Angelica, 132
Apples, 151–8
  bush trees, 152
  care of, 158
  cordons, 153–6
  espaliers, 157–8
  forms, 152
  picking, 206–7
  showing, 213
  soil, 152
  storage, 207
  varieties, 151–2
Artichokes *see* Chinese
    Artichokes; Globe
    Artichokes *and* Jerusalem
    Artichokes
Asparagus, 109–10
  forcing, 109–10
  from crowns, 109
  from seed, 109
Asparagus Peas, 89
Aubergines, 127–8
autumn Cauliflower, 76
awkward corners, 30

bag fertilisers, 20–1
  potting composts, 25
  sowing composts, 25
Balm, 132

basic techniques, 15–32
Basil, 132–3
Beans, 89–95
  Broad, 89–91
  Butter, 95
  climbing French Beans, 95
  crop rotation, 30
  dwarf French Beans, 36, 94
  growing in pots, 36
  Haricot, 95
  ornamental, 95
  Runner, 30, 40, 91–4
  showing, 212
  sowing in pots, 26
Beetroot, 57–8
  crop rotation, 30, 31, 32
  cultivation, 57–8
  forcing, 37
  intercropping, 32
  long Beet, 58, 213
  main-crop, 58
  showing, 212, 213
  storing, 60
  thinning, 29
  under cloches, 40, 57
  varieties, 57
Black Currants, 184
  care, 184
  ground preparation, 181
  propagation, 184
blanching, 107–20
bone meal, 21

Borage, 45, 133
brassicas, 71–6
  crop rotation, 30, 31
  planting out, 30
  sowing in pots, 26
  see also individual forms
Broad Beans, 89–91
  early sowings, 90–1
  ground preparation, 90
  sowing in open ground, 91
Broccoli, 72
  crop rotation, 32
Brussels Sprouts, 71–2
  early crops, 71–2
  ground preparation, 72
  intercropping, 32, 72
  main crops, 72
  planting out, 72
Butter Beans, 95

Cabbages, 73–4
  Coleworts, 74
  Couve Tronchuda, 74
  Savoys, 74
  spring, 30, 73
  summer, 73
  winter, 32, 73
  see also other types of brassica
Calabrese, 74
Cantaloupes, 200
Capsicum, 128
Caraway, 133, 208

Cardoons, 116–18
  blanching, 117
  sowing, 116
Carrots, 58–60
  Carrot fly, 60
  crop rotation, 30, 31, 60
  forcing, 37
  ground preparation, 60
  hotbeds, 36
  intercropping, 32
  showing, 60, 212, 213
  sowing, 60
  storing, 60
  thinning, 29, 60
  under cloches, 40
  varieties, 58
Cauliflowers, 75–6
  autumn, 76
  crop rotation, 32
  early summer, 75
  growing in pots, 37
  showing, 213
  storing, 76
  under glass, 75
  winter, 76
Celeriac, 61
  cultivation, 61
  sowing, 61
  storage, 62
Celery, 115–16
  blanching, 115
  crop rotation, 30, 31, 32
  frost protection, 116
  planting out, 115
  saving seed, 208
  showing, 213
  sowing, 115
  trench preparation, 115
chalky soils, 15–16
Cherries, 163–5
  bush, 163
  fans, 164
  forms of plant, 163
  Morello, 165

planting, 163
showing, 213
under glass, 164
Chervil, 134
Chicory, 108–9
  forcing, 108–9
  non-forcing, 108
Chinese Artichokes, 56–7
  cultivation, 56
  lifting, 57
Chives, 50
  cultivation, 50
  sowing, 50
clamps, storage, 205–6
clay soils, 15
climbing French Beans, 95
cloches, 40
  suppliers, 217
Clover, green manure, 23
cocktail Onions, 103
coldframes, 37
Coleworts, 74
Collards, 74
Comfrey, 23
compost, garden, 22–3, 96
  potting, 24–5
  sowing, 24, 25
cordons:
  Apples, 153–6
  Gooseberries, 182–3
  Plums, 169
  Red and White Currants,
    185
Corn Salad, 51–2
  cultivation, 52
  sowing, 52
Courgettes, 123–4
Cress, 50–1
  cones, 51
  cultivation, 51
  green manure, 23
  sowing, 50–1
  see also American Land Cress
crop rotation, 30–2

Cucumbers, 45–6
  bush varieties, 46
  greenhouse culture, 45
  greenhouse varieties, 45
  hotbeds, 36
  outside culture, 46
  ridge varieties, 46
curly Kale, 76
Currants, 184–6
  showing, 213

Dandelions, cultivation, 107–8
digging, 16–20
  alternatives to, 20
  double ridging, 18
  mock trenching, 17
  ordinary, 17
  reasons for, 16
  ridging single spit, 18
  trenching, 18
Dill, 134
drills, drawing out, 28
Dutch hoes, using, 99
dwarf French Beans, 94
  early crops, 94
  growing in pots, 36
  outdoor sowings, 94

Egyptian Onions, 102
Endives, 110–11
  blanching, 111
  broad-leaved, 110
  curly-headed, 110
espaliers:
  Apples, 157–8
  Plums, 168

farmyard manure, 20–1
  hotbeds, 35
  mulch, 20
  soil improvement, 15, 20
Farmyard Spinach, 81–2
Fennel, 124–5
  see also Florence Fennel

fertilisers, 20–1
  bone meal, 21
  dried blood, 21
  fish meal, 21
  hoof and horn, 21
  nitrochalk, 21
  potting composts, 25
  seaweed, 21
  soot, 21
  sowing composts, 25
  spent mushroom compost,
   21
  suppliers, 216
Figs, 174–6
  care, 174
  outside, 175
  in pots, 176
  propagating, 176
  restricting roots, 174
  siting, 174
  under glass, 176
fish meal, 21
Florence Fennel, 82–3
forcing vegetables, 35–40,
   107–20
  Cauliflowers, 37
  cloches, 40
  coldframes, 37
  French Beans, 36
  hotbeds, 35–6
  Peas, 36
  pot grown, 36–7
  Potatoes, 37
frames:
  coldframes, 37
  hotbeds, 35
French Beans, 94–5
  climbing, 95
  dwarf, 94
  growing in pots, 36
  under cloches, 40
fruit:
  farmyard manure mulches,
   20

showing, 211–13
storage, 203, 206
see also soft fruit; fruit trees
fruit trees, 143–8, 151–176
  bare-rooted, 148
  container-grown, 148
  heeling-in, 147
  liquid farmyard manure, 23
  planting, 147
  post and wire for, 146
  pruning, 148
  supplier, 216
  wiring walls for, 145

Gages, 166–9
  care, 169
  cordons, 169
  espalier, 168
  form, 166
  planting, 168
  pruning, 168
  showing, 213
  varieties, 166
Garlic, 135
Globe Artichokes, 83–4
  cultivation, 84
  from seed, 84
  winter treatment, 84
Good King Henry, 81–2
  cultivation, 82
Gooseberries, 181–3, 213
  bushes, 182
  care, 183
  cordons, 182–3
  fan-trained, 183
  ground preparation, 181
  planting, 181
  standard, 183
Grapes, 191–6
  cultivation, 191–2
  pollinating, 193
  pruning, 192–3
  storing, 195
  summer care, 193–4

syringing, 193
thinning, 196
training, 192
winter routine, 195–6
green manure, 23
  crop waste, 23
greenhouses:
  Cucumbers, 45
  Tomatoes, 43, 44
grit, soil improvement, 15
grow bags, Tomatoes, 44

Hamburg Parsley, 135
Haricot Beans, 95
heeling-in fruit trees, 147
herbs, 129–40
  storing, 208
  suppliers, 215
hoof and horn, 21
Horseradish, 136
hotbeds, 35–6

intercropping, 32

Jerusalem Artichokes, 55–6
  cultivation, 55–6
  siting, 30
  varieties, 56

Kales, 76
  intercropping, 32
Kohl Rabi, 62–3
  cultivation, 63
  varieties, 63

Lamb's Lettuce, 51–2
  cultivation, 52
  sowing, 52
leaf mould, potting composts,
   24–5
Leeks, 103–4
  cultivation, 104
  lifting, 104
  planting out, 104

second sowing, 104
showing, 213
sowing in a coldframe, 104
sowing under cloches, 103
Lettuces, 46–8
crop rotation, 30, 31, 32
cultivation, 46
forcing, 37
intercropping, 32
planting out, 29–30
showing, 213
sowing in pots, 26
successional growing, 46
thinning, 29
under cloches, 40
varieties, 46
lime, 21
liquid farmyard manure, 23
loam:
potting composts, 25
sowing composts, 24, 25
sterilising, 25
Loganberries, 186
long Beet, 58, 213
Lupins, green manure, 23

manure, 20, 23
crop rotation, 30, 31
farmyard, 15, 20–1, 35
green, 23
hotbeds, 35
liquid, 23
soil improvement, 15
Marjoram, 136
Marrows, 123–4
crop rotation, 31
hotbeds, 36
under cloches, 40
measuring rods, 29
medium-loam soil, 16
Melons, 196–200
cantaloupes, 200
suppliers, 216
under glass, 196–200

Mint, 136
Morello Cherries, 165
mulches: farmyard manure, 20
leaf mould, 24
Mushrooms, 118–20
easy methods, 118
picking 120
suppliers, 215
traditional methods, 118–19
Mustard and Cress, 50–1
cones, 51
cultivation, 51
green manure, 23
sowing, 50–1

Nectarines, 173
care, 172
moving trees, 170
pests and diseases, 173
planting, 169
pruning, 172
showing, 213
soil preparation, 169
thinning, 172
New Zealand Spinach, 80
Niton Buckley Pea, 95
nitrochalk, 21

Onions, 99–104
beds, 99
Chives, 50
cocktail, 103
crop rotation, 30, 31
early crops, 99
Egyptian, 102
from sets, 100–1
Leeks, 103–4, 213
lifting, 101
main crop, 100
ropes, 101
Shallots, 31, 102
showing, 213
Spring, 50
thinning, 29

Welsh, 102
Oregano, 136
out-of-season vegetables, 35
cloches, 40
coldframes, 37
hotbeds, 35–6
pot grown, 36–7

Parsley, 136–7
Hamburg, 135
Parsnips, 63–4
crop rotation, 30, 31
cultivation, 63–4
showing, 213
thinning, 29
varieties, 63
Peaches, 169–72
care, 172
moving trees, 170
planting, 169
pruning, 172
showing, 213
soil preparation, 169
thinning, 172
Pears, 158–61
care, 161
picking, 206–7
pruning, 160
soil, 160
storage, 207
training, 160–1
varieties, 160
Peas, 87–9
Asparagus Peas, 89
crop rotation, 30, 32
early crops, 88
ground preparation, 87
growing in pots, 36, 88
main crop, 89
mid-season crop, 88
Purple-podded Peas, 89
second earlies, 88
showing, 212
sowing, 88

sowing in pots, 26
Sugar Peas, 89
tall varieties, 87
under cloches, 40
Winged Peas, 89
Perpetual Spinach, 79–80
crop rotation, 31
pests and diseases, 173
planting out, 29–30
Plums, 166–9
care, 169
cordons, 169
espalier, 168
form, 166
planting, 168
pruning, 168
showing, 213
varieties, 166
Portuguese Cabbage, 74
Potatoes, 64–6
buying seed, 64
crop rotation, 30, 31, 32
cultivation, 66
early cropping, 65
follow-on crops, 66
forcing, 37
ground preparation, 65
growing in pots, 36
intercropping, 32
planting, 65–6
seed, 64, 208
showing, 212
storing, 66, 203
varieties, 64
pots:
forwarding plants in, 36–7
sowing seed in, 25–6
potting composts, 24–5
pricking off, 27
composts for, 25
Prickly Spinach, 79
pruning, fruit trees, 148
Pumpkins, 123–4
Purple-podded Peas, 89

'Purple Sprouting' Broccoli, 72

Radishes, 49
crop rotation, 30
cultivation, 49
intercropping, 32
sowing, 49
varieties, 49
winter varieties, 49
Raspberries, 179–81
care, 179–81
ground preparation, 179
showing, 213
Red Currants, 185–6
bushes, 185
care, 186
cordons, 185
ground preparation, 181
standards, 185
Rhubarb, 111–12
cultivation, 111–12
forcing, 112
ground preparation, 112
lifting, 112
picking, 112
siting, 30
Rhubarb Chard, 81
ridging:
double, 18
single spit, 18
root vegetables, 55–68
lifting, 204
storage, 204–6
Rosemary, 139
siting, 30
Roundleaf Spinach, 31, 79
Rue, 139
Runner Beans, 91–4
crop rotation, 30
early crops, 92
ground preparation, 91–2
open-ground sowing, 93
supports, 92, 93–4
under cloches, 40

wigwams, 93–4
Rye Grass, green manure, 23

Sage, 140
siting, 30
salad crops, 43–52
Salsify, 66–8
sandy soils, 15
Savory, 140
Savoys, 74
Scorzonera, 66–8
Seakale, 112–14
forcing, 114
from seed, 113
from thongs, 113
suppliers, 215
Seakale Beet, see Swiss Chard
80–1
seaweed, 21
seed:
saving, 208
storing, 208
suppliers, 214
seed beds:
preparation, 28
sowing, 29
seedlings:
planting out, 29–30
pricking off, 25, 27
thinning out, 29
sets, Onion, 100–1
Shallots, 102
crop rotation, 31
showing, 211–13
at the show, 212
faults, 213
judging, 212–13
planning, 211–12
preparation, 212
soft fruit, 177
suppliers, 216
soil:
chalky, 15–16
clay, 15

composts, 22–3
digging, 16–20
fertilisers, 20–1
manures, 20, 23
medium loam, 16
sandy, 15
seed beds, 28
sterilising, 25
for tomatoes, 44
types, 15–16
soot, 21
Sorrel, 140
sowing, hotbeds, 36
sowing composts, 24, 25
sowing vegetables, 24–9
composts, 24, 25
ground preparation, 28
hotbeds, 36
in situ, 28, 29
out of doors, 27–9
pots and trays, 26
pricking off, 27
seed beds, 29
small seed, 26
thinning out, 29
timing, 25
under cover, 24–7
out of doors, 27–9
spent mushroom compost, 21
Spinach, 79–82
crop rotation, 31
Good King Henry, 81–2
intercropping, 32
New Zealand, 80–1
Perpetual, 79–80
Prickly, 79
Rhubarb Chard, 81
Roundleaf, 31, 79
Seakale Beet, 80–1
Swiss Chard, 80
winter, 79–80
spring Cabbage, 73
crop rotation, 30

cultivation, 73
modern forms, 73
spring-heading Broccoli, 76
Spring Onions, 50
cultivation, 50
sowing, 50
varieties, 50
sprouting, 72
Sprouts *see* Brussels Sprouts
Squashes, 123–4
sterilising soil, 25
storing, 203–8
Strawberries, 186–8
crop rotation, 30, 32
cultivation, 186
planting, 186
propagating, 186–7
showing, 213
under cloches, 40, 187
under glass, 187–8
Sugar Peas, 89
summer Cabbage, 73
suppliers, 214
Swedes, 68
Sweet Corn, 95–6
cultivation, 96
early crops, 96
making compost from, 96
outdoor sowings, 96
Swiss Chard, 80–1

Tarragon, 140
thinning seedlings, 29
Thyme, 140
siting, 30
Tomatoes, 42–5
crop rotation, 31
feeding, 45
greenhouse culture, 43, 44
outdoor culture, 43–4
pollination, 44
soil for, 44
sowing in pots, 26
varieties, 43

trays, sowing seed in, 25–6
tree fruit *see* fruit trees
Trefoil, green manure, 23
trenching, 16
mock, 16
tubers, 55–68
Turnips, 68
crop rotation, 30, 31, 32
showing, 212
sowing, 68
thinning, 29
varieties, 68

vegetables:
basic techniques, 15–32
blanching, 107–20
crop rotation, 30–2
forcing, 107–20
intercropping, 32
out-of-season, 35–40
planting out, 29–30
seed suppliers, 214
sowing, 24–9
storing, 203–8

walls, for fruit, 145
Welsh Onions, 102
White Currants, 185–6
bushes, 185
care, 186
cordons, 185
ground preparation, 181
standards, 185
Winged Peas, 89
winter Cabbage, 73
intercropping, 32
winter Cauliflower, 76
winter radishes, 49
winter Spinach, 79–80
Winter Tares, green manure, 23
wireworm, 23
wiring for fruit trees, 145–6
woodlice, traps, 120